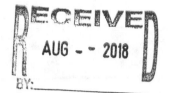
THE CLIMB FROM SALT LICK

THE CLIMB *FROM* SALT LICK

A MEMOIR
OF APPALACHIA

◆ ◆ ◆

Nancy L. Abrams

◆ ◆ ◆

VANDALIA PRESS

MORGANTOWN 2018

Copyright © 2018 Nancy L. Abrams

First edition published 2018 by Vandalia Press, an imprint of

West Virginia University Press

Printed in the United States of America

ISBN:

Paper: 978-1-946684-18-9

EPUB: 978-1-946684-19-6

PDF: 978-1-946684-20-2

Library of Congress Cataloging-in-Publication Data is

available from the Library of Congress

Book and cover design by Than Saffel / WVU Press

Cover photograph by Ray Wong

CONTENTS

Prologue   vii

SECTION I: A HOME

1   Carpetbagger   3

2   Salt Lick and Calamity   11

3   *Non Compos Mentis*   16

4   Embedded   20

5   I Grow Fond   32

6   Take Me Home, Country Roads   37

7   Real Life   43

8   The Move to Salt Lick   49

9   Through Calamity   51

10   A Doctor! And He's Jewish!   58

11   Ramps   61

12   The Commune Down Salt Lick, Part 1   67

13   Pot Roast   71

CONTENTS *continued*

SECTION II: A MATE

14   Switching Gears   81

15   Judy Judy Judy   93

16   Diamonds Are a Girl's Best Friend   95

17   Disaster Practice   100

18   West Virginia Brigadoon   106

19   The Commune Down Salt Lick, Part 2   116

20   Civil War   125

21   Deer Dear Friend   135

22   Happy Daze   138

23   Why Is This Night Different?   145

24   Black Power   149

25   The Murderer and Me   156

26   Buckwheat Baby   166

27   Apple Cider   173

28   Busted   178

29   Dilettante   189

30   The Nesting Instinct   195

31   Experiments with Utopia   206

32   Changes in Altitude   216

33   The Cheat 1   222

34   The Cheat 2   232

35   The Climb from Salt Lick   241

Acknowledgments   245

PROLOGUE

WITH YOUR RIGHT HAND, make a fist, thumb to the right. Extend your thumb and middle finger. This is the shape of West Virginia. My story takes place in your bent pointer finger, in Preston County, bordered to the north by Pennsylvania, to the east by Maryland, and dissected diagonally by the Allegheny Mountains.

Section One

◆ ◆ ◆

A HOME

1

CARPETBAGGER

"HOW WOULD YOU LIKE to spend the summer in Terra Alta, West Virginia?" My professor's powerful baritone filled his office. It was spring 1974 and I was about to finish my junior year at the University of Missouri in Columbia.

Bill Kuykendall had been my teacher for two semesters. He seemed to think I could actually become a photojournalist. His question was thrilling. I had just come from a darkroom and squinted under the fluorescent lights. "Two of my friends own a newspaper in the mountains," Bill said. His thick mustache and bushy eyebrows animated his sales pitch. "They need an intern."

I inhaled, smelled the photo chemicals on my hands. "Terra Alta?" It wasn't really a question. I understood some Latin. "High ground." I was interested. I liked high.

"I'll go," I said.

Bill told me he had met the owners of the paper when he was a student at West Virginia University and he admired them. I was flattered that he wanted me to work for his friends. That meant he approved of my work. He didn't care that my portfolio was the result of instinct

3

more than intent. Almost all the other photojournalism majors at the University of Missouri were male, cocksure of their abilities. They talked about the technology and chemistry of photography with easy familiarity. The guys also had lots of equipment: cameras, lenses, and tripods. They carried them like tools. My Nikon was more of an accessory, a necklace; my camera bag substituted for a purse. But the photographs I made were good. I was observant and had an eye for composition. And I was short, which gave my work a less-seen angle.

◆

A few days later Bill handed me the phone in his office. "Meet Jerry Ash, editor of *The Preston County News*."

"Let me tell you about our newspaper." Jerry's voice was friendly. "My partner Rich and I liked teaching, but we wanted to practice what we preached. And we've done it." His voice lowered, as if he was sharing a secret. "We need a summer intern because our part-time ad paste-up person wants the summer off to spend time with her new baby." I'd have to do her job one day a week, he said, and devote the rest of my time to photography. "Our black and white reproduction is great. And we're just an hour away from Morgantown, where West Virginia University is." He cleared his throat. "Still interested?"

I agreed to a salary of eighty-five dollars a week. Jerry said his wife Michele would find me a cheap place to live.

He sent me a few issues of the paper, a weekly. It was striking. The photographs were printed well and the body copy was set in Helvetica with ragged right margins. The design was clean and simple, with respect for white space. I hadn't considered that *The Preston County News* would be unlike any newspaper I had ever seen. It would be a fine place to display my work. I imagined the portfolio I would build, a collection of images that would win admiration and job offers.

"West Virginia!" my friends exclaimed with surprise and just a little pity when I announced my summer plans. My fellow students had more conventional internships in cities and suburbs. My only connection to West Virginia was that my maternal grandmother had once spent the night in Wheeling. I had studied the Farm Security Administration

Depression—era photos of poverty-stricken Appalachians. I knew that coal mining was the state's main industry. I vaguely remembered television coverage of poverty in Appalachia. The theme song from the *Beverly Hillbillies* played in my head. I knew they were from Tennessee, but . . .

◆

To prepare for my trip East, I went shopping. I bought a quarter of a pound of pot from students across the street (thirty-five dollars in their end-of-the-school-year close-out sale) and a hundred hits of Dexedrine in the form of white crosses—enough pot for a mellow summer and enough speed for attentive driving.

On May 9, 1974, just two days before I left for Terra Alta, the United States House of Representatives voted to initiate impeachment proceedings against Richard Nixon. On the day I left Columbia, Missouri, it was rumored that Nixon was on the verge of announcing his resignation—a great omen.

I didn't want to spend my limited funds on a hotel room; buoyed by optimism, I planned to drive straight through to West Virginia. Dexedrine and moderate marijuana intake would offset the tedium of eighteen hours in the car. I drove through the vowel states—Illinois, Indiana, and Ohio—and listened to Jesse Colin Young, Joni Mitchell, and the Beatles. At two in the morning, just east of Columbus, the road began to climb. The terrain change energized my senses. The steering wheel became a living thing; the motor strummed through my body. I had never been out of the Midwest, not east of Lexington, Kentucky, or west of Topeka, Kansas. The hills loomed before me in silhouette, dark and romantic. Here was the divide between the Eastern Seaboard and the Midwest. My chin rose with the horizon like a supplicant. After crossing the Ohio River into Wheeling, West Virginia, I whooshed through a tunnel gilded with artificial light. This shining cave made me laugh out loud.

The laughter didn't last long. West Virginia's less-than-fifteen-mile section of Interstate 70 was pocked with potholes so big that they wrenched the steering wheel, my introduction to a state so poor that it couldn't maintain this important highway. I turned south into Pennsylvania and was greeted by a warm May morning, all sunshine and humidity. The light, a diffused gold, coming at an angle, highlighted the high-low contours of the land. The air glowed; the foliage was a magic quilt in shades of green, tints blurring in the frames of the car windows.

When the still-under-construction four-lane ended, a two-lane road wound through the countryside. A small sign, "Wild, Wonderful West Virginia," welcomed me to my new state. I crossed the Monongahela River (which I would eventually learn to pronounce muh-NON-guh-HEE-luh) and an enormous, concrete spaceship, round with a scalloped roof, surprised me. The West Virginia University Coliseum, according to a sign. In his directions Jerry had called Route 7 a highway, but buildings crowded close when I looped through downtown Morgantown. Just east of town the road ended without warning in a muddy construction site. Confused, I turned the car around and pulled into a doughnut shop, the only place that was open.

"Where's Route 7?" I asked the sleepy clerk.

She looked at me, eyelids half lowered as if to proclaim I was obviously stupid. She pointed to the road in front. "There it is."

"I know. But it ends just up the hill."

Her face softened. "Oh no. They're building a new highway. Just keep going and you'll pick up the hardtop in a bit."

"So I'm supposed to drive through the construction site?"

She shrugged. "Everybody does."

I motored under the skeleton of a massive overpass, past piles of concrete and metal that would eventually become Interstate 68, and finally, just as the doughnut girl promised, the hardtop resumed. The road curved over a narrow creek and skirted rows of look-alike houses. (I would learn that these were the remnants of a coal company town.) A ramshackle bar's sign said "Pioneer Rocks." To the right, evergreen bushes tumbled down a rocky cliff. The musical, churning creek below splashed crystal water. The woods were close and lush. I caught my breath. I would have pulled over for a picture, but the road was narrow and without a shoulder. Too dangerous for my first day in West Virginia. Small towns, little more than a row of houses and a couple of businesses, sat hard against the road. A dozen miles east I came to Kingwood. A courthouse, wider streets, and some grand houses were evidence of the town's status as county seat. As were the two stoplights. Years later, when I drove there with my two sons, they would shout, "The city, the city!" when they saw those lights.

Beyond Kingwood, the hillsides were covered with trilliums— grand, white, three-petaled flowers. Water trickled off a high rock shelf and fell into a natural basin next to the road. I slowed to admire this curiosity and felt cool air coming off the stone. Just afterward I came to the bottom of the hill and the Cheat River. Jerry had warned me about the one-lane iron bridge that crossed the river. It was solid, he said; it just looked scary. Its beams and iron spikes offered a staccato percussion when I drove across. My car whined on its ascent of Caddell Mountain; my ears popped with the change in altitude. I passed a watering trough left over from horse and buggy days but didn't know that the spring there flowed continuously with cold, sweet water. At the summit, I coasted through a small glade and rounded a serpentine curve. The sudden vista, an up and down rhythm of trees and mountains, stretched for miles and miles. I gasped. Who knew West Virginia was beautiful? It was famous for poverty, for coal mining, for hillbillies. I felt as if I had discovered an unknown world, a never-ending panorama of ridges and valleys, scenery that filled my heart with joy. When I could climb no higher, I realized that the small town to my right was Terra Alta, population fourteen hundred.

◆

Jerry had told me that the newspaper office was next to the post office on a small street parallel to Route 7, but somehow I missed the turn and ended up driving through the entire town. It took about a minute. Puzzled, I slowed to turn around. The smell of fried food hung in the air, and in that instant, I realized I was famished. The sign on the restaurant said "My-Own Chicken." The reddish-brown building was no bigger than twenty-four feet by twenty-four feet. Large windows revealed people in booths.

When I walked in, the buzz of conversation paused. Diners looked up from their plates. Some openly stared. All the customers looked as though they were heading to or from church. My long red hair, jeans, and wrinkled flannel shirt shouted hippie. The waitress called me "Hon" and led me to a booth. Her pink uniform looked like it might be itchy. Bacon, eggs, and fried potatoes appeared in minutes. As I ate, I could see into a small, separate dining room in the back of the building. The tableau looked like Leonardo da Vinci's *The Last Supper*, with a row of men paying rapt attention to the person seated in the middle of the long table. In time I would learn that he was Jim Teets, a member of the West Virginia House of Delegates and the chief Republican in a Republican town. I would also learn that Preston County was then one of just a few Republican counties in West Virginia. Jim's brother Bob would run the town's general store and years later buy *The Preston County News* and become my boss; his mother, Ruth, ran Teets Oil Company. The Teetses were Terra Alta high society. At that Sunday morning meeting, those men no doubt were plotting political maneuvers. Politics, in Preston County, meant jobs—jobs at Hopemont State Hospital, a former tuberculosis sanitarium turned into a facility for the chronically ill, the state road department, the schools. But I didn't know that then.

The waitress brought me the check.

"Where's the post office?" I asked, digging for my wallet.

"Honey, the post office is closed on Sunday."

"I know," I said, handing her cash. "I'm actually looking for the newspaper. I'm going to be working there this summer."

The din of conversation suddenly died. Now it seemed that everyone was staring at me. I smiled nervously. This was my first encounter with the citizens of Terra Alta; I felt exposed and strange. I rested my forearms on the Formica tabletop, fought to keep from slumping. The waitress tucked the tip in her apron, pointed west, and precisely described how to find the newspaper office. "Good luck, Hon," she said.

Washington Street was a few short blocks of two-story brick and frame buildings: a five-and-dime discount store, a furniture store, and the Terra Alta Library. Why was I surprised to see parking meters? I knocked on the door to *The Preston County News*. Jerry, a big man in his mid-thirties, opened the door. His thick beard had a sprinkling of gray. He pumped my hand with enthusiasm and introduced me to his wife, Michele, who stood behind him. She was round with dark, round glasses. Her voice was loud and friendly.

"How was your trip?" Her short, brunette bob glistened as she shifted from foot to foot.

"I drove all night," I said. "I was in a hurry to get here."

Jerry beamed at me, his face alive with enthusiasm. He moved quickly and grabbed my bags. "You'll be staying with us for a couple of weeks." He headed upstairs and called over his shoulder. "Then you can move into a trailer that we found."

I followed him. A trailer? I had never even been in a trailer. Jerry put my stuff in a small bedroom at the top of the stairs, then observed me, hands on hips. A white German shepherd padded over. "Not afraid of dogs?" Jerry's eyebrows rose in question, animated his face. I shook my head. "Good. This is Cleo." I stroked the dog's shoulders, looked around. Two huge tanks of fish dominated the long, rectangular living room. I walked over to look at a couple of large photos on the wall.

"Those are Bill's," Jerry explained. "He's really talented." I nodded; I had seen Bill's work and admired it. Jerry turned toward me and I felt his focused attention. "Get settled a bit, then come on down," he said, heading downstairs. "Michele and I are doing a little work on this week's paper."

Several minutes later, I stood before Jerry again. When he gave me another intent look, I realized he had noticed the Star of David hanging from a thin gold chain around my neck. "You're Jewish?" he asked.

I nodded, a little puzzled. Should I admit that I was more interested in the symbol, the tribe, than the religion? I kept quiet.

Jerry rocked back on his heels. "That will be interesting." He folded his arms and rested them against his slightly protruding stomach. "After we talked, I was worried you might be black. After all, you're from St. Louis." He quickly added, "Not that that's a problem for me. But this is a pretty white town."

I'd like to think that my shock didn't show. But I'm sure my face betrayed my emotions. It always has. As I followed Jerry and Michele through the building, I sniffed the air, smelled ink and paper. A huge press, "Heidelberg" painted on its side, dominated the back room. Jerry gestured. "The Pioneer Press, our commercial printing business, is

Rich's baby," he said. "The newspaper's printed down the mountain in Keyser." At the back of the building, a door stood open to a small dock and train tracks. In the basement, a large, rectangular machine dominated a brightly lit room. It beeped and chattered as it devoured what looked like ticker tape. "Mergenthaler VIP" was spelled out on its side. Michele patted the beige plastic. "Setting copy," she explained.

Back upstairs Jerry steered me toward the darkroom. I admired its neatness and smelled the familiar sharp odors of Dektol and hypo. Suddenly, fatigue hit me like a weight. I leaned against the door.

"I'm sorry," I said. "I might have to take a nap."

Michele made a clucking sound. "Go rest," she urged. "We'll finish our work."

"When you wake up," Jerry said, "we'll go to Deep Creek Lake, Maryland, about half an hour away. It's your first day here; we'll take you out. A restaurant over there has great stuffed lobster."

I brightened. "I love lobster," I said. Michele beamed her approval. We would bond over food.

I pulled myself up the stairs and collapsed on the double bed. Dust floated in an amber glow beneath a skylight. A loud whistle pierced the air and the building shook as a train rattled by. I closed my eyes and let the rhythmic sound of wheels on tracks rock me to sleep.

2

◆ ◆ ◆

SALT LICK AND CALAMITY

———

I HAD BEEN IN TERRA ALTA less than a week when Jerry gave me an assignment. He rubbed his hands together and bowed toward me, his large frame suddenly graceful. "Here's a great story." He grinned. "Man, you are so lucky." He said that the Olympic whitewater trials were being held in Preston County on the Cheat River. Canoeists and kayakers from across the country would compete for spots on the U.S. Olympic whitewater team. "A national story right in our back yard, less than half an hour from here." Excitement lit his eyes. "Here are directions: Go down Salt Lick to Rowlesburg, then take a right and follow the river until you come to a place full of cars." He told me to watch the river for Calamity Rock, dark gray, the size of a Volkswagen, guardian of a challenging slender passage in the river. "One more thing," he added. "I hate to keep warning you about our bridges but the bridge at the bottom of Salt Lick is only a little less scary than the bridge you crossed over the Cheat past Kingwood." He seemed ashamed.

Calamity Rock. Cheat River. Salt Lick. The place names rolled off Jerry's tongue as if he was saying "Main Street" or "Downtown." Did he know that these names were evocative and musical?

Salt Lick Road started at a rattling railroad bridge in Terra Alta and wound down a steep hill. Scattered houses perched precariously on tiny flat plots that arced like commas next to the angled blacktop. At the valley floor I looked up to the bordering hills, turned glowing green by the morning light. The road straightened a bit and passed a pond. A blue heron stood, one leg crooked out of the water, and I slowed to consider a photo. But I was worried about screwing up my assignment and stepped on the gas. I had a great car for this road, a 1969 BMW sedan.

◆

Cars were one of my father's great passions. He scoured the classified ads, bought neglected gems, restored them, played with them, then sold them. He particularly loved convertibles. When I was in high school we had a series of sports cars: a Triumph, an MG, and an Alfa Romeo Spider. The first time I drove that Alfa, I was giddy with joy. (A car just like one in *The Graduate!*) My father seemed relaxed in the passenger seat as I guided the sleek vehicle through the curves near our house, then took off on a straight stretch. My father leaned over to look at the instrument panel.

"Aren't you going a little fast?" His voice was calm.

"I'm only doing forty!" I shouted over the wind.

"Nancy, that's the tachometer."

He loved to tell that story.

◆

Salt Lick Creek and Salt Lick Road dropped down the valley, past spread-apart farmhouses, barns, and trailers. Clusters of buildings marked family enclaves. The road swooped up and down hills, entered shady, deep woods and emerged into sunlight. It curved along steep banks and played peek-a-boo with the creek and the railroad. If landscape has gender, the valley was definitely female, cleft and voluptuous. Cows buried their noses in new grass. Wildflowers paraded their glory. The valley separated mountains that rose and fell—like breasts, like thighs—closed in, opened up. West Virginia has the history of a woman's hard life: divorced from the more prosperous Virginia at the dawn of the Civil War, raped for her natural resources, damaged and abandoned with her impoverished children. West Virginia is like a woman scorned for her wild appearance and independent ways. Part of her begs for rescue; part of her looks at any offer of help with suspicion. She is so beautiful, a tossed quilt of many colors.

My seduction began that May morning as I followed Salt Lick's fourteen miles—from Terra Alta, half a mile high, to Rowlesburg, fourteen hundred feet above sea level. The sequence of curving road, sudden vistas, and sparkling creek was both new yet familiar.

◆

Salt Lick Valley resembled Wild Horse Creek Valley, the idyllic site of my tomboy youth. From the age of ten until I graduated from high school I had explored the area around our thirteen acres in St. Louis County, in the narrow watershed between Babler State Park and the Missouri River. The western part of the county was wild then, unincorporated, undeveloped. I was particularly fascinated by the natural world. My mother taught me the names of wildflowers and birds. I carried a hammer with me to crack stones in search of fossils and geodes. I particularly liked to visit a small glade two farms over. Our neighbors told me it was a hundred-year-old slave cemetery. They pointed out rough headstones nearly invisible in the vegetation. I spent hours there among violets and gray rocks, touched by imagined history and the graves beneath me.

I was happy in that valley. My sisters and I took care of a small domestic zoo: dogs, cats, horses, chickens, an occasional lamb. We had a Tennessee walking horse that had been retired from the show ring and given to my mother. She joined half a dozen horses owned by various neighbors and pastured on the land next to ours. My sisters and I explored the bluffs overlooking the Missouri River on horseback. Local legend said the outlaw Jesse James had ridden there; the hilly terrain was still sparsely occupied. In a small clearing along an old dirt road, a single Civil War–era grave marked the death of a wounded soldier on his way home. Pine needles hushed our steps in that sacred spot. Wild Horse Creek Valley had history and beauty. Its spaces nurtured me.

When my parents had announced during my senior year of high school that, after I graduated, we would leave Wild Horse Creek Valley and move to Kansas City, I was heartbroken. I understood why we had to move: my father had been commuting between Missouri's two biggest cities for two years. But I mourned the loss of my home, that place.

On the drive down Salt Lick I was thrilled to once again wander through a valley, green hills close above me, blacktop parallel to a creek. This world felt like a larger version of my childhood valley.

◆

As Jerry had warned, the bridge at the bottom of Salt Lick *was* scary—a spindly, narrow hundred yards of wood and iron hung precariously above railroad tracks and the creek. The approach required a ninety-degree turn, and I stopped to make sure another car wasn't heading toward me. The rhythm of tires on planks echoed my pulse.

The Cheat River at Rowlesburg was placid and shallow; its green waters reflected the steep mountains on either side. Past the sleepy town, hillsides closed in to funnel the river through the Cheat Narrows. The terrain compressed the wide green water, threw it against massive boulders, turned it to silver foam. As the river narrowed and curved, bursts of white-capped waves spotted its surface; canoes and kayaks carrying one or two people bobbed in the current. I parked behind a line of cars at the first gravel pull-off. "Is this Calamity Rock?" I asked the first person I saw, a man dressed in a black rubber suit. He looked both ridiculous and serious. He pointed downstream. "Calamity is further. You'll see lots more cars."

I slowed when I saw a group of vehicles in a gravel half circle on my right. I parked and the roar of whitewater announced that I was in the right place. Far below the road, two narrow channels split around an elephant-sized gray boulder. Waterfalls on either side emptied into a churning pool. Boaters approached, one at a time, greeted by whoops from the crowd perched along the banks. The waves heaved the kayaks and canoes toward jagged rocks and the power of the water forced furious paddling. Good pictures! I carefully inched down a dirt trail that plunged over the side of the hill, the camera bag on my shoulder causing me to list dangerously to the left, toward shiny vines with a triad of dark green leaves—poison ivy.

When I reached the river I asked a clipboard-carrying race official for information. He explained the difference between canoes and kayaks. Canoes were open boats; their paddlers knelt. Kayakers stretched their legs in front of them, wore their boats around their hips. He pointed to a ring of fabric at a kayaker's waist. "Keeps water out of the boat," he said.

I perched on a rock opposite Calamity, hoped I was out of range of the spray, and began shooting pictures. I had shot sports before. Football, baseball, and basketball required luck; photographers had to be in the right place at the right time. This was more like shooting wrestling; the action was right in front of me. And this sport held artistic merit, a composition of diagonal boats against a background of water, rocks, and trees.

A shout from the crowd interrupted my concentration and I turned to see a man in the water upstream, his empty boat bearing down on him. He bobbed in the foaming whitewater and was swept over the waterfall. I gasped, but no one else seemed too concerned. Buoyed by his lifejacket, the swimmer broke the surface of the water, grinned, and made his way to the riverbank, waving away the rescue kayak in the eddy beyond the rapids. I turned to see the reaction of the girl who was on the rock beside me. "Maybe it's not as dangerous as it looks," I said.

"I think they're having fun," she said. She clambered off the rock and headed downstream. I turned back to the river.

Through my viewfinder a canoe made a perfect diagonal. The Cheat River danced with energy, the whitewater incandescent.

3

✦ ✦ ✦

NON COMPOS MENTIS

MY FAVORITE SPOT TO READ when I was a sulky teenager was a soft green chair with an ottoman. I don't remember the book I was reading—*Catch-22* or *The Beastly Beatitudes of Balthazar B*, *Man O War*, or *Wuthering Heights*. I do remember that I put the book down because I was hungry, then wandered into the kitchen.

"When's Dad coming home?" I asked.

My mother looked up from washing lettuce. "Nancy, he said 'hello' to you a half an hour ago." She shook her head. "Non compos mentis." Her voice was a singsong deepened by cigarettes. She had uttered those Latin words before. I thought they meant "not paying attention." Years later I discovered the literal translation: not of sound mind.

Words are important to me. I had announced when I was six that I would be a writer. I would live on a farm and write about animals. My favorite writers wrote about horses, and dogs, and donkeys. Their books were like friends, their pages worn soft by touch. A friend of my mother's had given us her old copies of books by Albert Payson Terhune and Walter Farley. Marguerite Henry's books came to my sisters and me on birthdays. Volumes were grouped by author in our walk-in closet.

When I finished devouring my library books, long before they were due, I returned over and over to *Misty of Chincoteague*, *The Black Stallion*, and *Lad, A Dog*. *Brighty of the Grand Canyon* was one of my favorites. Its donkey hero might have been a factor in my becoming a Democrat. Logos are powerful. Then I discovered Louisa May Alcott and the Brontës. Romance, glorious and tragic. My mother, also a passionate reader, shared her library books when she thought I was old enough to read them: Leon Uris, Joseph Heller, Anne Morrow Lindbergh, Truman Capote. I curled up in a soft, green chair and lost myself in words. I tried to drop my expanding vocabulary into everyday conversation, not always with success. My mother caught my errors. "Miss Malaprop!" she chortled. I was also, according to her, "a walking garden of infinitesimal knowledge." Criticism that was tempered with pride.

I don't have any of my early writing—the novel about a young pioneer girl I began at the age of ten, the short stories that won prizes in junior high. And I don't remember when my parents, wary of my ability to earn a living as an author, suggested that I consider a career in journalism.

My family held journalists in high regard. In the 1960s my father ran the St. Louis Press Club. It was a fancy restaurant in the hotel owned by my grandfather, maybe twenty tables with white tablecloths and heavy tableware. Famous front pages anchored the decor. Headlines screamed: "McKinley Shot"—"Titanic Sinks"—"War!" My mother, sisters, and I ate in the coffee shop that shared a kitchen with the Press Club. If I was allowed, I darted into the big restaurant, rounded the room, read all those stories. I absorbed the lessons of type, image, and history.

◆

My journalism career started with my high school newspaper. In 1968, when I was a fifteen-year-old sophomore, the St. Louis *Post-Dispatch* invited me and a hundred other teenage journalists to a press conference with John Danforth, then running for state attorney general. We gathered in a swanky hotel, nicer than my grandfather's hotel. I wanted to ask Danforth whether he supported a proposal to bus inner city black students to suburban schools, a hot topic in St. Louis, where racial strife simmered. My voice and knees shook when I stood to ask Danforth my question. He responded; his deep and rhythmic voice held echoes of his previous calling as a divinity student. Danforth spoke for several minutes about the value of education; he never answered my question. I was outraged. If politicians evaded controversial issues how could voters make educated choices? The role of a journalist was to seek the truth, reveal how the world worked. It was my duty to make the world a better place.

When I was a junior, my high school journalism teacher recognized my passion and proposed journalism camp. I spent the summer before my senior year at the University of Kansas (KU) in Lawrence. The teenagers at Midwestern Music and Art Camp in 1970 were band geeks, singers, painters, and writers. Some were aware that radicals had set the KU student union on fire in April. For months racial unrest had created a war zone in the community. People died. Campers were told to avoid certain areas in town. But I was on the side of hippies and black militants. It was that summer that I went into my first head shop, inhaled patchouli incense, and bought a rainbow patch to sew onto a shirt. (In those days rainbow said hippie, not gay.) Back at camp, deep in the photography lab, I inhaled photo chemicals, developed film, made prints. The camp had loaned me my first 35mm camera, a Pentax, a simple, heavy, metal box. To determine the correct exposure I manipulated a separate device crowded with numbers and dials, a light meter. I struggled with these new tools, so different from my family's cheap Kodak Brownie. But slowly I began to understand the process, to master my new tools.

One afternoon on the way from the lab to the dorm, the camera clunking against my nearly flat chest, I wandered through married students' housing. A small child on a tricycle halted before me on the sidewalk. She looked at me, then the camera, and raised a small dirty arm to block the sun from her eyes. I fumbled with the light meter, clicked to the correct f-stop, and took her picture. The shutter opened and closed with a satisfying clunk. The spontaneity of the moment thrilled me. Back at the dorm among fellow campers I put the camera to my eye and immediately people did what I asked. "Move over there." "Back up." "Sit down." What power! In the darkroom, images rose from liquid as if by magic, a fusion of silver, chemistry, paper, and light. I loved it all: the mechanics, the fumes, the art of composition.

I had been primed. A few years earlier, my grandmother had observed me with a Brownie camera and saw my delight. She recommended that I read Margaret Bourke-White's autobiography. I checked it out of the library and read it straight through. I was captivated by the story of *Life* Magazine's first female photographer, by her powerful photographs. I wanted her life—full of adventure and art. Well, except for the unhappy ending: Bourke-White suffered from Parkinson's and died alone. No children, no husband. When camp concluded, I thought about Margaret Bourke-White. I made an announcement. "I want to be a photographer," I told the head of KU's photojournalism program. He barely looked up from his desk. "Get a Nikon," he growled.

Midwestern Music and Art Camp's journalism division awarded its highest honor, the William Allen White Award, to two students that summer. A journalism professor handed copies of *The Autobiography of William Allen White* to Kurt Andersen and me. I would grow to admire William Allen White, a small-town editor who had a national voice, a man who won the Pulitzer Prize and managed to be a loving father. That was the balance I sought: success with words, photos, and family. I don't know if the book influenced Kurt. He went on to an Ivy League school and built a stellar career in New York as a writer, editor, and public radio host. It was fun to come across his name in a magazine. "I went to journalism camp with him," I'd tell anyone within earshot.

4

❖ ❖ ❖

EMBEDDED

SHORTLY AFTER THE OLYMPIC TRIALS in that summer of 1974, a soldier walked into *The Preston County News* and stood at the counter, a green silhouette against the doorway. He nodded, held out a sheet of paper, and spoke.

"I'm from Camp Dawson. We want this in the next issue of the newspaper." He paused. "We want people to know what's going on when they see armed soldiers in the woods or on the roads." I took the news release. "War games," he said. "We do this every year."

The document was written in all capital letters. Soldiers are coming, it seemed to yell. "Real guns?" I looked up at him. I am short. He was tall.

"Real guns. Fake bullets." He relaxed his posture and leaned against the counter. He had a pleasing countenance. High cheekbones framed a strong jaw, now used for a smile. Friendly. Not like soldiers I had imagined. I didn't actually know any soldiers. The boys of my youth had been determined to avoid Vietnam, a war that haunted my high school and college years. A friend we called Tall Tom abused amphetamines to become too thin for the Army. When another friend, Mike, blew out his knee playing tetherball everyone celebrated. Boys my age disappeared when their school deferments failed or when they lost the draft's birthday lottery. Vietnam was the boogeyman. It was still a quagmire that summer.

"You're new here?" the soldier asked.

"Yes. From Missouri."

He stood at ease while I read the press release. For two weeks, in a pretend war, United States Army Special Forces "guerillas" would fight "invaders" who had penetrated from the East Coast to the Ohio Valley. The guerillas' objective was to disrupt the invaders' supply lines.

"Which side are you on?" I asked.

He smiled, sly and charming. "Confidential." Did he wink at me?

Preston County's small military compound, Camp Dawson, where this soldier worked, hosted the training mission because Briery Mountain resembled Central America, where the next conflict was anticipated. At the time I couldn't conceive of wars to come, guerillas in deserts and barren lands.

◆

Yellow ribbons were everywhere that summer. Both bright new bands and pale, tattered shreds decorated trees along every country road, fluttered in dozens of yards. Without words, they meant, "I love a soldier," or "I support our troops," and, sometimes, "I hate hippies." "America: Love It or Leave It" was a popular slogan then.

Jerry no doubt was amused by the prospect of sending me to cover the war games. "Are you a hippie?" he had asked soon after I started work. He examined me from head to toe, took in patched jeans and embroidered top. "You dress like a hippie." Jerry seemed to know about costume. When dressed in a casual, checked shirt, he oozed a folksy persona, but he could also play serious businessman in a coat and tie.

I denied being a hippie. True hippies don't have jobs, I told Jerry. I didn't admit that I was a wannabe hippie. My favorite shirt was decorated with that rainbow patch I'd bought while I was at journalism camp in Lawrence, Kansas. I often paired it with an ankle-length skirt pieced together from old blue jeans. I thought I looked radical and cool, but in Terra Alta, the outfit made me an object of curiosity. When the Terra Alta garbage men pointed at me and laughed, I realized that my clothing branded me an outsider.

◆

It wasn't the first time in my life that clothing had caused trouble. Miniskirts were the fashion when I was in high school in the late 1960s and early 1970s. It was a struggle to stay decent as hemlines rose. Girls weren't allowed to wear pants and I didn't understand why. Boys wore jeans. It seemed unfair. I had been paying attention in civics class. History too. Civil disobedience might pay off, I thought. On a fall morning in 1969, my junior year, I wore a pair of wide-legged blue pants. Hip-huggers. White polka dots. Really cool. My friends wore their best trousers. We thought jeans might be too provocative. The word had gotten out. Two hundred girls showed up that morning wearing pants. Before the morning bell the intercom came to life: "Nancy Abrams, please come to the office."

My mother had been called in that morning to be a substitute teacher; she stood next to the vice principal. I had told her that he reminded me of Richard Nixon. She subbed often enough to know all the characters involved.

"You're violating the dress code," the vice principal said. "You need to change your clothes."

"I can't take her home," my mother said. "I have to teach."

"The dress code *specifically* says girls *can* wear pants under their dresses in the winter. It doesn't say they can't wear them at other times," I said. I had done my homework.

The vice principal pointed to a page in the small pamphlet. "The principal can make revisions to the code as needed," he quoted. "He did that this morning."

My social studies teacher pushed into the room. She was blonde and petite and fashionably dressed. Her hemline was above her knees. All of the boys had a crush on her.

"That's an ex post facto law forbidden by the United States

Constitution." My voice filled the crowded space. I can be loud when I need to be.

"She's right, you know." My teacher nodded at me. "She's right!"

We lost. My fellow revolutionaries had brought skirts to school. I had not. I had to wait in the office until my father brought me a skirt. Our group of radicals crowded into the restroom and altered our hemlines with masking tape. I taped my green dirndl too. Our skirts were so short that we couldn't sit down without being lewd. We stood next to our desks all day: young, vertical feminists. Early the next spring, the dress code was amended and jeans became the new school uniform. A few weeks after that, on May 4, 1970, Ohio National Guardsmen at Kent State University killed four students during an antiwar protest. Antiwar demonstrations spread across the country. When students at Washington University joined that tide, I wanted to be there. A group of us tied black bands around our arms and tried to sneak out of school. The vice principal ambushed us in the parking lot and marched us back to class.

◆

Now, four years later, Jerry was sending me to "war." The newspaper apparently had a role in these games. We were on the guerilla's side; our job was to support and document their mission. I would spend as much time as possible with the soldiers, although I would not stay overnight in their camps.

On a warm June evening, the sky filled with parachutes as hundreds of paratroopers, "reinforcements," according to the game rules, joined the guerillas. The exercise, called a night drop, was ostensibly secret, but dozens of spectators showed up at Camp Dawson to gaze skyward. The billowing chutes erupted in bursts from noisy planes; the moonlit white silk swelled and swayed above us. Enchanted by this shower of men and fabric, I was troubled: What kind of pacifist gets stirred by military spectacle?

A plummeting object and a loud smack prompted a flurry of activity, and unease rippled through the crowd. Had a parachute failed? Was a soldier hurt? Someone yelled that it was a loose helmet and spectators exhaled. Men continued to rain from the sky; boots thudded as they hit the ground. Shadowy figures clustered together then merged with the dark woods surrounding the camp.

The next morning I joined the guerillas on Caddell Mountain in the Briery range. In their green uniforms, faces smeared with black paint, the soldiers blended into their surroundings, spidery underbrush scattered beneath immature timber. Some of the men wore the green berets and insignia of the Special Forces. A popular ballad that praised "the brave men of the Green Beret" had been all over the radio. My friends in the antiwar movement hated the song, but its catchy staccato beat immediately came back to me. Here among men I had considered the "enemy," my cameras were my shield; behind them my stance on the war was hidden. "Do you want us to pose?" a soldier asked. "No," I said. "Ignore me." The guerillas moved uphill, their eyes sweeping the woods, their expressions alert. The weapons they carried were unfamiliar but these men slung them casually across their shoulders or held them close. Even loaded with blanks, the guns seemed threatening. I was fascinated. When we paused to rest, I asked for a closer look. "Folding stock carbine" and "M-16" were uttered in explanation, the guns held out for me to inspect. When I grasped each weapon, I kept my fingers on the stock and avoided the cold metal, the barrel, and the trigger. I knew a little about guns. My father had taught my sisters and me how to shoot. We had picked off clay pigeons with a .410 shotgun and blasted holes in beer cans with a .22 pistol. But these weapons were different; they had no hint of sport. Had any been used in Vietnam? I picked up my Nikon, held it to my eye, and, with a shudder, identified the parallel between gun and camera: find your prey, aim, then shoot.

A soldier squatted nearby and unfolded a rectangular piece of white plastic covered with squiggly concentric circles. I could see it was a very strange map—I leaned forward to touch it. The men gathered around. "Topographic," one explained. "These circles indicate altitude." He pointed to our destination, an inner ring marking the top of the ridge. A young soldier, his face smeared with greasy black and green paint, crouched away from the others, his expression blank. I remembered hearing his soft southern voice earlier. I raised the camera and squeezed the shutter. My heart beat faster; I knew that I had made a strong portrait. I asked the soldier for his name. "Phil," he said, and spelled the name of his home town. I took more pictures, wrote more names, and in this way, became acquainted with the group.

They climbed through the woods. The slanted ground was scattered with rocks. Briars pulled at our pants, piles of leaves amplified our steps. The soldiers settled into their game. They moved cautiously, alert, looking for the "enemy"—military teams pretending to be invading forces. The guerillas feared the shame of capture and "incarceration" in the county jail. We made our way uphill, the walk interrupted by their questions:

"Where are you from?" a soldier asked.

"Missouri." I shifted the heavy camera bag to check my film supply.

"I've never seen a girl photographer." This soldier seemed perplexed. "Why do you want to be a photographer?"

I didn't think I should talk about Margaret Bourke-White, the photographer in the book my grandmother recommended; I couldn't imagine that this soldier had heard of her. Instead I said I had always been interested by photographs in newspapers and magazines.

Another soldier dropped back to walk beside me. Richard was mustached and muscular and he leaned toward me, intense. "So, are you a woman's libber?" he asked, a drawl revealing his southern West Virginia roots. Although his voice was kind, I heard a challenge in it.

"Yes," I admitted. I suspected this would also peg me as antiwar, and by association, anti-soldier. Instead Richard cracked a crinkly grin, and I noticed how green his eyes were. Was he coming on to me? A tickle of attraction threatened my professional mien, so I knelt to dig through my camera bag. I didn't want to flirt back. I knew how susceptible I was to seduction. I loved sex, its irresistible mixture of sensuality and physicality. The feel of bare skin. But this was not an appropriate setting for flirtation. I straightened up, took on what I hoped was the aura of a professional journalist, and rejoined the group. When we paused again, I pulled out my notebook. "Tell me about the war," I said, a request I had never made of my own father, a veteran of World War II.

Richard started talking first. "Jumping out of a plane is better than sex," he said. He raised an arm over his head. "Falling free, then whump!" His arm fell. He ducked his head and a blush crept up his neck. A chorus of agreement from his buddies bolstered his confidence. "Every man here is a Vietnam vet," he announced. "West Virginia has more enlistees per capita than any other state." He spoke with pride. "Each of them, every single one, went to Vietnam a patriot."

The other soldiers nodded. These men were just a little older than I was but the gulf between us seemed vast. I thought a summer internship in West Virginia would be an adventure. The soldiers next to me had been halfway around the world fighting in jungles and rice paddies. They had returned to a country that seemed to have no use for them. A couple of the guys seemed more like schoolteachers than soldiers—bespectacled, eager to share their skills. One man could have come from a vintage war movie: the gregarious city boy with dark, wavy hair and an Italian last name. Then there was shy Phil, captured by my camera. And Richard. They talked about the friends they had made "in country," the intensity of their experience, the damp heat of Vietnam, the terror, and the excitement.

I wanted to ask these questions: "Are you still patriots?" "What do you think of a country that does not welcome its soldiers when they return from war?" "Do you know that some people call you baby killers?" Instead I picked up my camera and shot pictures I knew I wouldn't like. The sun was high in the sky and filtered by leaves that cast mottled patterns on the soldiers' faces. I knew any print I made would be ugly, its whites too white and blacks too black. This high contrast turned faces sinister. I put the camera down, quickened my steps. I wasn't afraid that these soldiers would harm me. I was afraid I would insult them. I decided I could masquerade as a sort of mascot, the tomboy little sister following guys through the woods. I wouldn't ask the hard questions.

As the hours passed, the quality of light improved and so did my mood. The Green Berets had turned out to be nice guys. By the time we reached the top of the mountain, our banter had turned teasing and friendly. A vast hayfield lay below us and the wind arrived in waves of dancing grass. The openness after the shelter of the woods felt like freedom. Just inside the woods line, the soldiers set up "camp," tarps strung from trees. A few shared C-rations: cans of some sort of meat product, covered by a film of grease, fruit cocktail, crackers. I gratefully accepted a candy bar. Some of the men went to forage for food, and one soldier returned successful. He held a box turtle by its tail and asked for butchering help. The turtle's legs paddled in the air. It didn't have the sense to withdraw into its shell; instead the head stretched up, with alert eyes and a mouth that seemed to smile. I shot a photo of a disembodied hand holding the small reptile, then turned away. A hypocrite, I could not watch the butchering. Later, when the turtle had been roasted, a soldier offered me a small piece. It was chewy and tasteless. "Not bad," I lied.

As I prepared to leave their camp that evening, the soldiers surrounded me. "We want to take a picture of *you*," one said. The Italian held out a green Army jacket for me to put on. "No, no, no," I weakly protested. "*I'm* the photographer." Outnumbered, I handed over my camera. Richard plopped a cap onto my head and tucked a gun under my arm. I faced the woods and heard the shutter release, a loud, metallic sound.

◆

A few days later I followed a guerilla on a scouting mission. He strode across an old railroad bridge that jutted over the Cheat River. Creosote-soaked ties spaced ten inches apart framed rectangles of whitewater. The height, the pervious base beneath me, rendered me helpless. My heart thrummed and a wave of panic brought me to a stop. The disguised soldier moved farther away. I raised my camera and shot two frames. One was published in the newspaper; it shows a broad-shouldered man in a plaid shirt walking away, hands hanging at his sides. The tracks stretch in front of him and the riffles in the water below are visible. It is an aesthetically pleasing image; my distress is utterly absent. After I took those photos, I dropped to my knees and crawled back to solid ground, shamed and shaken. The soldiers in these war games were fierce and brave and proud. And I, the pacifist, was felled by a fear of heights.

◆

Jerry had arranged my rendezvous with a guerilla officer at a beer joint on U.S. Route 50. A couple of old pickups sat in the gravel lot of the

Blue Moon, a wood-frame building not much bigger than a chicken coop. A crescent moon cut into the door made it look like an outhouse. Captain Jesse Jennings was easy to spot in the dim interior, where every light fixture advertised beer. He sat erect amid men slouched over the sticky bar. It seemed unnecessary to use the code word I had been given. Instead, I nodded at Jesse. He touched the brim of his hat in introduction, leaned toward me, and in a low voice asked if I had been followed.

"I don't think so." I shook my head, ashamed that I had not uttered the password Jerry had shared. "I hope not." We walked outside and Jesse gave me an update on the war. So far the guerillas had resisted the invading force. They had attacked supply lines and enlisted local sympathizers.

"Like your newspaper," he said. His voice was that of a teacher. "Remember, if you get captured you could go to jail." He didn't smile.

"I hope not," I said.

We headed west on Route 50; Jesse steered with casual grace, an elbow angled out the window. Crew cut, small features, a serious look. Like the soldiers on Caddell Mountain, Jesse was probably a Vietnam veteran. If I asked, I thought, he might not be able to tell that I belonged to an antiwar tribe. Jesse broke the quiet. "Where are you from?"

"Missouri," I answered.

"Missouri? I thought you were from New York." He was not the first person that summer to say that. At first I didn't get it. My accent was Midwestern. Then I realized they saw the Star of David around my neck and recognized that I was Jewish. To them Jewish equaled New York.

"No. St. Louis," I said. "The Midwest." I touched the small, gold star, a nervous habit.

Jesse kept his eyes on the road. We headed east and quickly turned onto a dirt road. "I need to stop up home," Jesse explained. Huge boulders, gray and textured, jutted out of the ground; a house and barn nestled in flat spots. Three towheaded children surrounded the truck. They grinned at me. Jesse's wife came out of the house, projected the same smile, and introduced herself.

"Want to come with us to feed our calf?" The two older children, a boy and a girl, shifted from foot to foot. "He's a market steer. Going to the Buckwheat Festival in September," the boy told me. They walked barefoot through the field on the way to the barn, the boy carrying a metal bucket with a rubber nipple the size of my middle finger jutting from the bottom. In a small corral, a calf ran up and butted his head against the bucket. He began to suck the nipple. Loudly.

"Bad manners." I laughed. "Excuse you."

The children laughed. The girl stroked the calf's sleek brown neck while the boy struggled to keep the calf from wrenching the bucket from his hand. I wondered that these kids could have a relationship with an animal whose fate is to be food. A market steer is beef—hamburger, steak, roasts.

At our next stop, Jesse's brother's farm, we found a band of soldiers "liberating" a pig behind a weathered barn. The hog squealed as the men tied its feet to sturdy poles.

"We actually bought it." Jesse bent to my ear and whispered. Like the market steer, this hog was bred to be food. He struggled against the ropes but quieted when four soldiers hoisted him into the air. They headed uphill at a brisk pace.

It started to drizzle; the low, gray sky promised heavier rain. I wrapped my camera gear in plastic bags and followed the men across a barbed wire fence. The pig bearers took a zigzag route up the steep mountain. Brambles grabbed at me as I struggled to keep up with the brisk pace, my heavy gear insignificant compared to the soldiers' burden. When at last we reached the summit, the rain gathered force. Big drops fell fast, quivering off of leaves and soaking the ground. Soldiers had constructed a shelter of tarps among huge thickets covered by surreal, grapefruit-sized clusters of white blossoms. These flowers were totally unfamiliar, spectacular domes of small white flowers with pink centers. I reached out to touch one. "Rhododendron," Jesse explained, "the West Virginia state flower." He smiled at my surprise.

While I was looking at flowers, a soldier killed the pig, slit its throat and belly. I turned to see bright blood spilling over the ground and steam rising from the blue-gray entrails that fell in a ropy cascade. The sight and the smell were a shock. I put the camera in front of my face, and pursed my lips to control my breath. I pressed the shutter and took several pictures that I knew I would never print.

Under another tarp, soldiers squatted around a topographic map. Fingers traced a proposed route. These guerillas were going to "destroy" a railroad switch along Raccoon Creek, a few miles away. They rose, ready for the assault. I followed them down the hill, now slick from the rain. We climbed into the back of Jesse's pickup truck, its camper top offering cover from both enemy and elements. Raccoon Creek turned out to be a trickle of water framed by orange rocks. I later learned that acid mine drainage had poisoned the area. The rusted skeleton of an old coal tipple loomed above us; the ruins of an old deep mine lay buried close by. Huge, asphalt-like chunks of coal mining waste were mounded everywhere.

"Gob piles," Jesse said. The words were as ugly as the landscape.

The rail bed followed a narrow swath of flat land next to the creek. During the Civil War, the Confederate Army eyed vulnerable rail sites like this in Preston County. Their goal was the same as the guerillas': the disruption of supply lines. The mountains had not been scarred by coal mining then. The soldiers probably could have filled canteens in Raccoon Creek. Not anymore. The soldiers proceeded cautiously along the track, close to the cover of the woods, wary of capture. Something in their posture, the way they moved, triggered memories of the television show *Combat*, my father's favorite series. He had served in the Army Air Corps during World War II, but all my father said about his experience was that he raced sports cars on the airstrips of France. He taught my sisters and me the French he had learned: *Cherchez les femmes;* look for the women. On Tuesday evenings, the black and white images on our little television taught me more about war than the man next to me on the couch. My sisters and I understood that the topic was off-limits. The men in front of me following the tracks might have been willing to answer questions had I inquired. But my father had made me afraid to ask, afraid any query would cross a forbidden line.

We reached the rail switch, and the soldiers tied ribbons to the metal to mark their successful "strike" against the enemy. I expected a celebration, but the group was nonchalant. Maybe the victory was anticlimactic compared to their real war experiences. Or maybe they thought it would look silly to applaud a ribbon on a railroad spike. Still, there was pride in their thrown-back shoulders, in Jesse's approving nod. They had won this battle against the invaders.

◆

At the end of the week, the soldiers returned to Camp Dawson and invited me to join them for a postwar party. We drank beer and played poker and I continued the flirtation with Richard that had begun in the woods. Most of the other soldiers were married; they encouraged our amorous pursuit. I liked Richard's green eyes, the way he moved. He had gone to college, was an engineer in the coal industry. He had a cool car, a Datsun 240Z. My seduction was sealed when he told me he was a widower, that his wife had died suddenly when a blood vessel burst in her brain. He had a son, Richie, who was two. Richard's eyes gleamed with need, or lust. I wanted to wrap myself around him. Later that night I did. We undressed in my trailer and I noticed areas of inflamed skin at the top of his thighs, spilling toward his crotch. In bed, I ran my fingers over the red patches.

"Jock rot," Richard said, his drawl beguiling in spite of those unseemly words. "Started in Vietnam. Can't get rid of it." He held himself above me on strong arms. "It's not catching," he said.

◆

When the war games ended, I processed my film, made prints, and wrote a story. My contact sheets were heavily marked with red grease pencil squares. One outlined picture, though, was not for publication. I made a five by seven inch print of the photo of me that the soldiers had shot. The image was remarkably similar to the portrait of kidnapped heiress Patty Hearst that had been on magazine covers that year. There had been much public debate about that portrait, taken by the Symbionese Liberation Army. Some thought it proved that Hearst's abductors had brainwashed her. Others believed that she willingly became a militant radical. I made another print and mailed it to my parents. They were amused by the reference to Patty Hearst. But months later, back in Missouri, the picture still made me uneasy. I looked at my face, at the gun I pointed out of the frame. I thought I knew who I was: a liberal, a pacifist. But this woman, her mouth on the verge of a smile, seemed to be someone else entirely.

5

◆ ◆ ◆

I GROW FOND

———

In July, Rich, Jerry's business partner, burst into *The News* office; he waved a small sheaf of paper above his head. "A quiz! I have a type quiz for you!" He came around the counter and with a grand gesture laid a beige rectangle on my desk. Sentences were stacked underneath a small flourish, a spot of art he called a dingbat. I picked up the paper: "The quick brown fox jumps over the lazy dog" in repeated lines down the page. Each slightly different, but how? I examined the serifs, felt letters as imprints in the thick paper. Rich shifted his weight from foot to foot, nearly dancing with glee. I had aced the last test, but this one was tough. I peered again at the paper, frowned.

"Give up?" Rich turned to walk away and pivoted. "It's Caslon, all Caslon," he cackled. "Different foundries!"

Rich's hobby wasn't much different from what he did for a living. He arranged type and subjected it to ink, paper, and pressure. Although computers and offset presses had taken over his work life, he could always retreat to the basement of his house, filled with beloved letterpresses and a world-class collection of type. When he saw that I was interested in type and design, he became my personal professor. He invited me to his home for dinner with his family and led me into his basement. I pulled out trays of old type: wood and metal, familiar, obscure; pleasing in its lines and curves, its communicative shapes. I showed off, proved that I knew the California job case, the wooden tray that organized the type. It had been the subject of a test in a graphic design class the semester before. Rich's enthusiasm felt like praise.

◆

Rich and Jerry also enthusiastically pointed me toward stories and pushed. *The Preston County News* provided an extravagant canvas. A four-page tabloid (a publication the size of a folded-in-half newspaper) for the war games. An eight-page tab about the doctor shortage in Preston County. That was the biggest project of the summer. Rich, Jerry, and Michele all contributed stories. I followed Terra Alta's general practitioner for weeks. I photographed him in his office, on house calls, at the hospital. *Life* Magazine and W. Eugene Smith had already done the ultimate country doctor story in 1948; I knew my efforts would disappoint in comparison. But I was pleased by my photos, proud of *The Preston County News*. Rich and Jerry were determined to show me that publishing was a noble business, that words and pictures arranged on paper mattered. They knew what they were doing. Before they taught journalism, both had served as information officers for the Army. Their mission in Preston County was equal parts journalism, printing, propaganda, and profit. In the mid-1970s, the Arab Oil Embargo had created a demand for a coal. West Virginia was still a poor state but the economy was improving.

◆

Jerry was the salesman in the partnership. He sold ads for the newspaper, sold printing to businesses. The Pioneer Press turned out forms, brochures, flyers, and creative publications. Jerry had hustle. He had charisma. He had ambition. He was chairman of the upcoming Preston County Buckwheat Festival, a fall county fair that brought thousands of dollars to the area. He promoted the event with P. T. Barnum-like zeal and spoke of the festival as if you'd be a fool to miss it. Jerry had become enamored of the hammered dulcimer, made and played by local brothers. To promote the festival he took his dulcimer on the road—to schools and civic groups, to radio stations and senior citizens meetings.

He practiced in the office, delicate mallets in large hands dancing across strings. The music he coaxed from the gleaming instrument echoed through the building, off the wood floors, hovered in air flavored by the smell of ink. Tinkly, old-time music that sounded like a confluence of banjo and harpsichord. Vibration and sweet tone.

Jerry celebrated the mountain culture. I didn't know it then—and I'm not sure that this was a deliberate calculation on his part—but he was laying the groundwork for a career in politics. We often talked about politics that summer. I crowed with delight when Nixon was forced to hand over the Watergate tapes. Jerry called himself a Democrat, but his opinions sounded Republican to me. He was not ashamed to have voted for Richard Nixon. He was skeptical about environmental laws. He kept a sharp eye on government: town councils, the school board, the county commission, and state lawmakers. Jerry was unafraid to voice his views on the editorial page. He thought government mattered and that his opinion counted. Jerry clamored for better schools, better roads, and better services. Politics delighted him; powerful people interested him. He could be charming, which helped him sell ads for *The Preston County News*, printing for the Pioneer Press, and rural journalism to me.

Jerry also was a good writer, an authentic storyteller. His folksy tone softened his editorial scolding and won him fans. His coverage of a Memorial Day celebration in a small, mountaintop cemetery showed me he was a talented photographer. Writer, photographer, editor: he did it all. Jerry had me cover the Terra Alta Fourth of July—the oldest, continuous celebration in the state, he said—and Good Neighbor Days in Bruceton. Their parades were the only traffic jams I witnessed that summer. Keening fire trucks, convertibles bearing politicians, and marching bands. Girls in gowns on floats of varying sophistication. I was particularly drawn to the aesthetically pleasing: handsome faces, interesting buildings. It was as if in defiance I photographed pretty things. Sure, I took pictures of poor West Virginia. It's what people expected. But they wouldn't expect pretty West Virginia. Jerry didn't mind that I shot roll after roll of film. "Film is cheap," he said as he peered at my negatives, evaluated my prints.

◆

In addition to Jerry and Rich, I also grew to really like Annie, the office manager who was a year older than I was and knew everybody in Terra Alta. She had lived there her entire life. When she was born, not in a hospital but on the family dairy farm, she was so small that they feared she would die. "They put me in a shoe box and kept me in the oven," she told me. Her family hosted a picnic for me, an old-fashioned corn roast, on their farm. The tables sagged from the weight of food—hams and turkeys and salads and sweets in endless variety. A boy fished from a dock that jutted into a pond a little removed from the food and bustle around the picnic tables, his line the source of spreading ripples.

I also made some friends in my neighborhood. One afternoon early in June two little girls, one of whom I'd seen mere minutes before, stood on the steps to my trailer. "Pia told me you gave her a cookie." The speaker had cropped blonde hair and enormous blue eyes in a heart-shaped face. She looked like a doll. "I'm Ellie. I live over there." She indicated a house up the hill. "My mom won't mind if you give me a cookie too."

This pair of girls would wait for me to come home from work. Once they figured out what I did, they'd perform for me.

"Look, look!" Ellie demanded. She struck a purse-lipped pose that rendered her beauty grotesque. She called it her "fish face."

"Ellie! Pia!" A woman's voice would summon the girls.

Ellie would lean out the door. "We're at this lady's house," she said. Lady? She was referring to me as a lady? Did this mean she thought I was a grown-up? I didn't feel like a grown-up.

◆

When I had free time, I drove down Salt Lick. The valley never failed to enchant me. I would find a wide spot to park my car, then I'd wade in the creek. I spread a blanket on top of sun-warmed stones and opened a book. It was so quiet, so lush. I was sure I had discovered paradise. I loved my job, the people I met, and this beautiful place.

6

✦ ✦ ✦

TAKE ME HOME, COUNTRY ROADS

———

WHEN I DROVE OUT OF TERRA ALTA on a warm August day in 1974 and headed west, Richard Nixon's face was on nearly every television in nearly every house I passed, a blue, flickering light. I could scarcely contain my joy. Resigned! Nixon had resigned! I despised Tricky Dick—his sad dishonesty, his shiny ambition, his disdain for my tribes: hippies, Jews, journalists. I had hated him for years. He *was* a crook. Watergate happened while I was majoring in journalism. To me, journalists were heroic, especially those involved in exposing the Watergate story—righteous truth tellers. And this was my chosen profession.

Nixon be damned and gone, I thought.

As I headed away from Terra Alta, wave after wave of forested mountains filled the horizon, a view that just months before had been foreign. To my left, Terra Alta nestled in a shallow dip in the hills. I cranked open the sunroof of my car and tears started. The wind turned them cool on my face. In the passenger seat, my beat-up portable cassette player blared *Elephant Mountain*. Jesse Colin Young's high, pure voice prompted more crying. I was sad to leave the newspaper and the mountains. But my summer in West Virginia was over. The work I had done from May to August was captured in sheets of newsprint, silver gelatin prints, negatives filed in translucent glassine sleeves. I was headed back to Missouri.

In a farewell column for the newspaper, I confessed I had expected West Virginia to be full of "hillbillies and moonshine and people who would as soon shoot at me as talk to me." But, I wrote, "I was wrong. I have found nothing but wonderful people who are more than willing to tell the girl from Missouri interesting stories about life in Mountaineer country." I praised the beautiful landscape. "I can't imagine what I'm going to do back in Missouri when I look out a window and don't see a mountain."

What I didn't say, what I didn't know to say, was how the beauty of those mountains affected me. The green hills, undulating forests, and the music of water as it tumbled over rocks felt like nourishment. The aesthetics of the landscape brought me joy. I had come to Preston County to build a strong portfolio, one that would set me apart from other aspiring photojournalists. My objective was to shoot pictures that would win me a coveted job on a good newspaper. Rich and Jerry let me take my negatives, a generous gift. Stacked in pink envelopes, these magic strips of emulsion contained my future.

My reverie as I was leaving was interrupted by a glance at my dashboard. The car, an old BMW, had been overheating all summer, the gauge rising suddenly into the red zone every time I drove up a mountain, which was often. The local mechanic didn't know what to do. "I don't know much about foreign cars," he said. He raised the hood, then raised his ball cap to scratch his head.

"I can pull the thermostat," he offered. "It won't hurt anything, since you don't need your heater. But if that don't fix your problem. . . ." He shrugged apologetically. "Just make sure you keep the radiator filled so you don't crack the block."

Ever since, I'd kept a couple of gallon jugs filled with water behind my seat. That summer, when the gauge did its accelerated rise, I'd pulled over to the side of the road, waited a while for the steam to dissipate, then refilled the radiator. This lesson in patience was easier to take in Preston County, where the roadside view was pleasant and the traffic unthreatening. But the trip west across Interstate 70 was less charming. In Indiana, in the middle of a downpour, the gauge rose soon after I had already refilled the radiator and again I pulled onto the shoulder, the empty gallon jugs rattling on the floor. The traffic splashed by as I poked my head out of the sunroof, an umbrella in one hand and a hastily scribbled sign pleading for water in the other. Finally, a trucker stopped and we used his empty soda cans to ladle water from the roadside ditch into my radiator.

I was unnerved. I called my parents. I needed to get back to their home in Kansas City in time for my older sister's wedding. Thankfully, my father still had "car friends" in St. Louis who promised to fix the car. While it was in the shop, I stayed with a friend from high school. She was already a wife and a mother with a neat brunette bob shaped by rollers. My hair was lanky and long. We were a 1970s study in contrasts: grown-up versus flower child. Across a living room filled with early American furniture, the old rhythm of our relationship faltered. I was shocked to hear that my friend considered herself a Republican. Two years later, on an election night trip through St. Louis, she would (slightly in jest) slam the door in my face when I announced that I had voted for Jimmy Carter. Despite this incident we have remained friends into what I call our perigeriatric years: an age not quite geriatric but circling it.

◆

At my older sister Julie's wedding that August in a Kansas City hotel, I was both bridesmaid and photographer. That dual role—participant and observer—was difficult. I couldn't wholly inhabit either character. I didn't know then that this dichotomy would be a challenge throughout my professional life. The wedding was a happy occasion; my parents loved Julie's new husband. A cousin asked, "Will you be next?" I shook my head. "I'd need a boyfriend first," I said. I thought about my brief summer romance with Richard, the soldier, and the passion I had felt with him. I wanted to be in love, to find my mate. I wondered who it would be.

During my stay in Kansas City, I couldn't shake the feeling that I no longer belonged in the Midwest. The landscape of shallow hills, strip malls, and subdivisions offered none of the excitement I had found in West Virginia. And the people, including my own family, seemed cut from the same fabric—white, middle class, predictable.

Right after the wedding I returned to college for my senior year. It felt anticlimactic, an intermission before real life. The only thing that mattered to me was my portfolio, a collection of images that would determine my fate. In April 1975, I huddled with other photojournalists on the verge of graduation. We hunched over contact sheets, requested critical opinions, and outlined the negatives we would print with red grease pencil. I pulled several all-nighters in the darkroom. Accompanied by Joni Mitchell's pure voice, I rocked chemical-filled trays until the images rose, a process that never ceased to thrill. Here were the images from my summer in West Virginia. I welcomed them like old friends. Hypo stains dotted my clothes, my nails were stained by Dektol, and the lights of the outside world seemed too bright.

I had spent my senior year working as an undergraduate teaching assistant in the photo lab and after nine months of regarding students' prints in dripping trays, I became both teacher and critic. My portfolio, the twenty prints that represented my best work, was good. I was good. Because of that summer in Preston County, my pictures were unusual: the whitewater race for my sports submission, rural scenes, portraits that resembled images from the 1930s, the country doctor story. My professors asked me and several other students to apply for internships with *National Geographic* magazine. The photo editor at the *Geographic* was a Missouri alumnus and usually awarded at least one of the three internship slots to a Missouri student. Just weeks before the semester ended, in the tiny office shared by all the teaching assistants, the professors announced that three of us—Charlie, Len, and I—were among the five finalists for the *Geographic* internship. Later, in the Heidelberg, the beer joint next to the journalism school, the three of us ordered fried mushrooms. These crunchy, juicy treats had sustained us through the school year. At this celebratory meal, we ate and drank and told each other that it didn't matter who got the job. I was delighted to be a finalist. But I thought Charlie and Len were better. They had hustle, more ambition. Squeezed into a booth and uncomfortable on the peeling vinyl seat, I heard the last notes of the Eagles fade on the jukebox. The early jangles of "Take Me Home, Country Roads" made me sit up. The guys nudged me.

"They're playing your song," Len joked. We were not John Denver fans. Still, when Denver warbled, "West Virginia, Mountain Mama," tears filled my eyes. What a summer I had had.

When I talked to my parents that weekend, they offered practical advice: if I could find a job now, then I wouldn't have to gamble on the internship. In fact, a professor had mentioned that the *Miami Herald* was looking for a woman photographer. But I hesitated. I didn't want to be a token, hired simply for my sex. And I didn't like hot, humid weather; the closed-in comfort of air conditioning made me claustrophobic. I thought of summer in Preston County—temperatures in the mid-seventies, an ever-present breeze, those mountains. My parents had infected me with their scorn for big cities, their hatred of traffic, and their fear of crime. When I had covered the Terra Alta Fourth of July celebration, I had left an expensive lens on a picnic table. Just minutes later, a young boy brought it to me and said, "This looks like it's yours." Another Missouri student interned in Cleveland and had all of his camera equipment stolen his first night in that city.

I realized that Miami held no charm for me.

Preston County did.

I wanted to use my talents to right the world's wrongs. I wanted the view out my window to sustain me. I wanted a life. I wanted to be a wife, a mother. I remembered again how my grandmother changed my life when she had me read Margaret Bourke-White's autobiography. Now, a decade later, I considered Bourke-White's success as a pioneering photojournalist and wanted more. Work *and* a life. At that moment I decided I would go back to Preston County. In that place, I thought, I could have it all.

The next morning I called Jerry, nervously twisted the phone cord around my finger. "I might be crazy, but I want to come back," I said.

He laughed. "You *are* crazy!" Then he stopped laughing, quietly asked, "Are you sure?" When I told him yes, he said he'd talk to Rich.

He called me back an hour later. ""Want to be managing editor? Michele and I both want to spend more time with the Pioneer Press. We'll pay you a hundred twenty-five dollars a week."

I accepted.

I had the highest title and lowest salary of my graduating class.

Len and Charlie won the *National Geographic* internships.

7

❖ ❖ ❖

REAL LIFE

IF I HAD ANY DOUBTS about my decision to return to Preston County, they were dispelled by a freelance job I did just after graduation in May 1975. During my senior year of college, a visiting photojournalism professor had taken a group of us to New Ulm, Minnesota, where we photographed many facets of that town and its surrounding farms for DOCUMERICA, a program sponsored by the Environmental Protection Agency. It was my first real experience shooting color slides, which demand precise exposures. Scary. During this field trip, I had spent time with a farm family in the nearby community of Sleepy Eye, and just before I graduated, DOCUMERICA contacted me asking if I would shoot more pictures of the family's activities. I agreed to their offer and decided I'd fit the job in before I headed East. My father took a photo of me before I left. In the photo, I have two cameras hanging from my neck, an overfull camera bag on one shoulder, a tripod on the other. I squeeze a large box of film against my hip. I am overburdened. The physical weight of the equipment was my first hint that the life of *National Geographic* photographers might not be so glamorous.

When I got to Sleepy Eye, the farm family welcomed me back. "Ignore me. Don't look at the camera," I said, and they followed those instructions. I was with them in the fields, the barns, and the kitchen, where I often gorged on homemade bread and jam. In spite of my travel alarm clock, I was usually the last one out of bed. The family's work ethic put me to shame. When I wasn't feeling guilty about that, I was worried about the photos, about my lack of experience with color film. The job took a week and that entire time I felt alone and under enormous pressure. When the work was done, I was glad to leave. As the plane rose over the flat fields of the upper Midwest, I leaned back in my seat and looked forward to my new life in the mountains, at *The Preston County News*.

◆

When I arrived at my parents' townhouse in Kansas City after my freelance job was complete, I was pleasantly surprised.

My mother waved her menthol cigarette in an arc. "Ta da!" My father stood next to a white truck, my new ride. The undependable BMW was gone.

"This is great!" I liked it, a girl-sized pickup truck, a Ford Courier with a cute camper top. I opened the back door. Everything I owned would fit in that space. "Thank you! Thank you!"

Days later, when I was packed and ready to leave, my mother and father stood together outside their townhouse in the bright June sunshine. Every building in their complex was painted the same bland beige. I thought the place lacked appeal but my parents seemed happy there.

"You could still look for a job closer to home," my father's usually deep voice was plaintive, a tone that broke my heart. I couldn't tell him that Kansas City didn't feel like home. St. Louis had been home. I had felt uprooted when they moved from one side of Missouri to the other just as I entered college. Now home was no longer defined by where my parents lived.

◆

My new home was in Terra Alta, West Virginia, in a tiny square house behind the trailer I had rented the summer before. Ellie, the little girl who had befriended me and charmed me with her fish face, was on my doorstep in minutes.

"I didn't think I'd ever see you again," she said excitedly. I waved at her parents; their doorstep was thirty feet from mine. How long until everyone knew I was back?

◆

When I went to work, I discovered that *The News* office had not changed. Fluorescent lights dropped from a pressed tin ceiling over desks grouped between a high counter and a back wall lined with the equipment for mailing the paper to each of our two thousand subscribers. Another fifteen hundred people would buy the paper on the newsstand. Our readers. When the paper came back from the printer in Keyser at noon on Tuesdays, almost everyone pitched in to get it ready for distribution. If we had an insert, even Jerry helped slide the thin, colorful ads into each paper.

I settled into my new routine as managing editor. On Mondays, I laid out the paper, pasting stories and photos on pages lined with a faint, blue grid. On Tuesdays I helped to mail the finished product to subscribers. If I didn't have a story to take me out of the office on Wednesdays, Thursdays, or Fridays, I was in the office editing copy. The paper's correspondents, women from communities across the county, wrote about 4-H, Future Farmers, and Homemakers clubs. They wrote about church activities, about the ambulance squads. Each column ended with the "Personals"—paragraphs about people "motoring" to Morgantown, visiting relatives, recuperating from illnesses. The names were exotic: Ora, Oakey, Nila. Or Biblical: Sarah, Ezekiel, Matthew. I wrote subheads for each story, fixed punctuation and spelling, and undangled participles. My standards were high and probably obnoxious, but through this exercise I became acquainted with the county and its residents. I read other weeklies from across the state. I worked on feature stories, rewrote press releases, and typed obituaries. I was invited into businesses, homes, and schools. Each visit offered clues about the people who inhabited Preston County. I photographed wrecks and fires and people handing checks to each other. I worked in the darkroom on Sundays, when the building was quiet. I turned on music and turned off the lights, still enchanted by chemistry and images.

If there wasn't a community event to cover on a given Saturday, I would drive to places I hadn't been to look for interesting pictures. Preston County had more than 750 miles of roads; most were unpaved. High on Laurel Mountain one evening when the late afternoon sun made the moist air luminescent, I turned onto a gravel road. It followed the ridge top then fell in tortuous curves. Thick trees shielded the rocky path; I didn't pass another soul. It was a little spooky, like I had driven through a wrinkle in time. When my truck finally emerged into sunlight, I slammed on the brakes. Giant satellite dishes glowed like small white suns, triangular antenna pointed skyward. What the hell! Etam Earth Station was quite a surprise, scientific eavesdropping on an enormous scale. Years later I would do a story on the installation of a new antenna in another area of Preston County, excited because my headline would read "Dropping a Dish."

◆

One day late in the summer, shortly after I had moved back to Terra Alta, I stopped by the courthouse to register to vote. A long counter divided customers and staff. "Which party?" a woman asked. "You have to choose one to vote in the primary election." I frowned. I didn't remember having to choose a party when I registered to vote in Missouri.

"Got any socialists?" It was a bit of a wise-crack. I wasn't sure I wanted to claim the West Virginia Democratic Party. The clerk stepped back and looked at me, eyebrows clenched.

"Ha ha." I saw that I had made a mistake, that the courthouse was not the place for an outsider to make light of politics. Were there other witnesses? The room was quiet; several women bent over paperwork. "Democrat." I said. "I'm a Democrat." I did not say that I became a Democrat in 1960 when a cute boy offered me a Kennedy for President campaign pin. I did not explain that my negative opinion of Richard Nixon had turned me against the Republican Party.

◆

Every Monday Michele punched numbers into a calculator. She added the number of advertising inches that had been sold and determined how big the paper would be. "Twelve pages," she announced most weeks. That was the norm. Ads would appear on each page except the editorial page and the front page. Mondays were our busiest day. A pair of typists turned copy into ticker tape that we took downstairs and fed to the Mergenthaler. It beeped and whirled and rolled paper coated with chemicals into a light-safe box. We fed the okay-to-expose end of that paper into a larger, light-safe box filled with stinky chemicals, took the output, and trimmed it into odorous columns of print. A small Compugraphic produced type for headlines and ads. Michele was a genius at typing to fit. We then ran copy and art through a waxer and wielded desperately sharp Exacto knives as we arranged squares and rectangles on pages. Black construction paper held spots for photographs. The printer in Keyser turned our photos into halftones, which used dots, a pre-cursor to pixels, to create images. I found paste-up to be a grown-up version of playing with paper dolls, with enough of a design angle to be interesting.

In every issue we left blank space for late-breaking news. The board of education and the county commission both met on Mondays in Kingwood. Eventually Jerry and I split reporting duties: he covered the commission, which met during the day, and gave me responsibility for the school board, which met in the evening. I would return from Kingwood late at night, write a story, typeset it, then fit it into the space we had left. My final responsibility was to count the pages, which would be picked up before dawn on Tuesday to be taken to the printer in Keyser. (We couldn't print the newspaper in Terra Alta; job presses like those at the Pioneer Press are completely different from newspaper presses.)

As a result of my late nights, I rarely came to work on Tuesdays before noon and often showed up just as the newspaper was delivered.

When the paper showed up, Annie, our office manager, took charge of the loud machine that stamped addresses on each of the copies that was to be mailed. The rest of the crew, myself included, sorted the papers by zip code and stuffed them into canvas bags, which we dragged next door to the post office. It was dusty, heavy, mindless work, but that finished newspaper was satisfying—a tangible record of one week, one time, one place. I longed for a perfect issue, but I always found something wrong: a typo I had missed, a mistake in a story, photographs that weren't up to my high standards.

"Birdcage liner!" I'd say, waving the paper above my head. "Better luck next week."

8

✦ ✦ ✦

THE MOVE TO SALT LICK

IN THE FALL OF 1975 a man came to the newspaper counter. "I want to put an ad in the paper." The man held himself at attention. Retired soldier? He was slight, with close-cropped white hair. "I have a house to rent. On Salt Lick."

Annie usually took the classified ads, but when I heard "Salt Lick," I waved her away. "I'll take this," I said. My tiny house in the middle of town was exposed; I had no privacy. Salt Lick would be much nicer.

"I love Salt Lick," I said. "I'm interested in the house."

"Carl Smith." The man offered his hand, which I shook with enough enthusiasm to confuse him. "It's just a little cabin." His voice was apologetic, but he smiled. "It *is* in the middle of two hundred acres."

"When can I see it?"

"I'm heading back to Bethesda now, but you can see it any time. I have a caretaker looking after it, Bob Shrout." Mr. Smith gave me Mr. Shrout's number and directions.

"If I don't take it, the ad will be in next week's paper," I promised.

Mr. Shrout agreed to meet me at the house that afternoon. I drove two miles down Salt Lick, as Mr. Smith had directed, and scrutinized the driveway. Actually, driveway is much too suburban a term. The road cut diagonally across the mountain, sliced across a wooded, rocky face. A steep bank tangled with mountain laurel bordered one side; the other dropped into air. I drove slowly, hanging onto the steering wheel as rocks wrenched the tires. Close to the top of the hill, the road made a horseshoe turn to the left and continued to climb; by then the woods had closed in and the drop-off was no longer a threat. A small cinder-block cabin sat in a clearing behind a row of pine trees. Beyond the house was a huge barn and a wide field. Fall had painted the landscape in vivid colors. It was spectacular. I gasped with delight. When I stepped out of the truck a flock of huge birds exploded from the pines. Black shapes drummed the air. I was startled, then thrilled when I recognized them as turkeys. Mr. Shrout pulled up as the flock winged away.

"Turkeys," he said. Was he growling? "Used to be scarce." He acknowledged me with a sober nod and went to unlock the door. He was stocky; dark hair stuck out of the sides of a worn John Deere ball cap. Maybe he just wasn't the friendly sort. His manner shouldn't have bothered me but it did. I'm generally a happy person. Have been my whole life. It's charming when it's not annoying. This guy seemed to be annoyed.

The cinderblocks were painted an ugly avocado green, but the cabin was neat and clean inside, the small space divided into two bed-rooms and a large room with a kitchen at one end and my future living room on the other. The bathroom was a bump-out and I was delighted to find a washer and dryer there.

"I'll take it!" I couldn't hide my joy. At the time I didn't have any idea that Mr. Shrout was worried that I was going to interfere with his plans to hunt on the property. I couldn't have known that our relationship would be fraught. I didn't even consider how treacherous the driveway would be in the winter. I was young and optimistic and naïve. I was unaware that visual beauty could sabotage rational thinking. I pictured myself in that cabin, in that landscape, and knew that I was a lucky girl.

9

✦ ✦ ✦

THROUGH CALAMITY

———

"THE RIVER'S UP. It's hit the three-foot line at Albright." Paul, the kayak teacher, couldn't stand still. He paced the riverbank, a compact, athletic man, then turned to address his class. "The good news is a lot of the rocks are under water now." He looked at me. "The bad news is that the current is strong and some of you are going to get wet."

I had signed up for Paul's September 1975 kayak class. In spite of his expert instruction and my inherent coordination, I was not a star pupil. When I had photographed the Olympic whitewater trials the previous summer the racers had made it look so easy. It was not. Paul usually put me in a sturdy kayak, an orange fiberglass taper built to run waterfalls. I would sit in its round opening, legs in front of me, feet pushing against blocks. I felt secure, like the boat fit me. I tried to emulate Paul on the water, his strong arms controlling the paddle, harnessing the strong current. He had taught me to recognize a rock below the surface by watching how the water bounced above it. But I found that I couldn't consistently steer with any accuracy. In spite of my vigorous paddling, the kayak seemed to have a mind of its own. Paul winced each time I scraped across a rock.

Paul was a teacher by inclination, not by profession. He was in his mid-forties and had lived by the Cheat his entire life. He went straight from high school to the railroad. M&K Junction below Salt Lick Bridge was his usual office. The wide flat spot in the valley where Salt Lick Creek met the Cheat River was a busy railroad yard. Coal trains, empty and full, stretched along multiple tracks. If they were empty, they were waiting to be sent to coal tipples. If they were full, they were waiting to be sent east. Salt Lick Grade is one of the longest, steepest climbs between Baltimore and Ohio. Heavy coal trains actually needed helper engines to get up the mountain. Paul's job required him to know where those helpers were. And all the other trains. He spent hours in that small brick tower waiting for trains and throwing switches. When he wasn't working he was outdoors. Like most men in Preston County, Paul hunted and fished. But he might have been the first local man to kayak or cross-country ski. He was so enthusiastic about those activities that he taught them. That's how we met— through the community schools program. Its schedule was a regular feature in the newspaper.

That morning, I looked at the river and knew Paul was right. The late September rains had increased the volume in the Cheat Narrows. On the river bank we strapped on helmets and lifejackets and pulled rubber spray skirts to our waists. I stepped into the O of my much-abused orange kayak and Paul adjusted my foot rests and pulled the skirt tightly over the lip of the opening. On the water, the boat moved side to side like a horizontal mermaid's tail when I wiggled my hips. All week the water level had been low, rocks thrust above the surface. But heavy rains the night before had altered the river. It was swollen, dark green, fast, and foaming.

While I was acclimating to the quicker pace, Paul drew his boat alongside of me and pointed ahead to the bursts of white spray. He meant for me to avoid those rocks. As I started into the whitewater, Paul shouted, "Right! Straighten out!" I dragged my oar against the current, backpaddled furiously trying to avoid both rocks and Paul's grimace. Paul's son David floated by, his wide grin a taunt to my flailing. David seemed born to the river. He threaded his boat through narrow channels with teenage nonchalance. He was like a seal, capsizing and righting himself, shaking water from the blond curls beneath his helmet. His control of his boat seemed effortless. I was in awe.

When we reached a calm section of the river, Paul said, "David will take your boat through Calamity. Unless you want to try?"

"I want to try." I thought I might be ready. In the preceding weeks I had adapted to the thrilling up and down ride through milder rapids. I had tipped over again and again, shed the boat, and floated to safety; my life vest enabled me to sit back in the churning water as if I were in a chair, using my feet to push off of rocks. What a rush. Paul had taught me to respect the river, not fear it, to look as far ahead as possible and try to steer around trouble.

That morning I felt as if my kayak was going more or less in the direction I was steering. I had made it through some rapids, through the scary "Herman's Hydraulic," a churning hole famous for toppling boats. Calamity was just ahead. I started my approach. My heartbeat echoed the roar of the river as I aimed for the chute to the right of Calamity. A big wave knocked me sideways, my boat flipped, and I shook free. The water boiled and foamed and forced me over the falls. I was terrified until my lifejacket popped me to the surface and I swam into the eddy below the rapids. Wow. Oh wow. Adrenalin still pumping, I climbed back into my kayak (retrieved by David) and with the class stayed upright through Rocking Horse and Wind rapids. What a thrill.

Three of Paul's children—Rick, his oldest, about my age; and twins David and Debra, five years younger—had joined our class that day. After we got out of the river, I followed them home to help stow the equipment in a shed behind their house. A redhead leaned out the back door. "You must be Nancy. Paul's told me about you. Please join us for dinner." I would learn over the course of our friendship that Betty, Paul's wife, enjoyed the indoors more than the outdoors.

We crowded into the immaculate kitchen and talked about our trip through the Narrows.

"Perfect level," Paul said. He practically vibrated with the success of our outing. Most of the paddlers had stayed in their boats through Calamity.

"It was great!" said Debra. Her voice was loud.

"Some of us got wet." David was a tease.

"Next time I'll stay in my boat," I vowed.

Betty shook her head. "You aren't going to get me out on that river," she said, nodding at the section of the Cheat that stretched wide and calm at the edge of their back yard. "Sometimes I think you all are crazy."

◆

Paul wasn't like most of the people I had met in Preston County. Both men and women seemed content to repeat their parents' lives. They didn't want to travel to big cities or explore other cultures. Paul was curious. He found outsiders interesting, not threatening. I had written a column about my trip through Calamity and he liked that I put his name in the paper. Soon he had an idea for another story—a camping trip to Dolly Sods—and he asked if I'd like to join him and his kids. "Wilderness," he said. "I've taken Boy Scouts there. The wind blows so hard the trees only have branches on one side." On an October weekend, Paul drove us all to a rocky plateau in the Monongahela National Forest. When we got out of the car, the wind overwhelmed me. It was a force, a constant. Spruce trees clung to a skim of soil, their branches thinned by unrelenting gusts. We were on the Eastern Continental Divide and it was a primitive place, fierce in its beauty. Autumn had added orange, yellow, and red to the green and white of pine and rock. I took in the view, exclaimed my delight.

"This is one of my favorite places in West Virginia." Rick stepped up to help me hoist my backpack. "You got it?" I staggered a bit under the weight. Rick was a redhead, a foot taller than me. Well built. Attractive. He grinned. "The more you eat and drink, the less it will weigh."

Before Paul led us down the Red Creek trail, he paused at the edge of a high meadow. I shot his portrait there. It's a wonderful picture: a handsome man, stylish in sunglasses and a plaid shirt, strikes an explorer's pose. Years later, a large, framed print of that photo would have a prominent place at Paul's funeral.

The path meandered through meadows and into the woods. We stepped to the side to let a Boy Scout troop pass, but when they were out of earshot, silence descended. We refilled our canteens at a spring next to the path. Paul laughed out loud when I asked if the water was safe to drink. "There's nothing above us to mess it up," he said. "Taste." I filled the collapsible cup I had in my pack. The water was cold and delicious. Better than any water fountain. After an hour or so of hiking, we made camp. I say we, but Debra did most of the work on our tent. Not that she minded. "It's good to have another girl around," she said. "I've had enough of my stinky brothers." She was nonchalant, used to tents and backpacks and the accoutrements of camping. I had never backpacked before and I hoped my enthusiasm would offset whatever mistakes I would make.

We changed into cutoffs and waded into Red Creek.

"It's cold!" I shouted.

"Thirty degrees!" David estimated.

"Thirty-three," I retorted. "Thirty-two is ice."

David showed me a room-size cave half hidden behind a large waterfall and I took some photos of him playing there. Then I put the camera down and explored the space. The flat stones were cold beneath my bare feet and the roar of water filled my ears, my head. The cascade was a rain of diamonds refracting the sun, a moving scrim between me and the world.

◆

I joined Paul's family for Thanksgiving. Early that morning Paul and Rick led me into the woods for my first (and only) deer hunt. We kept our voices low as we walked, the ground a carpet of dry branches and leaves. Rick climbed a steep bank, then turned to offer his hand. Strong and warm and dry. Nice. By the time we opened the door to the smell of turkey and pie we had figured out our first date. "We're going dancing this weekend," Rick announced to his family. I felt a blush warm my face.

◆

The roller-skating-rink-turned-dance-hall was so rickety that the walls vibrated to the rhythm of the bass. Until that evening, I wondered where all of Preston County's young people were. Now they were all around me, clustered in groups in the dim space. Rick introduced me to dozens of people. Then he introduced me to the members of the band, Fat Man's Face. Lean men with lots of hair on their heads and cheeks. They covered Grand Funk, Bachman Turner Overdrive, Lynyrd Skynyrd. Serious rock and roll. I danced with joy. Until I started dating Rick, I hadn't met many people who shared my sensibilities. I didn't know where to look. They didn't advertise in the paper. What would the ads say? "Hippies wanted for rock and roll. Drugs available."

For the next several months Rick and I followed Fat Man's Face as they made the circuit of local bars. When the members of the band asked me to take publicity photos for them, we agreed to meet at an old iron furnace built in the 1700s. They lined up in their tight jeans against the centuries-old stones, then across the creek on boulders tainted bright orange by acid mine drainage. Rick carried my heavy camera bag, acted as my assistant. He accompanied me to band practice when I delivered contact sheets from the photo shoot. I was beginning to feel like part of a group. Rick had delivered me to our peers. He was such a nice guy, smart and cheerful. He worked for the railroad, a good job. He was a catch. But I suspected our relationship was futile. I wanted heart-thumping, pheromone-fueled love. With Rick, what I felt was comfort—except when we kissed: he was too tall; I had to stand on my tiptoes. When I invited him to a Joni Mitchell concert in Pittsburgh, a couple of hours north, it was a sort of test. From high above the stage, we could barely make out Joni's face; she perversely wore a hat through most of the concert. Rick sat silent as I mouthed the words to each song. On the drive back to Preston County, Rick held the steering wheel at ten and two. The wheels hummed on the black highway. He was so dependable, so steady.

"I didn't like the concert," Rick finally admitted. He glanced at my face then back to the road. "That's not my kind of music."

Could I love a man who rejected Joni's soaring voice, her poetry, her mercury-slippery emotions? I could, maybe, but I didn't love Rick. This wasn't going to work.

"If you don't love Joni, you can't love me." The window framed the moving black emptiness.

"Well, shit." Rick took my hand. "Are you sure?" he asked, his voice plaintive.

"I'm sure," I whispered. I felt ashamed. Mean. Here was this perfectly nice guy and I didn't want him. What did I want? I leaned forward to eject the Joni Mitchell cassette. "Beatles?" I asked.

"Fine," Rick said. "We can agree on that."

10

◆ ◆ ◆

A DOCTOR!
AND HE'S JEWISH!

I HAD BRIEFLY RECONNECTED with Richard, the soldier, in June 1975. The spark was still there. The sex was wonderful. I was giddy. Lounging around afterward, I talked about my sister's wedding. I jumped up to show Richard the photos I had taken at the ceremony. A wary look crossed his face.

"I need to get back to Dawson," he said. And he made a quick retreat. I didn't see him again. I was crushed. I cursed my aggressive behavior. After all, my mother had told me how to catch a man.

"Men and puppies," she had said. "If you want them, run the other way."

Between Richard and Rick I had dated the high school principal, another redhead. Date here is a euphemism. We had sex. He was a good guy, a single father. Everyone in Terra Alta thought we made a perfect couple. We had fun, but he wasn't in love with me and I wasn't in love with him. We were in lust. Lust can be good, but love and partnership were my objectives.

After Rick, I had hooked up with two West Virginia University graduate students who had placements in Preston County. Smart men, fun. But they weren't committed to the area. I was.

✦

I met my next potential mate through a blind date. In response to the doctor shortage that *The News* had documented in 1974, a group of determined idealists created the Preston County Health Council. Government grants helped them open a clinic in the corner of the L-shaped Kingwood Plaza, the first shopping center in Preston County, and hire doctors, nurses, and staff. The Health Council opened clinics in Eglon and Newburg. The doctors came from the National Health Service Corps, a federal program that paid for students' medical education if they were willing to practice in underserved areas. Rich, Jerry, Michele, and I believed that the tabloid we had published helped all this come about, and *The News* celebrated each improvement in local health care with a story and photos.

My frequent visits to the Kingwood Clinic led to a friendship with its administrator. Beverly was just a little older than I was and had been a teenage mother who went on to graduate from the West Virginia University School of Social Work. She was bright, smart, funny. When the Health Council recruited a doctor for a new clinic in Bruceton, she thought that doctor, Simon, who was Jewish, should meet the only other unmarried Jew in Preston County: me. Beverly invited us to dinner at her home in Morgantown. Simon wore a white tunic; he looked like a hippie who had visited India. His hair fell past his ears into a renegade page boy. On one hand, he had a finger that ended at its first knuckle, the result of an accident at his father's printing company. He was California cool. We got along fine.

The town of Bruceton was also happy to meet Simon, its new doctor. Citizens greeted him with a ham dinner. Simon, who like me didn't follow the dietary laws of the religion he had been born into, made his way along tables laden with covered dishes—salads of potato, gelatin, or cabbage, beans prepared various ways, vegetables that until that morning had been growing in gardens, and a vast array of cakes, pies, cookies, and other sweets. Simon became the town doctor. He did not become my boyfriend. Although several people expected that Preston County's two Jewish professionals would end up together, that didn't happen. We went on a few dates, including another Pittsburgh concert. Linda Ronstadt this time. Simon fed me grapes as I drove. It was all perfect. So why wasn't I having more fun? Why wasn't *he* having more fun? The chemistry just wasn't there. We tried again; we went to Morgantown for dinner. We had spirited sex. But the relationship never took off. We liked each other. But we wanted more: love and passion and fireworks. So elusive.

11

♦ ♦ ♦

RAMPS

GIG WHITE WAS A BIG MAN with a big belly, six feet tall and dressed in overalls. He walked into *The News* office in the summer of 1975, put one hand on the counter, and leaned back on his heels.

"I need to run my peaches ad," he said. His voice was falsetto, halting, odd. His wattle wiggled as he nodded at me. Annie took a form out of her drawer.

"Same as last year?" she asked. "Peaches from Romney?" She turned toward me. "Gig gets the best peaches."

Gig was in his late fifties or early sixties, with a full head of white hair slicked back from a widow's peak. If a turkey gobbler could take human form, Gig would be it. He bobbed his head up and down as Annie wrote the ad. Everyone in Terra Alta wanted Gig's peaches, the first of the summer. They came from West Virginia's eastern panhandle where warm weather arrived weeks before it came to the mountains. Big wooden crates of peaches. That summer I canned eight quarts of Gig's peaches, the first food I ever preserved. Orange half-spheres that smelled of summer. So good.

◆

One April morning in 1976, Gig again strutted into *The News* office.

"Annie, I need to run my ramps ad," he said.

Paul, my kayak teacher, had just told me about ramps, pungent greens found in Preston County's mountains. *Allium tricoccum*—wild leeks—appear in March or April, an early spot of green in the colorless woods. "Ramps were a tonic in the old days," Paul had said. "After a winter eating buckwheat cakes and sausage gravy, they were a treat." He described them as a kind of cross between garlic and onions.

He said some people hated ramps. "They do have a particular odor about them and it sticks with you for a while." The smell oozed from your pores, he said. The stench was legendary. Kids ate ramps to get sent home from school. Men chased ramps with beer and had to sleep outside. Cooked ramps don't have such a bad effect: a little heat makes them sweeter.

Each spring, all over West Virginia, communities hold ramp dinners, fund-raisers where ramps are served alongside soup beans, ham, and cornbread, and fried up with potatoes. The most famous ramp dinner is the Feast of the Ramson in Richwood, West Virginia, home of the late newspaperman Jim Comstock. Comstock gained fame in the 1960s when he added ramp juice to ink and published a newspaper so smelly that the post office issued a reprimand. But it was public relations genius and the ramp dinner in Richwood funded the local volunteer fire department for decades.

At the newspaper office, while Annie got to work on Gig's ad, he addressed me. "I think you should come ramp hunting," he said. The rhythm of his speech struck me again. I interpreted the gap between words as a sign of shyness. "We're going down Wolf Creek Saturday and you should come along."

It sounded like a good story. Good pictures. I agreed to come.

◆

That Saturday Gig pulled up in front of *The News* and got out of his truck. Ralph, Gig's usual sidekick, sat in the passenger seat. Ralph nodded at me when he got out to hold the door, a gallant move that ensured that I sit in the middle. The old truck smelled of petroleum products and the stick shift was uncomfortably close to my knee. The three of us were wedged together on the bench seat. We headed out the Aurora Pike, a two-lane road that hugged the ridge top between Terra Alta and Aurora.

"We're going to follow Wolf Creek to the bottom of Cheat Mountain," Gig said. "Last night, we parked Ralph's car in a little pull-off there." I looked out the dirty windshield and tried to keep my knee from knocking the truck out of gear. Snow still covered the north-facing slopes. Cattle looked miserable in their muddy pastures. I hugged my camera bag on my lap. We didn't talk much. Close to Route 50, Gig took a right down a gravel road. We bumped past scattered farmhouses and pulled off in front of a gate. I was dressed for hiking, an activity I enjoyed, even while carrying twenty pounds of camera equipment over my shoulder and two cameras around my neck. The sun was out and the temperature had settled at around fifty degrees. Although I appreciated the sun's warmth, the bright light didn't make for good photos. Still, I figured the day would be fun.

The hike was mostly downhill. We followed little runs, damp, rocky ditches filled by springs and melting snow. The mud was slick and there was no path, but as long as I stepped carefully, it wasn't dangerous. I didn't think we could get lost. I knew the mountain we were descending.

Cheat Mountain rises more than a thousand feet from the Cheat River. Route 50 winds east-west following the mountain in curving switchbacks that provide views of a sharp hollow. The mountain rises on one side of the road and falls off the other. Nothing to see but trees and brush. No one bothers to build on ground that steep.

The men soon spotted the first clump of ramps, a ten-foot-wide wash of green against the brown and gray woods. They leaned over and began digging, using mattocks to free the plants from the hillside. They shook off clods of mud before putting the ramps in their "pokes" (what they called burlap bags). On the side of the hill, the ramps resembled lilies-of-the-valley—they had leaves like fat bunny ears pushing the carpet of brown leaves aside. All similarities to these fragrant flowers ended when the white bulbs were freed from the dirt. I sniffed. The smell wasn't as bad as I expected; it reminded me of the wild onions I used to eat as a child. Gig brushed dirt from a ramp, trimmed it with a lethal-looking hunting knife, and offered it to me. It smelled sharp, and green. I took a bite and my mouth filled with a particular taste. Not like garlic, with its heat. Or like a green onion, with its bite. This had less acid, more flavor.

"I like it," I announced. The men grinned. I grinned back, certain that I had entered their fraternity. The next couple of hours unfolded slowly as I followed the men from patch to patch. I took pictures; Gig preened for the camera and swaggered a little as he walked.

When we paused for lunch, we sat on rocks warmed by the sun. Gig unwrapped thick slices of homemade bread, heavily buttered. He carefully cleaned ramps, then stacked them on the bread. These stinky sandwiches were delicious. Ralph slipped off to pee and Gig and I packed up our trash. Gig cleared his throat. I turned toward him, curious. He seemed to be having a hard time finding words. His wattle twitched.

"My wife has female troubles," he said in his halting falsetto. His blue eyes blinked rapidly. "She had an operation but she doesn't want relations no more." I stopped breathing as he propositioned me, assured me that his wife understood his needs and didn't mind his adultery. I stood up, my feet planted on ground that suddenly felt dangerous.

I was horrified by the thought of having sex with Gig White. He was older than my father, unattractive, and desperate. I forced myself to take some deep, rampy breaths. I was in the middle of nowhere with a randy old bird. Where was Ralph? Had they planned this?

I couldn't claim a boyfriend. I am a terrible liar. My mother made it clear that lying was a major offense. So I never honed that skill. The few times I had tried I couldn't keep my stories straight. I had lived in Terra Alta for nearly a year. Most of the residents knew where I lived, where I ate, and that I drove a little Ford pickup truck. For a moment, I considered telling Gig that I had a fiancée in the Midwest.

After a pause that seemed to go on forever, I came up with a story. "I'm flattered, Gig," I said, "but I always promised myself I would never get involved with a married man." I avoided eye contact.

Gig bobbed his head, unintentionally becoming even more turkey-like. "If you change your mind, the offer stands," he squeaked. He slung his bag over his shoulder and walked off.

I tried to disguise my distress by fiddling with the cameras. Shielded behind the viewfinder, I pointed the camera at Gig's back and pushed the shutter. My hands shook. Gig didn't scare me but his proposition had unsettled me. Ew. I shuddered. How could I have said I was flattered? And why was I worried that I had hurt his feelings?

The men were twenty yards ahead of me when I fell. I was picking my way carefully across a wide run when my boot slid on a slimy rock. I managed to catch myself in a push-up position, my hands in the ice-cold water. With horror I realized that one camera was submerged and probably ruined along with the photos I had shot that day. I struggled to my feet, determined not to cry. The bottom of my camera bag was damp, but the rest of my equipment was safe. I waved off Gig and Ralph.

"I'm fine," I lied. I wanted to curse and wail. Instead, I concentrated on breathing, willing my chest to rise and fall slowly. I scrambled over rocks and through mud. I twisted the lens off the camera and water poured out, a very bad sign. I had just bought that camera. Even used, it had cost me two weeks' salary. No one would be able to resurrect its complicated mechanics. I closed my eyes and softly groaned. My hands hurt. I was muddy, cold, and miserable. But there was no escape, no easy route out. I clambered after the men.

I heard the roar of Wolf Creek before I saw it. To our left was a five-foot-high waterfall. In front of us, the creek was fast-moving, clear, cold, and twenty-five-feet wide. I could see the rocky bottom. There was no bridge, not even a fallen log. Downstream, the creek looked wider and deeper.

"I didn't think it would be this high," Gig said. "Must be all the melting snow." He shrugged. "I don't think it gets any better below."

Ralph shook his head and waded into the water, holding his sack of ramps over his head. Gig and I watched him slowly make his way to the opposite bank. His pants were wet to the crotch. I knew the water would reach my waist. Gig looked at me.

"I'll carry the bags across, then come back to get you," Gig said, failing to look me in the eye. I just nodded.

I handed over my camera bag, noted his surprise as he registered its weight, and watched him make his careful way across, my bag held aloft like something offered at auction. His bag of ramps rested over the other shoulder. At its deepest, the water came to the top of his thighs. He dropped the bags on the opposite bank and came back for me.

I watched him in the water and realized with horror I would have to jump onto his back. He'd never be able to get up from a squat carrying me. I was short, but I was solid, five feet tall and every bit of 125 pounds. I looked around to find a rock to serve as a mounting block. Ralph watched with interest from the other side as I climbed a boulder. Gig turned his back to me and I put my hands on his squishy shoulders and leapt. He groaned softly, took a step forward, and caught his balance. I tried to hang on tightly without pressing my body against his jacket. The cameras around my neck were a lumpy barrier between us.

Gig stepped into the water. I hung on, my knees pressed to his sides as I rode the old letch across Wolf Creek, hoping that if I held my breath, I might weigh less. The bottoms of my boots skimmed the water. Ralph was silent as he waited, but he couldn't hide his grin. When we got to the other bank, I slipped off Gig's back, shouldered my bag, and said "thanks" in what I hoped was a dignified voice.

"We're almost to the car." Gig bobbed his head. We headed downhill through mud, both men's boots squishing with each step. Fifteen minutes later, we came upon Ralph's Ford in a clearing.

I chose to sit in the back, with the ramps.

12

✦ ✦ ✦

THE COMMUNE DOWN
SALT LICK, PART 1

***

NOT LONG AFTER my uncomfortable ramp hunt, a corona of red hair, a bright beacon in a car parked in front of the newspaper office, caught my eye. I stood to get a better look. The owner of those auburn curls sat in the back seat of a 1966 Chevy Malibu. A petite woman sat next to him, her head bent over a baby in her arms. Then two men returned to the car from the post office next door and just like that they were gone.

Annie was watching them too. "Those must be the hippies who bought the old Washington Lantz farm down Salt Lick," she said. "It's just a couple of miles past your place. They have Tennessee plates. People are talking about them. That long hair. Hey," she looked at me, "maybe you can make friends."

I longed to meet them. "Maybe I could drive up to the farm and introduce myself," I said. "I could say it's my duty as a reporter." But I didn't do it. I feared these exotic outsiders would see through my pose as a country editor, mock my overalls and work boots. They would discover that I was not a hippie, but a Midwestern suburbanite, a girl who had no culture to reject.

◆

That same spring a dog appeared at my house. She was small, a terrier mix, brown hair tufting in all directions, and she looked hungry. She bolted the scraps I gave her and looked up, her slightly protruding eyes begging for more. I mixed eggs with bread and milk and she licked the bowl clean. Then she curled up next to my rocking chair and fell asleep. Her now round belly rose and fell. I didn't know what to do with her. My parents had told me they were giving me a collie for my birthday in September. I had already named that puppy Mac after the first in a long line of collies my family had owned. My mother was passionate about dogs and people who loved dogs. Show dogs. She started raising collies in the mid-1950s and first focused on obedience competitions. She switched to Old English Sheepdogs in 1958, before the breed became famous in a Disney movie, *The Shaggy Dog*. Donnie, our first Old English Sheepdog, was a squared-off hairy guy who earned a championship and had a brief modeling career. Dreamy came next. She too earned a championship. My mom's kennel, Downeylane, was named after the street we lived on. My younger sister Laura got into trouble at school when she shocked her teacher with this answer about our pets at home: "We have two dogs and three bitches." My mother loved to tell that story. "She was right, you know," she'd say, her voice deep and tobacco-tinged.

We had never gone on family vacations; instead my sisters and I took turns accompanying my mother to dog shows in cities scattered through the Midwest: Quincy and Wheaton, Illinois; Cape Girardeau, Missouri; Des Moines, Iowa. Those trips turned me into a dog snob. I didn't want a mutt. I wanted a collie—beautiful, regal, and intelligent.

But the mutt at my feet looked needy. I rationalized her adoption this way: Mac was not just the name of my first (and next) collie, it was also the nickname of the head of photojournalism at the University of Missouri. His wife was Betty. I patted the mutt's wiry head. "I guess you're Betty," I said out loud. "Mac will be here soon." She didn't budge.

Betty rebounded quickly from spaying and immunizations. Her rabies tag jingled as she romped around the yard. Sometimes she took off and stayed away for days. My accidental dog. I didn't really own her; my house was probably just one of the stops in her circuit, but she played a crucial role in my introduction to the folks on the Washington Lantz farm.

◆

When the phone rang one Saturday afternoon in August, an unfamiliar voice spoke. The man said he had my dog. He said he lived down Salt Lick, on the old Washington Lantz place. The hippies. My dog had found the hippies. I told the man that I knew where the farm was and that I would be there soon.

I knew where I was going because when Annie told me about the hippies, I had driven down Salt Lick to note the farm's location. Not an hour after I got the call, I turned onto the gravel road, which soon crossed Salt Lick Creek. I steered through a hollow where steep forested hills absorbed the light. I drove through two gates, carefully shutting each behind me, finally emerging in the bottom of a bowl-shaped pasture, a sudden wide-open space where the sun burst free of the tree cover. A white farmhouse perched on the side of the hill far above me. By the time I pulled up, Betty was bouncing with excitement. I squatted to pet her, then stood to meet the group of people gathered around a crude fire pit next to the worn house.

A short blond man stepped forward and introduced himself. "I'm Dale. I'm the one who called." His eyeglasses glinted in the sun as he gestured at the tall redhead, petite woman, and baby I had seen outside the post office. "The Verlendens." I nodded at them. Another man, slight, with a piercing gaze, said that he and his wife and daughter were visiting from New York. The wife was lithe with close-cropped hair. The August day shimmered with heat. While I was thanking Dale for calling me about Betty, it seemed as if the group went back to a meeting I must have interrupted.

"The dancers need more space," the lithe woman pronounced in a high, musical voice. "We could use the barn," her husband offered. They spoke about "art" with an ease that sparked my envy. They seemed both wildly sophisticated and slightly ridiculous. The discussion was earnest and though I didn't feel unwelcome, I felt extraneous. I wanted to ask a hundred questions. Was this a commune? What did these people do? How had they arrived on Salt Lick? Instead I thanked them all for finding Betty and left.

❧ 13 ❧

✦ ✦ ✦

POT ROAST

———

HERE IS A LIST OF THE JEWS who lived in Preston County, West Virginia, in 1976: Out of a population of thirty thousand, there was Simon, the doctor my friend had tried to set me up with; one veterinarian whose wife wasn't Jewish; one family who lived there just long enough for their son's bar mitzvah to be a front page story in *The News;* and me.

Occasionally I made the hour's drive to Morgantown to attend religious services at the Tree of Life Synagogue. I was a curiosity there—a hippie-like journalist who lived in the mountains—but the congregation made me feel welcome. A family that lived in Morgantown had a farm near Terra Alta and made sure I knew they subscribed to *The Preston County News.* Then there was Mark, a single engineering student who was short, dark, and a little furry. Not really my type. Mark's accent revealed he was from Brooklyn. He spoke with intelligence and humor, even when he questioned the sanity of a nice Jewish girl living in Preston County.

"Where do you shop?" he asked. "What do you do?"

I described my home, a cabin high in the middle of two hundred acres. Surrounded by fields and forest. Turkeys nesting in the pine trees. A silence broken only by the wind and the sound of coal trains rumbling through the valley. The big sky full of stars. I talked about my job. "A couple of weeks ago I covered the Bruceton Mills Good Neighbor Days celebration," I said. "I took a photo of the Junior Deputies, kids who want to be cops, trying to be cool while they waited to march in the parade. It's one of my favorite pictures from the summer." I told him how much I liked the pace of a weekly newspaper. "Every week is different," I said, "but there's a rhythm to the work, to the schedule." He looked skeptical. This was a challenge. "It's beautiful there. You have to come up," I insisted. "I'll make dinner."

In August, Mark told me his brother was coming to visit. "That's it," I said. "We'll give him a West Virginia experience. My driveway alone will be an adventure. Come to the mountains. I'll make pot roast."

◆

Jews were rare in Preston County; Blacks were also scarce. Hippies were the next minority. Men with long hair and women who went braless beneath ethnic clothing, even those born and raised in the mountains, were viewed with suspicion, except by bar owners, who hired rock bands to lure their business. The Veterans of Foreign Wars post at the bottom of Caddell Mountain was a favorite hangout. When Fat Man's Face, the most popular local band in 1976, took a break from playing Lynyrd Skynyrd or Bad Company covers, the veterans stayed inside to play Freddy Fender and Mickey Gilley on the jukebox while the hippies gathered in the parking lot to smoke pot. In just such a circle, I passed a joint and looked at the faces around me. I realized that I had found my tribe. This was where I belonged. The group often included two charismatic men: Charlie and Eugene, both locals. Charlie was the band's lead guitarist; he aspired to be a bad boy. He had long, long dark hair and a mustache that drooped over a sweet grin. He made a living driving a coal truck, his hair nearly always drawing comments from the guys at the coal tipple. "Rock and roll," he'd growl good-naturedly in response. Eugene's expertise as a hairstylist was renowned although he couldn't seem to tame his own fuzzy halo of golden curls. He fluttered his hands in giddy enthusiasm when he talked and never attempted to pass for straight. Since he was related to nearly everyone in the county, he was rarely harassed. He looked like an angel. Charlie was the devil. At every dance, I flirted with him. "Come visit me," I said. "You know where I live."

The Saturday Mark and his brother came to dinner coincided with the Perseids meteor shower. I had read about this annual celestial event but had never seen it. The field beyond my cabin, far from city lights, would offer the perfect vantage point. "This will be a special night," I told Mark.

I made my mother's pot roast, one of those easy 1950s dinners that used mushroom and onion soups. To prove I was at least a culinary Jew, I grated potatoes for latkes and made my grandmother's cheesecake.

I heard their car making its tortuous way up my impossible driveway and walked outside to applaud Mark's arrival. "Is there another way down?" Mark's brother said, looking worried, then remembered his manners. He extended his hand. "I'm Eric," he said. "Where am I?" He was slightly taller and thinner than Mark. "You're in Salt Lick Valley," I said, "between Terra Alta and Rowlesburg. Almost heaven." I stuck my hands in my back pockets. "Dinner's not quite ready. Want to take a walk?"

They followed me past the house, past the barn. The road bisected the empty field and headed up another steep hill. My landlord leased the field to local farmers, who had just finished their second cutting of hay. The dusty, sweet smell hung in the air. The early evening sun turned the meadow golden.

"It's beautiful," Eric said. He sounded surprised. "This is not how I thought of West Virginia."

We hiked slowly up the hill, occasionally turning to admire the rolling mountains behind us. I was used to the walk, but Mark and Eric were panting. I stopped, set my heels against the hillside. I pointed to the ridge opposite. "Briery Mountain," I said. We were about half a mile high; far across the valley meadows like the one we had just crossed could be seen—large, lighter green squares punctuating the thick, green forest. I sighed with admiration. I never took the view for granted. I had come to understand that the mountains nurtured me. I waited for exclamations from my guests. Nothing.

"Are you interested in the Civil War?" I asked. Eric nodded.

"The B&O Railroad runs through this valley, and during the Civil War the train was a vital supply link for the Union Army." I pointed south. "Four sites near here were heavily guarded: the Amblersburg Trestle, the iron bridge over the Cheat River, the Tray Run Trestle, and the Tunnelton Tunnel. They were all built in the 1850s and were considered great engineering feats of the time." I paused. "Worth a visit." I didn't volunteer to be tour guide.

I could almost hear my aunt's voice. "Nice Jewish boys!" she would have said. But I didn't feel any attraction. No buzz. No romance. These brothers couldn't appreciate the landscape I loved, couldn't understand why I had chosen to live here. The three of us faced west and watched the sun move lower in the sky. "It is pretty," Mark said. He sounded unconvinced. "But I'm getting hungry."

Back at the house, I handed out beers, motioned the guys to the porch swing. "If you see a big black snake, don't freak out," I said. "He lives in the attic." Mark and Eric exchanged alarmed looks.

"You need any help?" Mark asked.

I laughed. "You can come in."

My entire house was three rooms, less than six hundred square feet. I thought it was tiny, but I had never seen a New York apartment. The table was three feet from the stove so it was easy to flip latkes right onto our dinner plates. The guys praised the pot roast and asked for more latkes. They ate with gusto, confessing that neither of them cooked.

I was just clearing the dishes when the sound of a roaring engine drew us outside. A Harley Davidson motorcycle pulled into the yard. As we watched from the porch, Charlie kicked his leg over the side of the machine, leaned against the seat, and took off his helmet. His hair fell almost to his waist.

"Hey," he said. Mark and Eric stared.

"This is Charlie," I said. "He's a rock and roll musician and coal truck driver." I introduced the brothers. "Hey Charlie," I said. "You're just in time for cheesecake."

The three men filled my little house. Charlie took a look at the leftovers. He sniffed the pot roast. "Can I have some of this?" he asked. "What are these?" He leaned forward, pointed to a latke.

"It's a latke," Mark said. Charlie looked confused.

"Potato pancake," Eric translated. Charlie relaxed.

We had Charlie try latkes plain first, then with sour cream, and then with applesauce. Eric launched into the tale of Hanukkah. Charlie helped himself to the rest of the latkes, furrowed his eyebrows. "I didn't know there was Jewish food." Then he looked at us. "I don't think I ever met any Jewish people before."

"That's okay," Mark said. "I don't think I've ever met a coal truck driver."

"Are you expecting anyone else?" Eric asked. We stopped talking; the noise of an engine grew louder. From the front porch, we watched a car make its careful way up the hill. From any distance, I would have recognized Eugene's blond halo.

If Mark and Eric had been surprised by Charlie, they really didn't know what to make of Eugene. His arms rose and dipped, bird-like as he entered the room. "A party!" he exclaimed. "How exciting! Is that cheesecake?"

I leaned against the sink. I only had four chairs and they were occupied. I used all four of my small plates to serve the cheesecake and put my own piece on a saucer. I poured coffee while the men quizzed each other. Soon the conversation turned to coal mining.

Eugene sighed, then leaned his long frame back in the chair. "Nance, don't you have some pot?" he asked. Then he covered his mouth with his hand. "Oops," he said. "Was that uncool?" He giggled.

I held my breath a second, immediately uneasy. I didn't know how the brothers felt about pot, but I didn't think they would call the cops. I had come to the conclusion that I wasn't interested in them romantically so any pressure to be a good girl was off.

"I'd smoke some pot," Charlie offered, pitching his voice low.

I looked at Mark, raised my eyebrows. "I don't smoke," Mark said. "But go ahead."

Eric nodded. "I'm not in law school yet. Don't mind us."

I rolled a few joints, lit one, and chose an album, *Brothers and Sisters* by the Allman Brothers, to play. I sat on the counter, legs swinging, as

Charlie, Eugene, and I passed the joint. We talked some more about coal mining. We talked about music. We ate more cheesecake. Around nine-thirty, I looked at the clock and shouted, "Oh my God! I almost forgot the Perseids!" Four sets of male eyes, two pairs bloodshot, looked at me. "A meteor shower," I explained. The guys shrugged their indifference, except for Eugene, who clapped his hands and trilled, "How exciting! Let's go see!"

Eugene and I left Mark, Eric, and Charlie in the kitchen, picked our way across the ruts in the road, and spread a blanket in the meadow. I lit another joint. We sat on the crunchy remains of hay, passed the joint, and pointed our chins to the sky. A few minutes passed.

"I want to lie down," Eugene said. He patted the blanket next to him. We stretched out on our backs. The sky was a vast ceiling of stars above us.

"Beautiful," breathed Eugene.

"Watch the north," I suggested. "I read that's where they're supposed to be." An easy wind stirred the warm mountain air. We could hear the stereo faintly back at the house.

A pale streak across the sky tickled my peripheral vision.

"Did you see that?" I asked Eugene. I doubted my own eyes, high as I was.

"No," Eugene whined.

Then a broad, white streak took a diagonal run just above us.

"Oh my God!" Eugene squealed.

"It looked like something Disney drew!" I shrieked.

Then we saw another, and another. Random white lines, some bright, some faint, dissected the sky. We giggled, then laughed out loud.

"There! There!" we pointed. And laughed some more. This was a show that needed to be shared, that needed witnesses. Who would believe such tales of a sky filled with shooting stars?

"I'm going to get the others," I said, and stumbled down to the house. I blinked as I entered the bright kitchen, used my hand as a visor to shield my eyes. Mark, Eric, and Charlie hadn't noticed that the record had stopped. They were deep in conversation, talking about the differences between Judaism and Christianity.

"It's magic!" I interrupted. "You have to see!"

They pushed back their chairs and followed me to the field. They leaned back on their heels and watched the sky. I waited for the shouts of glee.

"This hurts my neck," Mark said. He shifted from foot to foot.

Eric yawned.

Charlie's hair seemed even longer with his head back. "This is cool," he said, but his voice was flat, unconvincing.

"It's more comfortable on the blanket," I offered. Three heads shook no. Eugene flung his arms wide, not offended. We passed a few awkward minutes. The moon was rising and the meteors were harder to see.

"Well," said Mark, breaking the silence. "It's a long trip to Morgantown." Eric nodded in agreement. Both seemed relieved to be making their exit.

We watched their car slowly head down the road. I plopped back down on the blanket, looked at Charlie, patted the space next to me. "Join us," I prompted.

Charlie looked at me, then at Eugene. "Naw," he said, shrugging his shoulders. "Bad back." Where was the desire I had felt for him before? Not here. I followed him to his motorcycle, gave him a casual kiss, then watched as he disappeared around the bend. Eugene straggled down from the field, wearing the blanket like a cape. He twirled it off and tucked it around me.

"I had a wonderful time tonight," he said. "I'll never forget it."

I settled on the swing as this last set of headlights faded from view. A train, probably full of coal, made its slow way up the valley. The sound was musical and mournful. I sighed and leaned back against the oak slats. I hungered for a mate. My sister was married. My cousins were married. My high school friends were married. Would I ever find love? I lit another joint, hopped off the swing, and walked back into the field. I sprawled on the blanket and again tilted my face to the stars.

Section Two

✦ ✦ ✦

A MATE

14

♦ ♦ ♦

SWITCHING GEARS

———

MARY JANE GRABBED THE STICK SHIFT and pulled. For the fourth time that morning, ominous grinding sounds vibrated the truck as it lurched into reverse instead of second gear.

"Shit!" Mary Jane cried. I held my breath in a futile effort to control my giggles. Across the bench seat, Mary Jane gave me a look of exasperation and need.

"I'm such a Moats." Mary Jane sighed. "Let me try again."

In Preston County, Moats was a pejorative. The Moatses were known for their inbreeding, their lack of intelligence, their strange flat faces, and their poverty. Mary Jane had started working for *The Preston County News* in the summer of 1976. She sold advertising and often found herself overwhelmed by the task. "Come on, Mary Moats, you can do this," she'd say to herself as she paced the office.

Mary Jane had lived in Preston County her entire life. The day she walked into the newspaper, I knew we would be friends. She wore the same aviator-style glasses that I did (Gloria Steinem had them too) and she was close to my age. Her blonde bangs were a puffy fringe over high cheekbones and her slightly square figure was hidden by jeans and a flannel shirt worn tails out. An outfit nearly identical to mine.

Outgoing and enthusiastic, Mary Jane talked fast and laughed often. She added a burst of fun to the office.

The truck, a dirty blue Ford with *The Preston County News* logo on its side, idled in the parking lot of the Kingwood Plaza. When Mary Jane asked me to teach her how to drive a stick shift, we headed to the only spacious, flat, paved space in all of Preston County. A Pizza Hut sat in the front part of the county's first strip mall, built a couple of years before by a man who made his fortune in coal. L-shaped, anchored at one end by a discount store and at the other by an A&P grocery, the mall was hailed when it opened.

Mary Jane was flummoxed by the truck's "three on the tree" transmission. "Picture an H," I said. I drew the letter in the air and she nodded. "Reverse is at the top left with first below it. Second is at the top right. Third gear is below that. Neutral is in the middle." Mary Jane furrowed her eyebrows in concentration, put the stick shift in first and stepped on the gas while easing up on the clutch. The truck jumped forward and gained a little speed.

"Now shift," I said.

Mary Jane pushed in the clutch and brought the gear shift straight up. Into reverse. Again.

"Clutch, clutch!" I shrieked as the truck shuddered, coughed, and died. I rolled back and forth in the seat, hugged my sides, and laughed until I cried. Mary Jane frowned at me.

"Shit! I'm never going to get this."

I sat up, wiped away tears with the back of my hand, and caught my breath. "Mary Jane, hold your hand out, palm down." Mary Jane extended her right arm. I took her hand and pushed it down and away to her right. "Like this," I said. "Now turn your palm up. If you grab the gear shift like that, you're going to keep pulling it into reverse." She pushed up her glasses and nodded.

"Remember, down and out."

◆

So it was that I taught Mary Jane how to drive a stick shift and, in return, she helped me to infiltrate Preston County's youth underground.

Mary Jane seemed to know everyone. She and Eugene were close; the two of them created a party wherever they were, whether it was in a field in the middle of nowhere or at the Eagles Club in Kingwood. Fat Man's Face played somewhere every weekend. Charlie and the guys were local celebrities. We joined their fans, gyrated in front of the stage, and pulled out joints during the breaks.

One day in mid-August, Mary Jane came and stood in front of my desk. "I want to take you to a new place on Friday." She held a stack of paper, notes for the ads she had sold that week. "It's called the Top Joint and it's up near Cooper's Rock. Fat Man's Face is playing and I think my old boyfriend Mike might be there. I'd love to see him again. Maybe we could even get back together." Then she turned and headed downstairs to begin designing and pasting up ads.

That Saturday, we drove to the Top Joint, which was near the northern border of West Virginia, just below the Mason-Dixon Line. The low, unpainted wood building, a series of add-ons, sagged against the side of a hill. Coopers Rock State Forest, twelve thousand acres, was just down the road. During the Depression, the Civilian Conservation Corps used native chestnut and stone to build several structures in the park, including an overlook with a spectacular view of the Cheat River Gorge. But the Top Joint was a sad comment on this grand location. That night, I wasn't at my best either. On an impulse, I had gone to the local beauty shop and asked the owner to cut off all my hair and give me a perm. I looked like Little Orphan Annie; several people mentioned that. But I wore a favorite outfit that evening: a pair of white painter pants that followed the curve of my ass, and a tight, striped T-shirt.

I followed Mary Jane through the door, where she greeted two guys playing pool. Past her, down a dim hallway, two men, one dark-haired, one fair, stood with their backs to us facing an open space from which music erupted. Both men were long-haired and lean, which I found attractive. I looked at the blond, then the brunet, noted the nice asses on both, and thought, hmm, this is going to be fun.

The man with the light hair turned, looked at me, and began a sauntering approach. His hair fell past his shoulders, feathered back Farrah Fawcett-style, but not in a fussy way. The golden waves framed high cheekbones and a robust red mustache. The man looked like he could be in an alt country band except that he had an outlaw vibe of Keith Richards, that slightly intoxicated drooped body language. His eyes went to my hips and lingered a bit on my breasts. He sidled up beside me, close enough for me to see that his brilliant blue eyes were slightly bloodshot.

"Hey, my name's Wilford," he said. "You wanna sit on my face?"

I was shocked. But I recovered. "You want to come home with me?" I couldn't believe those words had come out of my mouth.

Wilford put his arm around my waist, guided me toward the band, and we began to dance. The music bounced off the wooden building, swirled through the fenced yard, and hung over the trees. The crowd pushed Wilford close. He was graceful and unselfconscious, the best dance partner I had ever had. I loved to dance. There's something primitive and satisfying about moving hips and stomping feet. Wilford matched me step for step, occasionally reaching out to twirl me in a circle. His hands on my hips felt comfortable, not lecherous. The band members nodded at me and grinned their approval. The guitars whined and the drums beat a rhythm that we echoed with our feet. Although the altitude of the bar kept the worst of the August heat at bay, our faces were shiny with sweat. We stopped only when the band took a break. Wilford offered me a red handkerchief that he pulled from his back pocket and I gasped with delight. The gesture reminded me of my father, who always carried a hanky. Wilford's folded, cotton square bore the symbolism of security. My attraction took on new significance. During that break, Wilford introduced me to his friend Todd, the man I had seen with him earlier. Mary Jane greeted both men; they appeared to be old friends. In fact, it seemed as though everyone at the bar knew everyone else.

We danced every set. We danced until the music stopped and the band started packing gear. I looked at Wilford in the sudden quiet. I could barely hear myself say, "You want to come home with me?" I knew Wilford's answer would be yes. Our attraction was like an electric charge in the air around us. I liked his looks, but in spite of his opening line, I also sensed that he was a gentleman. Wilford glanced at me with eyebrows raised in delight. He slid into the passenger side of my little Ford truck.

"What's your last name?" I asked.

"Feather," he said. He nodded his head, an old-fashioned gesture. "I'm Wilford Feather. From Glade Farms. Near Bruceton. Pleased to meet you." I took his hand and bowed toward him, felt gravity as a force.

As we pulled out of the parking lot, I noticed a pair of headlights behind us. They followed us down Route 73, then south on Route 26. Wilford told me to watch for the Prison Road. "It's a short cut to Terry Altie," he said, pronouncing the words as the locals did. "There," he pointed, and I veered left. When the headlights stayed with us, I realized we were being pursued.

"Do you know who that is?"

"No, Hon," Wilford said. "I can't tell what kind of car it is." In Preston County, people were identified by the vehicles they drove. When my younger sister visited and I loaned her my truck I told her to watch for waves from other drivers. "Wave back," I said. "Or they'll think I'm a snob."

Prison Road, according to the locals, had been built by prisoners. They must have been a bitter lot; the road is dangerously narrow with a couple of hairpin turns. I was driving fast, just this side of reckless. The high beams lit up the trees as we lurched around the first sharp turn and I braked hard. "Whoo-hoo!" Wilford yelped. "Git her, girl!" We picked up speed, then I gasped as the road ahead disappeared. I was forced to brake again as the blacktop dipped and turned back on itself. We slid through the curve, narrowly missing a tree that loomed close to the road. My heart was pounding from the danger and the excitement. The headlights behind us fell away.

But when we reached the Brandonville Pike, a road I was familiar with, the lights were back in my rearview mirror, and they stayed there through ten miles of alternating curves and straight stretches. "It's got to be someone we know," Wilford assured me. By now we were more puzzled than frightened. The car followed us when we turned onto Route 7, then Salt Lick. The lights were still on us when I turned up my driveway. Anyone who followed me up this road had to have been there before. I pulled in front of my dark house and Wilford and I jumped out of the truck.

"Hey," came a voice from the car idling in my driveway. "You sure drive fast."

"Who's there?" I tried to sound sure of myself.

"Well I'll be danged," Wilford walked toward the car and leaned in its window. "Hey, Doc. Hey, Bill."

Two men got out of the car. I recognized them both. The larger man was Doc Harriman's son, Bill Junior, also called Doc. He had been a medic in Vietnam. I had met his dad during my summer internship in 1974 when I did photographs for the doctor shortage tabloid. Bill Junior's friend, also named Bill, lived in Terra Alta. He was a regular at Fat Man's Face shows.

"Hippie, we thought you were a girl!" Doc laughed. "We thought we were following a couple of chicks!"

"Hippie?" I turned to Wilford.

"That's my nickname," he flicked his hair. "Hip." The four of us laughed at the folly of our road race.

"Hey, Hip, got any moonshine?" Doc asked.

Moonshine? I looked at Wilford, examined him again, the lean body, the relaxed stance. Who was this man? And what did he know about moonshine? All I knew was the stuff of legend: hidden stills, pursuit by the revenuers. I was intrigued.

"Nah," Wilford shook his head. "But I can get my hands on some." He glanced over at me. "Not tonight." The two men got back in their car and honked a farewell.

"Moonshine?" I asked as we headed to the house.

"I don't make it," Wilford said. "I just sell a little."

It was answer enough. I took Wilford's hand and led him to bed, where we danced the best dance.

◆

"Where's your lawnmower?" Wilford asked the next morning. He leaned against the kitchen counter, cradled a coffee cup in his fine, long fingers. Although it was August, mornings were cool in the mountains. "You haven't mowed for a while." This was an assessment, not an accusation.

We walked around the side of the house and I retrieved the old, rotary push mower I had bought for a few dollars at a yard sale. I didn't have much of a lawn and I had thought this gas-less machine would be less trouble than a modern lawnmower. And it was certainly less expensive. The couple of times I had tried to use it, though, I had given up in frustration. Mostly it chewed the weeds into strings that clogged the blades. Wilford squatted to examine it more closely. "If I had my tools, I could sharpen the blades," he said. "But it's never going to work very well." He stood up and put his arm around my waist in a gesture that already felt familiar. "Maybe I'll bring up a mower next time I visit."

After we'd finished our coffee, we drove back to the Top Joint so he could pick up his car, a battered Chevy Vega that sat by itself in the gravel lot. "Follow me to Todd's," he said. Todd was his dark-haired friend at the Top Joint. This chase was different from the previous night's adventure. Wilford's smoke-spewing Vega never came close to the speed limit.

I soon found out that Todd grew up in Florida, but he was spending the summer on his family's farm on Moyers Road, a road that bore his family's name. Wilford and I skirted a big, old farmhouse and made our way toward a tiny white house surrounded by small, unpainted buildings—an outhouse, some sheds. The barn was by far the biggest of all the structures. A clothesline between the outbuildings dipped under the weight of a neat row of jeans, T-shirts, and towels. Wilford and I entered the kitchen arm in arm. "Hey, you lovebirds," Todd said with a grin. "Hungry?" He wielded a cast-iron skillet. "I'm making some home fries." Bacon glistened on a plate. He took boiled new potatoes, chopped them, and scattered them in the skillet. When they were burnished and crisp, we ate.

It was a perfect summer day. We smoked cigarettes and pot. We talked and talked and ate some more. Todd and Wilford drank beer. I sipped cold well water from a canning jar. I explained my abstinence. "I've never been much of a drinker," I shrugged. "If I drink enough to get a buzz, I don't feel good." I pulled out a joint. "I prefer drugs, just enough to get high." I had a hard time understanding why kids my age wanted to get totally wasted on either intoxicant.

When Todd and Wilford's friend Chip showed up he nodded a disinterested greeting. Was I just another chick invading the clubhouse? I was too happy, too stoned, too sexually satiated to care. We lounged in a circle under the shade of a maple tree. When the talk turned to guns, I sat up.

"I know how to shoot," I said.

They looked at me. No one spoke.

"Really," I insisted.

They lined up beer cans on a fence and I watched from a distance, my fingers in my ears. Todd held the gun with assurance, as did Chip. Wilford's body language was more tentative. I could tell he wasn't an enthusiast, but the others seemed oblivious. When they grew tired of target shooting, they started throwing cans into the air so they could attempt to hit moving targets. I pointed to the laundry and suggested they throw the cans toward the open field. "Good idea," said Todd. They turned and started shooting again. The cans fell to earth, unmarred.

"Let me try," I said, stepping forward. "Please." I didn't tell them that my father made sure each of his three daughters knew how to handle a gun. One of his friends would toss clay pigeons across the sky so we could practice shooting moving targets. When I was Annie Oakley in eighth grade, chosen to sing four lines of "You Can't Get a Man with a Gun" because I was the girl with the loudest, deepest voice, I carried a real shotgun (not loaded) on stage.

Todd handed me a shotgun and I nodded at Wilford. He tossed a can high into the blue sky. I raised the gun, squeezed the trigger, and the can exploded with a flat, metallic thud. I hid my surprise; I hadn't really thought that I'd hit anything. I pointed the barrel toward the ground, shrugged in what I hoped was a modest gesture, and handed the gun back.

"Whee-hee!" Wilford cried. He danced a little jig. "That's my woman." We kissed with a loud smack. Todd gave me a cheer. Chip nodded.

◆

Wilford and I spent the rest of the weekend together. We discovered we were both born in September 1953. I was twenty-six days his senior. We lay in bed, a breeze skittering through curtains cooling our skin. We explored each other's bodies, our twin coloring: fair skin and freckles. His arms and face were a blanket of dots. My freckles were patterns across my shoulders, nose, and knees. Oh, I was happy. Here was my mate at last, I thought. But I had noticed a small area of decay in Wilford's top front teeth. Lying there, I fixated on the flaw, tried to assess its effect on my affection. I closed my eyes, ran my hands down his sinewy, smooth back. We'll fix his teeth, I thought, and snuggled against his side. I relaxed in his arms, my ass a perfect fit against his concave belly. The golden August seemed to bestow its blessing upon us.

The next Friday, I picked Wilford up from the lumber company where he worked. He had told me that he ran a chipper, but I was not prepared for the Rube Goldberg apparatus that filled a cavernous barn. Wilford fed scraps of wood and bark into a hopper that emptied into a great, spinning wheel eight feet in diameter. This screeching monster spit out mountains of mulch. My new love scurried up and down metal-grate paths high above me. He tugged rubber belts, pulled levers, moved quickly.

Finally, the monster stopped and Wilford climbed down.

"You mind waiting while I change knives?" he asked.

Wilford straddled the stilled chipper expertly and one by one removed and replaced the blades that fanned from its center. His grease-stained hands moved with expertise; the muscles rippled in his wiry body. Every once in a while he would look down at me and grin, a slow smile that deepened the dimple-like lines in his cheeks, that lit a source of heat deep inside me.

◆

Some new relationships are sealed with fancy dinners or flowers. On our third weekend together my new boyfriend brought me a lawn-mower. It was so old the red paint was just a suggestion over grime. But as soon as we got to my house, Wilford brought it to life with a quick, fierce tug. I sat on my porch swing and watched this sexy man tame my front yard in fifteen minutes. When he joined me, bits of grass and grease flecked his bare chest. He tucked a cold beer between his legs.

"When I was growing up, we mowed six acres of grass," I said, pushing the swing with my feet. "My sisters and I argued all the time about whose turn it was to mow. They didn't mind so much; they'd put on swimming suits and get a tan. But I burned. I was hot and miserable. I'd be happy if I never mowed another lawn as long as I live."

"Okay, Hon," Wilford said, patting my shoulder. "I'll mow."

We walked up the road behind my house and Wilford was quick to appreciate the view. We climbed to the very top of the hill and sat there, hand in hand, surveying the valley. My mountains. My man. On Sunday I took Wilford to work with me. He kept me company as I developed film and made prints. He understood the dark of the darkroom as an absolute. He understood making his way with touch. When I promised I would get him to work early Monday morning, he agreed to spend Sunday night with me.

"Should I pack your lunch?" I asked in the morning.

"Nah. Ma will send a bucket with Pap. He works at the mill, too. You'd have met him but he left before you got there."

It turned out that Wilford spent the entire week with me. Every day, his mother packed his lunch and sent it with his father. On the following Sunday, I finally took him home. He was eager to introduce me to his parents.

From the road, their house seemed barely a house at all. It was a basement built into a slight hill, its opening to the rear. It would take a decade for the Feathers to build what looked like a real house, and then only because the basement's flat roof had started to leak. The new structure had sides and a peaked roof, but the inside was an unfinished shell.

When we went inside the basement, the place smelled of dampness and cigarettes. Dripping plastic bags—the Feathers were early recyclers—were clipped to a clothesline just inside the only door. A large dog beautifully marked with silver and black whined and wiggled in greeting.

"Hey, Woman." Wilford knelt to pet the dog. "This is Misty," he said. "She's part white shepherd, part Doberman." I reached down to stroke her head and she wagged her tail. She didn't jump on me, which I appreciated.

Wilford's mother was at the stove. "Hello," she said. Her voice was soft and her hair shone white in the slant of sun coming in the kitchen window. "You must be Nancy. I'm Ellen." She pointed to a man in a recliner. "That's Guy." Wilford's father, a lean man like his son, nodded a greeting. The kitchen was crowded with food: plates of sausage, jars of homemade jelly, and a platter of soft molasses cookies that would later make me swoon. A box of peaches under the table added their sweet smell to the mix. The paneled living room was dark except for a row of high windows that bled dusty light through a row of succulents. The television blared and old newspapers and bundles of cloth were piled everywhere. A quilt in a frame took up a quarter of the space in the room.

Wilford had told me that his mother was a nurse's aide at Hopemont State Hospital. Hopemont, a former tuberculosis sanitarium, then a facility for the chronically ill, was just outside Terra Alta. I had covered several events there and knew Ellen probably worked hard. It was obvious that she spent her spare time cooking and quilting, not cleaning. I was not so good at cleaning myself; I could never please my immaculate mother.

Two large old photographs framed in raised oval glass drew my attention. I walked closer to take a look. Even in black and white, I could see the family resemblance in the portraits' pale eyes.

"The Feathers have been in these parts for way more than a hundred years," Wilford said. His tone was matter-of-fact, not boasting. A nonchalance of belonging.

"We're all family of Jacob Feather." Guy was a little hard to understand. He didn't have all his teeth.

"I hope you're hungry," Ellen called to us. "I'm making buckwheat cakes and gravy."

"I love buckwheat cakes. Can I help?"

"No, just sit and I'll red up." Red up? I had never heard that phrase.

Ellen cleared the table, a peninsula off the counter, by pushing several Ball jars of jelly to the side. "Mike," she said. "Go to the fruit cellar and get a jar of applesauce."

Mike? Who was Mike?

"Hey, Nance," Wilford said. "Come along." He headed out the door and I followed. How many names did this man have?

"Mike? I thought your name was Hippie. Or Wilford."

"My legal name is Wilford Mike Feather." Wilford strode across the yard toward a low shack. He called back over his shoulder. "Some people call me Mike; others call me Hip, but I am Wilford too." He took my hand so I wouldn't slip in the mud outside the fruit cellar, a springhouse lined with shelves of colorful home-canned goods. He handed me a jar of applesauce, then carefully latched the door behind us.

I stopped suddenly, my heart beating a wild rhythm in my chest.

"Mike?" I said. "Mary Jane's Mike?" I thought I might cry.

"Aw, Hon," Wilford said. He wrapped his arms around me. "Mary Jane isn't mad." He made clucking, consoling sounds. "Did she say anything to you?"

"No." I tried to remember any reproach. For the past two weeks Mary Jane hadn't even hinted that I had stolen her old boyfriend away. "He's a great guy," was what she had told me. "I'm happy for you."

◆

On Monday, I walked up to Mary Jane, hung my head, and whispered an apology. "I'm so sorry," I said. "I didn't know my Wilford was your Mike."

Mary Jane rested her hand on my shoulder. Her eyes found mine. "It's okay. He wasn't mine," she said quietly. She tilted her head toward me. "I saw that the moment you two met."

Within a year Mary Jane found a new job as a receptionist for a young doctor. She also found a new beau, a man who was impressed because she could drive a stick shift.

Within a year Wilford moved in with me. He brought the unreliable Chevy, some albums, several hats, and Misty, his beautiful dog. He brought tools and energy and he brought me a sense of belonging.

A CANOEIST passes Calamity Rock during the 1974 whitewater races on the Cheat Narrows.

RAY WONG, a friend from the University of Missouri, visited Terra Alta in 1975 and took this picture of me covering a parade. I miss that skirt but I still use that little Leitz tripod.

"A VERY SPECIAL VISITOR" is the headline over this portrait, the cover of a pullout section on the 1974 war games. Underneath: "His mission: To liberate Preston County."

THE CAPTION for this photo reads, "A small, but edible, turtle was none too pleased with its fate."

TOP: Do I look like a pacifist?
ABOVE: A "guerilla" scouts a bridge over the Cheat River.

DR. WILLIAM HENRY HARRIMAN JR. "Dr. Harriman makes one or two house calls a day," reads the caption, which then quotes the doctor:

"You can tell an awful lot about some people by going into their homes."

JERRY PLAYS HIS DULCIMER at a craft shop in Terra Alta.

SISTERS pose for a portrait outside of Rowlesburg.

MY FIRST FORAY into the world as a professional photojournalist.
(Photo by Bob Abrams.)

CORRESPONDENTS from throughout Preston County wrote weekly columns about their communities. Jessie Davis submitted the news from Sinclair Ridge on lined notebook paper. In 1976 I decided to meet and photograph all the correspondents.

PAUL, the leader of the hike, pauses on the Red Creek Trail
at Dolly Sods.

THE JUNIOR DEPUTIES wait for Bruceton's Good Neighbor Days
parade to begin.

WILFORD CARRIES MY TRIPOD as we make our way up the hill behind our cabin, seen in the background. The barn is no longer there; the wood was more valuable than the structure.

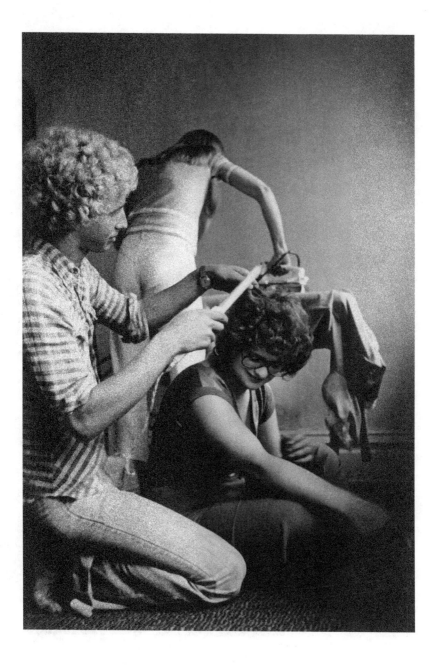

EUGENE helps Mary Jane get ready for her wedding.

JUDY, STYLISH SALES REP for *The Preston County News.*

15

♦ ♦ ♦

JUDY JUDY JUDY

––––––

IF MARY JANE AND I had shared the same flannel-shirts-and-jeans fashion sense, Judy, her replacement, was my fashion polar opposite. Judy wore classics: A-line shifts, sleeveless to show lithe arms, a vintage camel hair suit, carefully ironed white shirts. Her hair was cropped short with bangs that arched over her forehead. She smoked often and with enthusiasm. Where Mary Jane was friendly and laid back, great attributes for her new job in a doctor's office, Judy was serious, professional. She came to us in 1977 from a job at a Morgantown radio station. It was the newspaper's luck to snag someone who not only wanted the ad sales position but had the talent necessary to do a good job.

"Judy Judy Judy." Jerry, Rich, and I tried to mimic Cary Grant as mimicked by Goober on Mayberry: an exhaled emphasis on "Ju" and the briefest pause before "dee." Names interested me. Debbies, Lindas, Billys, and Bobbys were fellow baby boomers. So were Judys, Joes, and Kathys. Wilford's three names signaled three identities: Wilford, the old-fashioned gentleman, known only to a few; Mike, a school friend, a member of the family; Hip, the Hippie, long-haired and hard-partying. Judy met Wilford; she drank with Hip.

Judy was a social creature, at ease at the Preston Country Club or a crummy beer joint. She and Wilford would hold court, drinks lined up on the bar in front of them while I nursed one beer, slowly peeling the label from the bottle. Sometimes they would howl with the joy of alcohol and words. They told stories. I was an appreciative audience.

Michele and Jerry had moved out of the apartment upstairs from the newspaper and into their newly built house soon after Judy started work at the newspaper. Judy eyed the vacant expanse and convinced me that we should claim the abandoned living room for our office. She stood in our new space, sucked on a True cigarette, narrowed her eyes, and stared at the big, blank walls. "Paint," she said in a clipped, deep voice. "We need to paint." She blew smoke into the room. "Something dark and rich. Your photos will look great against that." She turned to me. "Do you paint?"

"Not well," I admitted. "But I'll try." I was flattered that she liked my photos enough to want to look at them every day. Until Judy, the photos had been stacked on a shelf in the darkroom, images ironed onto black cardboard rectangles. Days later, a dozen images striped mahogany walls. I admired the room, our work. Judy and I sat at our desks and smoked. I imagined sophistication entering through my pores. Judy was from Ohio; if she could project cool, maybe I had a chance.

Jerry pounded up the steps, stopped on the landing, and surveyed the room. "That paint's the color of diarrhea!" he exclaimed. Shit! He all but said it looked like shit. My satisfaction wavered. Judy stood up, crossed her arms, and walked to the front of her desk. She leaned against it and shrugged. "I like it," she said.

"Me too." And I would. Judy's confidence was a lesson: damn the critics. Please yourself. Under Judy's influence, I put away my overalls, paid attention to my wardrobe, polished my earrings. Distracted by trends and thwarted by budget, I found it difficult to live up to Judy's good example. But the effort propelled me toward adulthood.

❧ 16 ❧

✦ ✦ ✦

DIAMONDS ARE A GIRL'S BEST FRIEND

WEST VIRGINIA UNIVERSITY'S social work program cycled students in and out of Preston County. Many of them were from out of state. The graduate student in front of our group leaned forward on her chair. She clasped her arms between her legs as if she were afraid they would fly off if she didn't. Her untamed curly hair, her slender physique, and her confident attitude were clues that she was an outsider.

She started to speak. Her expressive hands, loosed from her grasp, fluttered and flew. Like a preacher. Like a choir director. The women in the circle around her were making history: the first consciousness raising group in Preston County. It was 1977 and across the country, women gathered to discuss their rights—to better pay, to abortions, to jobs previously closed to women. And, most important of all, the right to be safe. The vocabulary had grown. We now had terms like *domestic violence* and *battered women* to name the evil that haunted women's lives. We had finally realized that rape was a crime of violence. In the 1970s, women's lives had changed.

Just a handful of women showed up at each meeting: social work students; women like me, young professionals who had moved to Preston County; other outsiders. Marian had moved from Pennsylvania; Mickey from Maryland. Both were stay-at-home mothers with young children. We sat in a circle and nodded. We wanted equal pay for women; we wanted good childcare. We were confident that Congress would pass the Equal Rights Amendment. How could they not? Sure, there might be a battle, but we would win. Women had rights. Options.

The grad student told us that the Women's Information Center in Morgantown offered free pregnancy testing. (This was long before a woman could buy a chemical-coated stick in a drugstore: women had to go to a doctor or the health department to confirm a pregnancy.) She told us about a clinic in Pittsburgh that did abortions.

Our group wanted our own Women's Information Center. We wanted to help women who had unplanned pregnancies. We wanted to help victims of rape and domestic violence. We wanted to provide a safe place for women to speak openly. We met, ironically, at the county jail, in a carpeted room on the third floor, under slanted eaves. Our small group lamented our inability to recruit more participants. We sat in our circle and wondered what women in Preston County needed.

"Child care?" Marian guessed.

The grad student nodded. "That may be true." Then, in a strong, clear voice, she proclaimed, "I'm never having children." We gaped at her. "In fact," she announced, "I'm going to have my tubes tied." She leaned back in her chair, arms crossed defiantly across her chest.

"Are you sure?" Marian finally asked. "You're so young." She and Mickey exchanged puzzled looks.

"Yes, I'm sure," the student said. She quickly added, "My boyfriend supports my decision." She shrugged. "I guess I'm one of those women who don't want children."

I didn't understand. I wanted children. My first paid job had been babysitting for a young family. Their toddler, Sam, won my heart. I knew I would have a son, that I would name him Sam. With the certainty of youth, I had my life planned.

◆

Social work students from the university helped Preston County get much-needed services: options for victims of domestic violence, a new birth center at the hospital in Kingwood, and a daycare center. But serious feminism failed to gain a foothold. The county seemed to be stuck in the 1950s. Men aspired to good wages in coal mines or factories. Almost everyone believed that the man was the breadwinner, the wife the caregiver. Twenty years after Elvis came on the scene, his hairstyle was still copied. The typical Preston County man worshipped guns and vehicles and counted the days until hunting season. At one of my first Thanksgivings with Wilford's family, I put a bowl of mashed potatoes on the table and sat down. Other women emerged from the kitchen, serving dishes in hand, and stared at me. "The men eat first," someone said. I jumped from the chair and slunk back into the kitchen, embarrassed by my faux pas and confounded by the custom. Women in Preston County kept the house and tended children. Or they had traditional jobs: teacher, secretary, nurse. Many women never learned to drive. Husbands sat outside grocery stores, vehicles idling, while their wives prowled the aisles. That was the way things were.

At the ball field in Terra Alta, I photographed the men's slow-pitch softball game. The spectators, the women in particular, seemed to be enjoying themselves. They were there to support boyfriends and husbands on the field, but this was obviously a social event for them.

"Do any of you play?" I asked. They shook their heads.

"The high school has a team," said a woman whom I recognized as an elementary school teacher. "But there's nothing for girls after they get out of school."

"I'd like to play," I offered. Other women nodded.

The teacher organized a scrimmage between two groups of women. And another. Mickey, my friend from the Women's Information Center, organized a team in Kingwood. Word spread.

That fall, a dozen or more women sat around two tables on the second floor of the Terra Alta Moose Club. The dim room smelled like scuffed wood and spilled alcohol. But the women, a raucous group, loud and animated, were oblivious. They had come from all over Preston County—Masontown, Rowlesburg, Kingwood, and Terra Alta—and they were going to do something radical. They were going to start a women's softball league. I was not there just to cover the meeting for the newspaper; I was an enthusiastic booster of the project.

◆

My father was a ball player. Some of my earliest memories are of his fierce Sunday morning softball games. The glorious, silky dirt of the infield. The wondrous, sweet, animal smell of a baseball glove. The song of a wooden bat making solid contact with a ball. Sweaty men threw themselves on the ground, spikes up, sliding toward second base. I don't remember any spectators at these games. My mother never came. I'm sure she enjoyed the morning's solitude, husband and children at play. I'm sure she sat in her favorite chair, one leg tucked beneath her, a cigarette in one hand, a book in the other.

I was ten when I started playing softball. My sister Julie and I were short, fast members of the American Legion girls' team. Our uniforms, thick, soft blue cotton, had knickers that belted just below our knees. Julie was more competitive than I was, though I enjoyed the game. I loved being in the outfield, solitary, alert, my face tipped to the sun. Ready to sprint and throw.

◆

The joy of play, of team, never left me, so it was natural that I joined Terra Alta's women's team, the First National Bank Follies. I played center field. My teammates were all more talented: a right hander who hit the ball down the right field line, the steadiest infielder I've ever seen, and our captain, whose lack of speed was offset by her leadership and powerful swing. I recruited Judy, my coworker, who became a star pitcher. Unlike our teammates, Judy had not been an athlete in high school. She was not a natural runner, instead circling the bases in a series of graceful leaps. She defended her style and was aghast when one of the Follies slid into second base. "Why a grown woman would throw herself on the ground at a dead run is beyond me!" she cracked.

The Women's Information Center never gained popularity in Preston County. But the softball league thrived. Every spring and summer women gathered on fields to throw, bat, run, and cheer. Teams developed cross-county rivalries, grew familiar enough with each other to know whose throwing skills could be challenged and what batters deserved respect. It was socially acceptable for women to abandon their families to play softball. To do something for themselves. To join with other women in the sheer joy of athleticism.

Consciousness raising doesn't necessarily have to occur in a circle. Sometimes, it happens on a diamond.

17

♦ ♦ ♦

DISASTER PRACTICE

THE END OF THE WORLD began on a Friday in 1977. In the basement of the Preston County jail, static crackled from walkie-talkies then merged with voices and footsteps to form a cacophony that echoed off concrete walls. Fluorescent lights dropped from the gray ceiling, cast a green pall over gray furniture and cigarette smoke. Men scribbled on blackboards, spoke into radios, and huddled in earnest conference. Rich Wolfe, director of the Emergency Operations Center and the man in charge, sat in the middle of the room, his chair tilted back. One hand cradled the back of his head. His shaggy white eyebrows lifted slightly and his sharp features carried a look of satisfaction. The disaster—a practice drill—was going well.

It was a big one: a nuclear weapon had been launched from Russia and was headed toward Washington, D.C., just 180 miles away by air from Preston County. Refugees would be headed toward our mountains. Camp Dawson, the military installation by the Cheat River, was on alert. So were the rail lines and the power plant. Thick, black phones rang in the gray room. Volunteers from fire departments and ambulance companies joined professionals from law enforcement agencies, businesses, and the government to prepare for the fallout, both literal and figurative.

Preston County regularly faced smaller disasters: car crashes, fires, train derailments. Until a trucking company's owner put a warning sign at the top of Caddell Mountain, paid for it himself, an occasional truck would burn out its brakes and plummet to the bottom of the steep grade, ending in death and a pile of twisted metal and broken glass on the down side of a sharp curve. Occasionally the Cheat River claimed an unwary swimmer or unlucky whitewater rafter.

I don't know what federal honcho chose this specific disaster scenario. In the mid-1970s, we were still spending too much money on the Cold War. Rich Wolfe believed in the cause. His posture said soldier but his hair said Elvis fan. Rich was a calming force in the busy room. He listened to deputies and firemen, nodded his head, and dispatched instructions in a still voice. Was this a show for me, for the newspaper? If so, it was well rehearsed. Rich was kind to me. Like a teacher, he stood before the chalkboard and explained the lesson. One corner of the board had the heading "Dead and Wounded." The volunteer fire departments and ambulance squads had their assignments. Rail traffic was being monitored. Rich handed me a small booklet, a guide for surviving nuclear war. I've saved it for years, not because I think it would be useful, but because it is cool. The design is straight out of the mid-1950s, with sans serif type and swirls of turquoise. The section on food safety contains line drawings of loaves of bread and canned vegetables.

I flipped through the booklet. "I'm not so sure it's right about post-nuclear-war food safety," I said. Rich shook his head. "Plastic wrap will protect food from radiation," he insisted. He pursed his cheeks and demonstrated how he would blow the poisoned dust off of packages. He brushed his palms up and down, as if they were cymbals. "Now it's safe," he declared.

◆

When I was growing up, my parents must not have believed nuclear war was worth surviving. Maybe that's why we didn't have a bomb shelter.

Or maybe they didn't want to spend the money. Probably they didn't have the money. But some friends did. We often visited a couple who had built an underground world. A model train setup occupied their entire basement. Several trains moved across bridges, through tunnels, and past miniature buildings. I could watch the trains circle for hours. I didn't like the bunker in the back yard, however. We had to descend a steep hatch to get to what felt like a concrete closet filled with supplies: canned food and batteries. Both the basement and bunker smelled the same, like metal parts, dusty cardboard, and dampness.

In October 1962, during the Cuban Missile Crisis, one of my mother's "doggy friends" sought refuge with us. Lesley, an heiress to a St. Louis department store fortune, lived across the highway from McDonnell Douglas, where behind high fences and walls secretive workers developed space capsules and fighter planes. One of those planes was used to photograph Soviet missiles in Cuba, so the manufacturing facility was alleged to be on Khrushchev's list of targets. Lesley showed up at our house, dogs in tow (a couple of Shetland Sheepdogs, a Bedlington Terrier or two, a Whippet), and took over Julie's room since it had the nicest furniture: a canopy bed and matching dresser.

Lesley looked like a French schoolgirl. But a little off. She wore pleated skirts, white blouses, and knee socks with saddle shoes. She was thin and stood with her shoulders hunched. Wiry gray hairs peppered a geometric dark bob that framed cats-eye glasses. Her voice was high and whiny. It sounds bad but everyone loved her, me included. She was weird and charismatic.

While the Russians threatened from the skies, our new collection of non-neutered, non-spayed dogs posed other problems. The scene at home was nearly as scary as the news. The canines claimed territory, growling and flashing sharp teeth. The six of us: my parents, my sisters, Lesley, and I, navigated a maze of baby gates and crates. The gates were about crotch height for my older sister and me; crossings necessitated a coordinated hop. I'm still convinced that I damaged my virginity when an encounter with a baby gate went awry. During the missile crisis we watched flickering black and white images of world leaders on television, and studied two daily newspapers. People were scared. I was young and skeptical. The "duck and cover" exercises we practiced at school seemed futile. But shouldn't grown-ups be smart enough to prevent annihilation?

Lesley brought us a coloring book that poked fun of Jackie Kennedy's quest to redecorate the White House. "Color me chartreuse," read the caption under a pillbox hat-wearing first lady. I flipped through the pages and looked up at my mother. "This is mean."

"That's politics," my mother said. "We can talk about it later." I was confused. I liked Lesley. I liked the Kennedys. How could this be? I didn't understand the missile crisis either but when that threat ended, Lesley packed her dogs and belongings and returned to her home. I bet she blamed Kennedy himself for her inconvenience.

I wonder if Kennedy's assassination changed Lesley's opinion. On that terrible November day in 1963, my fifth grade teacher, a sour, feared woman, walked slowly into the classroom and crumpled into her chair. Through tears, she explained that the president had died. A student ran to her side and the teacher pulled her onto her lap. The rest of us sat stunned, sobbing. We watched our teacher cry and rock and clutch our friend. My heart was broken.

◆

Decades later, in 1992, an article in *The Washington Post* revealed that West Virginia had played a vital role in planning for nuclear holocaust. During the Cold War, the federal government built a secret, underground complex for Congress at the exclusive Greenbrier Resort in southern West Virginia. In the event of nuclear war, our representatives could board a train and in just a few hours be deep under a mountain, sheltered safely behind thick, steel doors. The bunker is now a draw for tourists who step from rooms decorated by Dorothy Draper in shades of pink and green into the buff, metal paranoia of the late 1950s and early 1960s.

On the other hand, Preston County's bomb shelter was no secret. Refugees were to come via rail to a dusty limestone mine next to the Cheat River near Rowlesburg. Rich Wolfe imagined terrified citizens fleeing cities for the forests of Preston County. He seemed delighted by the opportunity to serve as their host. I watched the activities of the day-long disaster with skepticism. How could these men (and a few women) face this mythical calamity with such élan? Yes, their role-playing games offered unusual, dramatic opportunities. They were like peacetime soldiers finally sent to war, let loose with weapons, but with no fear of casualties. I understood that this practice was necessary.

But did anyone really believe we could ever be ready for nuclear war? People rarely recognized the real threats that surrounded us: the asbestos in the floor and around the pipes in the ceiling. The lead paint. The cigarette smoke. We're still surrounded by poisons. And we're still spending too much on weapons and soldiers and spies. Today I believe that satellite television played a huge role in changing the world. American capitalism looked pretty comfortable to foreign eyes: big houses, big televisions, fancy cars.

I was seven years old when the United States discovered missiles in Cuba. Ten when John Kennedy was murdered. Fourteen when Martin Luther King Jr. and Bobby Kennedy were gunned down. Sixteen when four students were shot at Kent State. And twenty-something and skeptical that day in the Emergency Operations Center. I focused my camera and took notes. I bore witness to the effort to control what followed calamity. The story that I wrote would be full of praise for Rich and his crew. I was genuinely impressed by their performance and grateful that they believed society was worth their efforts.

◆

I wonder if the people at the Emergency Operations Center would have bothered to save the crowd I was with later that week? Kenny's Steakhouse, a squat bar next to one of Preston County's two-lane highways, was packed with hippies and outlaws. A family overflowed one booth; a toddler stood on the seat, his arm slung over his mother's shoulder as she nursed a beer and a cigarette. A baby was propped on the table; glasses and overflowing ashtrays circled its bouncy seat. The juke box ricocheted from country song to pop hit. Kenny's booming voice welcomed his customers, even the lowlifes he might later threaten with a shotgun when arguments fortified by alcohol grew into fistfights. Kenny was short, rotund, and powerful. Old enough to have a son my age. Smart enough to know rock and roll was good for business.

Fat Man's Face mounted the stage—a plywood platform eight inches above the floor. The low ceiling and close space amplified their loud chords and echoing bass. Wilford handed me ear plugs. His pockets always contained marvelous things: a handkerchief, a handful of loose firecrackers, marijuana, peppermints, a pocket knife. A little money, enough for a quart of beer. He pulled me onto the dance floor, lifted my arm, and twirled me in a slow circle. The movement of his slender body gracefully echoed the throbbing rhythm. He shifted weight from foot to foot and I mirrored his actions. He changed steps, flung his arms toward the sky and I followed. Our synchronicity made us grin; it was as if the Gods had paired us. We danced the vibration of the bass, for the pleasure it brought to our bodies. It was a joyous mating ritual. When the music slowed, Wilford pulled me close. My head rested in the crook of his collarbone. My hands felt taut muscles through his thin shirt. Oh the memory of young skin. His hands gently steered me back and forth. It was bliss to be with such a partner.

My mother had admired dancers: Gene Kelley, Gower Champion. I recognized talent. At Kenny's a dark, doe-eyed woman, Wilford's brother's girlfriend, moved with extraordinary grace. I tried to imitate her style, arm flung high making a pleasing arc from toe to finger. I don't have a dancer's line, but that didn't stop me from trying. Friends joined us on the dance floor. We danced in the smoky, close cave of a club, music like an anthem to our survival. Wilford tipped his chin toward the ceiling and howled, a rallying cry, an exhalation of ecstasy. We all howled back. We danced and we danced. We danced until the lights came on and revealed a new day.

18

❖ ❖ ❖

WEST VIRGINIA BRIGADOON

TWO HUNDRED THIRTY-SEVEN INCHES of snow fell in Terra Alta during the winter of 1976–77. Nearly nine feet of snow fell in January. Snow masked the world like a scrim. The landscape turned simple: black and white and gray. The mountains were beautiful and terrible, cold and high. Snow erased the roads, halted commerce, isolated families, attracted the national media.

Jerry had predicted that the state would not be prepared for a bad winter and it wasn't. West Virginia had just a few snow blowers and the one assigned to Preston County was down for repairs. Miles of roads remained impassable. Jerry was filled with righteous indignation. Local folks knew to get ready for big storms, he said, but they also expected the state to be prepared.

As the situation worsened, Jerry rallied help: several coal operators sent front-end loaders to move the snow. Soon after his January 1977 inauguration, West Virginia's brand-new governor, Jay Rockefeller, activated the National Guard. Thousands of residents were stranded in their homes. They needed medicine and food, help feeding their livestock. Some were out of coal, their only source of heat. In Kingwood,

Rich Wolfe, head of the Emergency Operations Center, coordinated an army of volunteers and the real Army. On the ground, the West Virginia National Guard would use six-wheel-drive Gama Goats to deliver coal, groceries, and medicine. In the air, helicopters could drop hay for animals.

◆

This all sounded like a great story for the newspaper. I was psyched to go with the National Guard on a mission. On a frigid day in early February, I climbed aboard a Gama Goat and found a perch on the cold metal shelf between two seats. When the two guardsmen got in, we were shoulder to shoulder in the tight space. The Gama Goat lurched forward and I lurched with it, arms wrapped around my camera bag. The Gama Goat was the vehicular equivalent of a Gila monster: low and threatening but slightly ridiculous, a cut-off Jeep front and a four-wheel wagon. The Army designed it to move cargo across Vietnam's rough terrain. Our mission was to deliver coal to the Rutherfords, a family on Laurel Mountain. The twenty miles of two-lane highway we covered on our way to the coal yard were torture. The vehicle's top speed was thirty miles an hour. It had no heater and its canvas sides, while little barrier against the wind, formed a tent filled with noxious fumes. The engine roar was an assault; we couldn't hear one another so we didn't try to talk. I had to pee. I saw no restroom at the coal yard; I prayed for continence until we arrived at the Rutherfords. Their farmhouse was visible from U.S. Route 50, one of the first highways to cross the United States. At its eastern end, it passes from Ocean City, Maryland, through Washington, D.C. To the west were St. Louis, Kansas City, and, finally San Francisco.

The driver pointed the Gama Goat toward a depression in the snow, certain that it was the driveway. We ground up the side of that mountain, broke a trail, and coughed to a stop at a white farmhouse. The Rutherfords stood outside. They smiled and waved. As soon as the guardsmen were out of the Goat, I scrambled out. The soldiers asked Mr. Rutherford where to dump the coal. I approached Mrs. Rutherford and asked if I could use the bathroom.

"We have an outhouse," Mrs. Rutherford said. My reaction must have determined what happened next. Mrs. Rutherford led me into the wood-frame house, to a plain room, and asked me to wait. Her footsteps echoed across the bare wood floor; she returned with an old saucepan. She handed it to me and went outside. My breath was visible in the cold air. I dropped my pants, squatted over the pot, and peed and peed. Sweet relief stopped when I imagined the pot spilling over. Satisfied it would not, I emptied my bladder, tried to shake off. I pulled up my long johns, zipped my jeans. Now what? No etiquette lesson covered this situation. I found Mrs. Rutherford, my hostess.

"What would you like me to do with the pot?" I asked.

"Just leave it," she said. She wore a thin coat, shoes that wouldn't keep out the snow, and her legs were bare. Outside, I photographed the farmer and soldiers as they shoveled coal out of the Gama Goat. I took a photo of Mr. and Mrs. Rutherford standing by the shiny black pyramid. That image exists, its negative carefully filed. The image in my head is a pot of pee steaming in a cold, gray room.

◆

Finally back at *The News* office, I shed my outer layers and slumped in a chair near Annie, the office manager. She sat up straight. I could tell she had news. "Budgie's got frostbite." Annie's voice betrayed some irritation. Budgie was the town drunk. He lived in a slanted shack off the Brandonville Pike, less than half a mile from the Terra Alta city limits, just past Jerry's house. The Brandonville Pike was closed most winters. The wind was fierce there. Jerry had to use a little snow blower to tunnel out of his driveway. Two people had died in a car on that ridge top one terrible winter years before. Annie had told me that story. As she told me Budgie's tale, she knew I would be disappointed to have missed the excitement. "They took him out by helicopter," Annie said. "All the TV stations came." Her eyes rounded in sympathy for me, then narrowed. "That's just great." Her tone, usually kind, was sarcastic. "Budgie puts Terra Alta on the map." She shook her head and I echoed the gesture. The only time West Virginia was in the national news, it was bad news: mine disasters, poverty stories. Still I envied the national media, the airborne reporters. I coveted their vantage point, their machinery, the ease of their mobility. I had traded my bad-in-snow little truck for a four-wheel-drive vehicle, a Jeep. It bucked along icy roads bordered by banks of snow so high that it was like driving through frigid, narrow canyons. When two vehicles met, one would back to a wide spot, often a driveway. I usually shifted into reverse before the other driver. It seemed appropriate. Natives earned the right of way, I thought. That winter, I was grateful that my father, who loved to drive, who was a teacher by profession and by instinct, had taught me how to steer out of skids in wintry, suburban St. Louis parking lots. He taught me to navigate that thin space that lies between control and lack of control. He taught me how to change tires and put chains on them.

That winter, I crisscrossed an endless white landscape. I photographed dead cattle and ruined beehives. So much snow. I understood this was big news, historic news, but I was often more concerned about my last challenge of the day, getting home. Every day I wondered how far I would make it up my driveway.

Salt Lick Road was plowed. In those days, road crews spread more cinders, waste from the Albright Power Plant, than salt. Gritty, toxic traction. Sometimes Salt Lick was the only access to Terra Alta from the west. The main highway, Route 7, closed when wind carried waves of snow across the long, bare ridge top and filled in Evans Curve, a sunken comma that arced around a steep bank. On Route 7, a mile from Terra Alta, the world ended. I joked that I could leave a white square on the front page with a caption underneath: "Evans Curve, Terra Alta." Readers would accept it as truth. Even when Evans Curve was "open" I spent terrified hours inching across the mountain, blind in the snow. It was almost a relief when the road was officially closed and I ended up on Salt Lick. Close to home.

Even on days when I didn't use chains on my Jeep anywhere else, I put them on before I headed home. I would lie in the slushy street and tighten the chains with thick rubber straps; struggle to secure S hooks into opposite sides of the crude necklaces that gave my tires more traction. At the bottom of my driveway I revved the motor, popped the clutch, and hit the tracks I had made the day before, or the day before that. The Jeep would grind thirty feet, forty feet, wheels flinging clods of snow into the air, then sink with a shudder of failure. If I wanted to wage another assault, I had to back down the road, lurch toward the bottom, toward the emptiness on my right. However scared I was on the ascent, my fear was multiplied when I descended backward. Reverse is not my area of expertise. I worried that an oncoming driver would be surprised when my battered yellow Jeep burst from the hillside onto Salt Lick Road.

On a late February morning, I spent my lunch hour breaking a trail. When the office closed at five, the sun's absence made the driveway more ominous. I rarely made more than one bid to climb the hill then. The successive failures led Wilford and me to tie a toboggan to a tree where the tracks ended. We used it to haul necessities—milk, bread, eggs, butter, chocolate, dog food, beer—by slow steps up that long hill. On one foolish, optimistic day, I told Wilford, who finished his job at the lumber mill early in the afternoon and caught a ride down Salt Lick, to meet me at the house. He could hike up, let the dogs out, and get the fire going. I thought we had made enough tracks and I would at last be able to break through the snow and drive all the way up to the door. I went to the grocery store, where I loaded up on supplies, including a six-pack of Dr. Pepper. I sometimes heated the soda and as a special treat floated a slice of lemon in the steaming cup. But that evening the Jeep ground to a halt at its usual spot a third of the way up the grade. Even if cell phones had been around then, they would have been useless, their signals blocked by Salt Lick's steep hillsides. CB radios were popular then, but I never had one.

At least I had told Wilford to leave the toboggan by the driveway. Rope secured the groceries—a few apples, a head of lettuce (iceberg was the only variety available in Preston County), a bag of dried beans, dog food, and my precious soda. With each step uphill, my boots sank a foot into the icy snow, the crust making a sharp, crunching sound as it gave way. I plodded several yards and stopped to catch my breath, then struggled on. I sat where a breaker made a sort of icy bench and looked at the sled. I removed one bottle of Dr. Pepper and planted it in the snow over the edge of the road, then hauled the sled another twenty yards. I lifted another bottle of soda, left it by the side of the road, and continued in this pattern until the six-pack was empty.

I thought of the pioneers on the Oregon Trail who had abandoned their belongings, one family heirloom at a time, to lighten their load as they struggled across the great western mountains. As a child, I had been fascinated by stories of western expansion. St. Louis had constructed the Arch, the Gateway to the West, during my youth in the 1960s. Construction began when we lived in the suburbs and ended two years after we moved to Wild Horse Creek Valley in West St. Louis County. When my parents drove toward downtown, the Arch loomed on the horizon, two tall, thin, curved towers that bowed toward each other and slowly, over time, met in the shape of a croquet wicket. The heroine of the first book I tried to write, a redheaded version of Laura Ingalls, headed West with a wagon train. I had dreamed of exploration and bravery and adventure.

But standing there, out of breath on that mountain, I could only think how silly I was. Adventure was exhausting; I was no pioneer. If I let go of the rope and climbed to the house, Wilford would come fetch the groceries. But something in me enjoyed the struggle, thought growth evolved from pain. And I knew this tale would make a good story. I picked up the rope and plodded on.

◆

Because it was such a struggle to get home that winter, Wilford and I rarely left unless we had to. In those pre-satellite television, pre-VCR days, we invented our own fun. We made popcorn, played cards. We smoked pot. We had sex. We went sledding. We dragged the toboggan up the gas pipeline far behind our house, past an old foundation we found one spring when daffodils marked its boundary. Neighbors had told us that the farm wife who lived there decades before had hung herself one winter. I thought of her when we trudged past in the snow. No electricity. No telephone. No escape. Wilford pulled the toboggan and broke a path for the dogs and me. The gas company had cleared brush and trees from a wide path over its pipeline, a steep slope broken by terraces. When we reached the top of the hill, breathless in the cold, we stood to survey a winter landscape that stretched for miles and miles. The view brought me joy, a catch in my throat. I thought of that long-ago farm wife who looked at the mountains and felt despair. I sat on the sled, my feet against its curved front. Wilford settled behind me, wrapped his body around mine.

The only way to steer a toboggan is to lean and that doesn't offer much control. We made sure we were pointed straight and gravity took over. Snow flew over the front of the toboggan, filled our eyes, obscured the view. Faster and faster we descended, the wind and snow wild around our ears. The dogs barked and feinted. When the ride ended they jumped in our laps, all of us covered in snow, blinking wet flakes from our eyelashes. Then Wilford and I climbed back up the hill, did it again. And again. As the sled packed the snow, our velocity increased until it felt like flying, like skimming through clouds.

◆

One winter Saturday, I woke to a stillness particular to winter, the snow muffling all sound. The wind had sung all night but the sun now entered the bedroom and I rolled onto my side, reluctantly awake. I reached for my glasses. What challenges would the weather bring today, I wondered, peering outside to gauge the snow. What I saw then caused my eyes to widen, prompted me to throw off the blanket, and heave myself out of the waterbed. What were those shapes scattered in the field behind the house? They looked like shimmering termite mounds, but I wasn't in Africa (I had never been in Africa). I was in West Virginia.

Wilford was in the other room poking the stove. Clouds of yellow, sulfurous smoke rose as he broke the crust of last night's fire and stirred the coals. Not long after we met, he had replaced the attractive but inefficient Ben Franklin stove in the house with a homely, cylindrical, efficient King O Heat. "Wilford!" I called.

"Yes, Hon?" I heard him drop sticks of kindling into the stove, then with a clunk, place a split log on top. I knew the room would soon be so warm that we would be comfortable wearing very little.

"Did you look outside?"

"No."

I made my words a command. "Look outside!" Wilford joined me at the window, which faced east across the large field. Bits of wood still clung to his hands; his long underwear sagged on his lean body. He took a long look. "Wow," he said under his breath. "I'll be damned. I think those are snow rollers."

"Snow rollers?" I said. "What are those?" The shapes stood like soldiers, like angels, in the field.

Today, if I came across such a mystery I would head for my computer. In seconds, I would know that a snow roller is "a rare meteorological phenomenon" formed when wind and snow converge in such a way as to mimic the making of snowmen. But in 1977, I didn't have Google. I had Wilford. I looked at him, raised my eyebrows in question.

"You don't see them often," Wilford explained. "I've only heard of them. They're caused by the wind."

As the coffee brewed, we dressed in layers, pulled on boots. Steaming mugs in hand, we headed outside to take a closer look at the snow rollers. The dogs bounded after us. The pasture glittered in the sun, the backlight a halo behind each snow roller.

I fell to my knees. Now I was the exact height of the snow roller in front of me. It was shaped like a wheel, concave on its sides. The layers of snow spiraled from an icy center. Like tree rings. I reached out to touch this mysterious object, gently nudged it with my pointed finger. I held my breath. Would it disintegrate, fall to powder? My finger met resistance. The snow was hard, solid in the way of papier-mâché over woven wire. I slid my palm over the top, down the sides; my gloves scratched across the rough, icy surface. Behind the snow roller, a faint track, a shallow indent in the snow, marked its mysterious journey.

"Hey, Nance," Wilford's voice rose in a teasing sing-song. He knelt on all fours, pretended to hide behind a snow roller twenty feet away. We laughed. I crawled over to him and leaned against his chest as we reclined in the snow sipping our rapidly cooling coffee. The dogs crowded us; they were less interested in the snow rollers than in the unusual behavior their humans were exhibiting. "Don't knock over the snow rollers." I wagged my finger. I looked at Mac, the collie. "And don't pee on them either." The dogs curled against our legs.

The shapes that had suddenly populated the field were varied. Some of the formations were tall and thin; others low and almost rectangular.

I didn't know much about art then. If I had, I would have pointed to one and said, "That could be a Giacometti." Or, "Look, a Brancusi." But I recognized nature's artistry, the unique construction. We sat until the cold worked its way through all our layers and into our skin. Wilford and I stood, stretched, and slowly zigzagged through the field circling the icy sculptures. We squinted to protect our eyes from the brightness.

I should have gone back to the house and grabbed my camera. But this scene—snow in the sun—would be particularly difficult to photograph. My prints would either be white, without detail, or gray, without magic. And I already had shot, processed, and printed the photographs I needed for that week's paper. If I wanted to include photos of the snow rollers, I would have to develop film again. I would have to leave my mountaintop and go to work. I would have to leave my cozy house and my sexy man. My ambition caved in the face of such comfort.

I'll take pictures tomorrow, I thought. When it clouds over. Or the next time I see snow rollers. Right now, today, I will simply enjoy them. Wilford and I waltzed in the field; the surreal sculptures were our audience.

I didn't take a single photo of the snow rollers. By Sunday morning, the icy statues had been whittled by the sun. Melting reduced each form to a crusty blob, and the field retained none of its enchantment. At the newspaper office on Monday morning, I tried to describe the magic of Saturday's scene.

"How many were there?" Annie asked.

"There had to be a hundred," I said. "Fifty for sure."

She looked at me, cocked her head in doubt. Her lifted eyebrow revealed skepticism and disapproval. At the post office next door, I sought information. Those guys were weather experts; they would know about snow rollers.

"I think there was one in Doc Harriman's yard," silver-haired Charlie said, adding, "They're really rare."

One, I thought. One! I had missed my chance to record history, to preserve, on film, nature's capriciousness. How could I have been so stupid?

The answer, of course, is I didn't recognize the extraordinary happening in my back yard. I didn't understand that life can veer into one-time-only moments. I couldn't imagine that I would never have another chance to capture snow rollers on film. But the images from that morning are in my heart, my head. I readily summon that astonishing daybreak, that dance across a sparkling field, those icy, doomed statues.

19

◆ ◆ ◆

THE COMMUNE DOWN
SALT LICK, PART 2

AFTER THAT HISTORIC WINTER, spring 1977 felt particularly welcome. I was in a good mood one afternoon when I spotted a smiling young woman at the top of Salt Lick, her colorful, hippie skirt a bright banner against the trees. Her thumb was out, her long, fair hair blowing in the wind. I decided to ignore my "don't pick up hitch-hikers" policy and stopped just past her.

"I'm Frances," she said as she climbed into my Jeep. "Thanks for the ride. I live down the valley."

I looked sideways at her. "The Washington Lantz farm?" I asked.

Frances shook her head. "No, but I know those folks. They're friends of my brother." Her voice was unhurried and faintly southern. "I live further down Salt Lick at Amblersburg. Do you know where that is?"

I nodded. "I've taken pictures of the bridge there." Amblersburg wasn't a burg at all. It was a bridge, two bridges really: a grand stone arch built for the railroad and a wooden bridge suspended below. Both striking and graphic.

"I just moved here from Atlanta." Frances said. "I'm going to grow and sell flowers." Her speech was languid. I glanced at her. She had closed her eyes and leaned back in the seat. I doubted whether she could make a living as a gardener, but I said nothing. She seemed unconcerned about hitch-hiking, about her new venture.

"My brother Gordon came to West Virginia because that's where the dart fell when he threw it." Frances sat up and turned toward me. "He and a bunch of his friends from Southwestern College wanted to get back to the land." She waved her hand at the green forest outside the window. "Gordon was the first of the group to actually buy a farm. He spent the summer of 1973 at Amblersburg listening to the Watergate hearings on the radio while fixing up the house and planting a garden." Frances twisted her hair into a bun that immediately collapsed. "When Gordo realized he wasn't a farmer, he invited some friends to stay in Amblersburg while they looked for a farm of their own. A couple years ago they found the Washington Lantz farm." My Jeep bounced across potholes. "Have you met the Verlendens? Or Michael?"

"I met the Verlendens," I said, and told Frances about my one trip to the farm.

"They don't live there now," she said. "But Michael does. You need to meet him. Come to dinner."

I agreed and offered to bring a pot of soup beans and some cornbread. I had told Wilford about my previous trip to the farm, how the hippies were polite, not friendly. "City folk," Wilford said. He was quiet as we drove to the farm, under trees, through an S-curve, up the steep slope. Wilford jumped out to open the gates. And to pee. We couldn't make it up Caddell Mountain without pulling over so he could pee. I accused him of marking territory like a dog. At the bottom of a steep cleared field, he waved me through and fastened the gate behind me. Barbed wire enclosed the space; a cow and calf grazed in the pasture. "We're in the boonies now," Wilford said. The farmhouse hadn't benefitted from any improvements, but the low-ceilinged kitchen had been prettied up with a Mason jar of wildflowers.

"Michael's up working on the tractor," Frances said. We shared a joint as we climbed a long hill to meet him. "He planted those trees." She gestured at a grove of pine trees to our left. She turned back and waved at the hill behind the house. "He planted an orchard there." A gate near the top of the hill offered an opportunity to rest and face a wide western view across the valley. The mountains repeated before us, held zigzag lines beneath the horizon. Wilford leaned against the locust post. "This is nice," he said, coming down hard on the *this*. We walked higher. Next to the barn, Michael stood by a tractor. He was golden, hair and skin kissed by the sun. He looked like Hemingway, barrel-chested with a round head and a handsome face.

A broad hayfield rose beyond Michael. We were surrounded on all sides by mountains and meadows. "This is beautiful!" I said. "I'm Nancy. This is Wilford."

Michael shook hands. "Good to meet you."

"Looks like you could use some help," Wilford said. He walked toward a hay rake; its metal fronds arched over high grass. He circled the manure spreader, touched its rough wooden sides. "These have been around a while."

"They came with the farm," Michael explained. He laughed. "We *could* use some help."

"Let's get higher." Frances turned to me. She indicated the top of the hill, the highest spot in the meadow. I followed her through waist-high grass sprinkled with Queen Anne's lace for a hundred yards. She stood, arms outstretched, and lifted her chin. We were circled by mountains, soft peaks of green, thousands and thousands of acres of mixed hardwood forest. As far as the eye could see not a structure in sight.

"Wow! Wow, wow, wow!" I cried. I echoed Frances's gesture, flung my arms wide, and started to run. I was in *The Sound of Music*. I sang, "The hills are alive!" I twirled and laughed. People talk about love at first sight and usually they mean with other people, but that day I fell in love with a place. That mountaintop. That particular mountaintop. Those views. That space.

Later we sat in the kitchen to share food and marijuana. I turned to Michael. "Frances told me how she got here," I said. "What's your story?"

"There was a group of us in Memphis," he said. "Into theater and art. We wanted a farm, and West Virginia was what we could afford. We almost bought a place in Lewis County, but while the Verlendens were staying at Gordon's in Amblersburg, they found this farm. A hundred and twenty-three acres." He ran a hand through his short hair. There were six of us. I gave them money without even seeing the place," he said. "Based on faith, optimism, and good vibes." He laughed. "When I got here in November 1975, the Verlendens were about to have a baby. They had bought a cow and some chickens." Michael shook his head. "We were totally unprepared for winter. I had a yellow 1966 Chevy Malibu and it was useless in the snow. And we had lots of snow. It was crazy."

In the spring of 1976, Michael said, he left Preston County for an acting gig in New York—Mabou Mines' production of *The Saint and the Football Player*, a play directed by Lee Breuer. "My friend Phil was also in the piece," Michael said. "He's a big guy, perfect for the part of a football player." Michael's face brightened. "We lived for a time in David Bowie's old place on 9th and St. Mark's Place in the East Village. My car was stripped." His voice rose. "I was mugged! I was walking home when a couple of guys stopped me. They wanted money. I had a sack of groceries in each arm and instead of putting them down, I lowered my head and rushed them, like in the football piece." His eyes widened. "They ran away. I couldn't believe it!"

He said the cast of *The Saint and the Football Player* came to the farm to rehearse that summer. "A different vibe from the city," Michael laughed. "We swam in the Cheat River, hung out here." The play toured Europe, its run partly sponsored by the government to celebrate the country's Bicentennial, Michael said.

"I wish I'd known," I said. A New York theater group's visit to Preston County would have been a big story for *The Preston County News*. I shook my head and sighed. Even though I lived a mile from the farm; even though I had been there to rescue my dog, I didn't know what was happening just down the road.

◆

I did recognize Michael's charisma. So did Frances. She and Michael became a couple. Wilford and I often joined them on the farm. He helped with the machinery; I cooked big meals. We sat in the rustic kitchen and listened to Michael talk about art and agriculture like a preacher talked about the gospel. He was an intellectual, a farmer, a philosopher, a scavenger, a teacher. He and Frances filled the house with inspirational materials: Wendell Berry, *The Whole Earth Catalog*, *Mother Earth News*, Henry David Thoreau, pamphlets from the West Virginia University Extension Office. Bits of detritus—metal parts, interesting stones, pieces of wood—were saved for art projects. Michael wanted to make art and live off the land, even if the thin, rock-strewn topsoil of Appalachia was inhospitable. Frances left Amblersburg and moved into the farmhouse. She bought a horse named Lily, whose form enhanced the landscape. The vegetable and flower gardens profited from applications of compost and manure.

◆

One spring morning, Wilford and I headed up the now familiar road to the farm. On the flat approach, before the road started to climb, we saw a figure in the road. A large figure. "I bet that's Phil," I told Wilford. I understood why he had been cast as a football player. He was huge—six feet four, 220 pounds. He towered over Wilford and me when we got out to make our introductions.

"Frances told us you were going to dig into the side of the hill here and build an underground house," Wilford said. Phil had narrow, tilted eyes and was losing his hair. He gazed at the steep bank, overgrown with rhododendron and laced by rock. He put his hands on his hips.

"A den," he said. "It could work."

It did not. A rented bulldozer only dented the hillside, which then threatened to collapse onto the road. But Phil shrugged off his failure and settled in the house. He decided he would become a farmer, and soon sheep dotted the pastures and challenged rickety fences.

◆

Early that summer we gathered around the tractor. Its red paint had long ago faded to a tint. Greasy parts lay on a rag spread beneath the engine. "Think we can fix it?" Phil asked Wilford. "We need to get the hay cut before the weather turns." Phil's voice was low and melodious;

he appeared unhurried. He and Wilford were a good team, both calm, easygoing men.

When Wilford and I went to the farm, we never knew who we would find there. Visitors cycled through. Some stayed. William, a temporary tenant, had a car filled with elite sporting equipment—squash and tennis racquets, golf clubs, cross-country skis—but he qualified for food stamps. I had more in common with the folks at the farm than I did with Wilford. Michael, Phil, Frances, and I were middle-class, college-educated ex-suburbanites. Liberals. Classic baby boomers with a hippie bent. Wilford had not spent much time with people like us; he had almost no knowledge of literature or philosophy. But he was a fount of practical knowledge. When Phil and Michael struggled to get the tractor running, or to repair the complicated farm equipment, they called on Wilford and his mechanical expertise. The three of them would stand around the rusty contraptions, their hands smeared with grease. When blue smoke roiled above their heads, it was a sign of success. A sputtering engine and clanking gears were the music of accomplishment. Wilford's repairs were sometimes transient, but he could always put a sharp edge on chain saws, mower blades, and knives.

Michael, Phil, and Frances never had any money. They occasionally found small jobs, but life was hard. When Phil decided to get a "real job" he applied for work at the only radio station in Preston County, a daylight-hours-only AM station. They were smart enough to recognize Phil's talent and hired him. They didn't pay him much, but the job allowed him to be both newsman and farmer. The radio proved to be the perfect forum for Phil's mellifluous voice, his natural talent for storytelling, and his keen interest in politics. WFSP broadcast a mixture of news, weather, farm reports, sports, and country music. I wish I could describe a typical broadcast but despite my friendship with Phil, I rarely listened to the station. The music and commercials annoyed me. I preferred rock and roll: records, tapes, and a Pittsburgh radio station. But it was Phil and Frances who eventually turned me on to public radio, which has turned into a lifelong passion, voices I turn to every morning.

◆

Phil and I covered the same events—the school board, the county commission, town meetings, community happenings—so we carpooled. Usually I drove. Phil's vehicles could be unreliable. Or they were crammed full of accumulated farm stuff: bits of greasy machinery, tools, and sheep supplies. Jumper cables. Phil had a passion for farming, celebrated its noble intent, its mystery, its rhythms. He also recognized its difficulties, the vicissitudes of weather, market, and luck. Because of Phil, I understood that meat was the result of sacrifice and that sheep were not the brightest of creatures.

In temperate months we often drove to Kingwood as the sun went down, headed west across the ridge of the Briery Mountain range, and snaked down Caddell. The gold light edged the horizon in gilt. We were—we are—nourished by that landscape. We would talk about our vision for Preston County: improved schools, expanded water and sewage systems, cultural opportunities. We talked about politics: national, state, and local. We talked about movies. We talked about our similar pasts—Phil's childhood in various Midwestern suburbs, mine in St. Louis County. And we talked about our present—my life with Wilford, Phil's dream for the farm.

Sometimes Caddell Mountain was shrouded in fog on the ride home, a thick gray mist that erased the road. One evening we crept along, blind. I had to drive with my door open, eyes down to see the yellow line in the middle of the road. Phil leaned his huge frame out the passenger side window, struggled to see the faded white line that marked the edge of the road. His calm was reassuring in that surreal atmosphere.

Winter also could turn the trip to Kingwood into a treacherous outing. One evening I hit a patch of ice at the top of the mountain and the car slid, gained speed, and turned sideways just as the road curved. Phil and I gasped in unison. I turned the steering wheel into the skid as my father had taught me and the car straightened. I pulled onto the shoulder and stopped. My foot tapped furiously, moved without my intent. I was unable to still my muscles. "That was fantastic!" Phil said. "Amazing! We could have died! I'll ride with you any time."

For the Preston County Commission's regular meetings, held during the day, we rendezvoused in Kingwood. The commissioners, all of them male, most of them the age of our parents, sat around a large wooden table in the courthouse. Phil and I, along with reporters from the *Dominion Post*, the area's daily newspaper, and the *Preston County Journal*, the county's other weekly, sat around a smaller table. The commission, a filter for state and federal programs among other activities, exists to manage the courthouse and dispense funds. Preston County had the sole remaining eight-member commission in the state; other counties had three-member authorities. Eight men, each representing a magisterial district, argued about water systems and what insurance company should get the contract for the sheriff's vehicles. They could take hours to decide how much money to give to volunteer fire departments and ambulance squads. The county clerk was a pitcher for the Kingwood women's softball team. She was required to take the minutes of each meeting. Sometimes she'd look to the press table and roll her eyes. Although Phil and I grumbled about the meetings, we looked forward to them, to the socializing they fostered. Phil, the other reporters, and I usually had lunch together. Since the commission often had a five-three split (Republicans outnumbered the Democrats), we followed the majority to a restaurant and sat nearby so we could eavesdrop on their conversations. After lunch, if the meeting was boring, we took turns paying attention. One reporter read mysteries. Phil often had a classic. I usually had a literary novel I'd checked out of the library. When the commissioners made a good decision, like the time they approved a public transportation project that put buses on the road for the first time, we applauded. Phil and I also cheered for the new county landfill, which provided the first local ecologically sound facility for solid waste. Here was progress. We believed that we were advocates for the public good.

◆

"I'm going back to school!" Michael had been awarded an artist-in-residency position at the University of Illinois in Urbana–Champaign. He would spend a month in Illinois each year from 1977 to 1980. During that time, he developed a following among the students and brought small groups to the farm. They built a magnificent fire pit during a school break and worked on other structures. They helped in the garden, fields, and orchard.

Michael's romantic relationship with Frances ended amicably soon after he announced his artist-in-residency. Within a few years, Frances had enrolled at West Virginia University; she would be an art teacher. She drove her rickety Datsun truck to and from Morgantown though she often spent the night at the "Earth House," a hippie haven next to campus. Phil began to court her. Both Michael and Phil suited Frances. Like both of them, she was committed to the land. Like Michael, she was an artist, motivated by beauty, found and man-made. Like Phil, she was spiritual (without religious dogma), political, and fun-loving. In West Virginia, a social life has much to do with who's nearby. Common interests are a bonus. We were good friends in a good place trying to accomplish good things.

✵ 20 ✵

✦ ✦ ✦

CIVIL WAR

———

PHIL PUSHED A COUPLE OF COUGH DROPS forward. "I raise you two. Three cards." The four of us around the table—journalists from the radio station, daily newspaper, and two weeklies—played cards as we waited for the board of education to emerge from behind closed doors. We suspected their discussion drifted past personnel issues (a legal excuse to bar the press from proceedings), but we could prove nothing. It was 1979 and Preston County's educational system had been hijacked by politics.

Phil had been covering the board for just a few months. But I was a veteran of the conflict. During our trips to Kingwood, I had talked to Phil about what I had learned about county politics.

"I wish you could have met R. Doyne Halbritter," I had said on one trip down the mountain. "He was a retired lawyer and amateur historian when I met him in 1974. He used to come into *The News* to pick up a stack of West Virginia weekly newspapers that we saved for him." I glanced at Phil. "I have a picture of him wearing a black beret. He was a great speaker. Really something.

"He said all the conflict in Preston County goes back to the battle for the county seat a hundred years ago," I said. "Kingwood won and now it has the courthouse, the hospital, the vocational center, and the jail," I said. "There are more voters along Route 7—Masontown, Kingwood, and Terra Alta—than in the rest of the county. The rural areas resent that control. You've heard people say, 'Kingwood gets everything?'"

Phil nodded. I continued. "So they fought back. For years the board of education had a three to two pro-consolidation majority, but last year, 1978, it reversed."

The board we were now waiting on was three to two against consolidation.

◆

Jerry had given me a lecture on the history of school consolidation when I made Preston County my permanent home in 1975. He had been in full professor mode as he paced the wide wood floors at *The News* office.

"We tried to improve the schools with bond issues in 1973 and 1974," he said. "Three separate plans and we couldn't pass any of them." Jerry stopped pacing. "The state requires two-thirds approval and Preston County is divided almost fifty-fifty between Route 7 and everyone else." Jerry enjoyed being a teacher. "You can't blame the folks in Tunnelton or Aurora for opposing consolidation," he said. "These roads are terrible. It can take forty-five minutes to get to Terra Alta from Aurora and that's in good weather." He became more agitated. "Some families have been here for generations. Their high school is the center of their community. Folks remember when the Tunnelton basketball team went to the state tournament. That was their moment of glory. They don't want to give that up."

I nodded assent. Jerry continued. "Just before you came back, the state admitted that a bond could not pass and funded a school improvement plan that consolidated eight high schools into five," he said. "Aurora students would go to Terra Alta, renamed East Preston; Fellowsville and Tunnelton students would go to Kingwood, renamed Central Preston; and Newburg students would go to Masontown, renamed West Preston. Rowlesburg and Bruceton would keep their schools. Of course opponents of consolidation hired lawyers and consultants to fight the plan."

◆

In June 1975, just as I returned to Preston County, the state had rebuffed the pleas of the anti-consolidation forces. But the protests didn't die. As the board of education moved forward with its plans, consolidation opponents continued to mobilize. They claimed "community schools" as their identifier. Nearly every week, *The Preston County News* carried impassioned letters to the editor protesting the upcoming changes. The writers attacked the pro-consolidation opinions that both Jerry and I expressed. They claimed there was a conspiracy to eventually have just one high school in Kingwood. "That will never happen," Jerry said.

Preston County schools were a shocking contrast to the bright, modern schools I had attended in Missouri. Most Preston County schools were built during a fifteen-year burst of prosperity from about 1915 on, but the county didn't have enough money to properly maintain them. The schools had coal boilers; some had leaky roofs.

The schools in Newburg and Tunnelton, red brick rectangles perched on hills, were the largest building in each town. Aurora, on U.S. Route 50 near the southeastern corner of the county, and Bruceton, next to what was then U.S. Route 48 in the northeast, had plain, white frame schools that looked like fire traps. But the Aurora school had a fine reputation. That community, at the summit of Cheat Mountain next to the virgin hemlock forest of Cathedral State Park, had been settled by Germans intent on turning the rolling green hills into rich agricultural land. The area had produced generations of excellent teachers.

But the curriculum didn't offer much more than the basics. College preparatory classes were a luxury. Still, each school had a basketball team and a marching band, identifying colors, and loyal alumni. Each school represented a tribe.

◆

I studied the textbook controversy in southern West Virginia. It had begun in the 1970s and drew national news coverage. Fundamentalists believed that books chosen by the Kanawha County School Board undermined Christianity and threatened their way of life. Mobs threw rocks; schools were firebombed and dynamited. Two people were shot. Among the books that evoked protests: *Lord of the Flies, Paradise Lost, The Great Gatsby, The Old Man and the Sea, The Crucible, The Good Earth, Crime and Punishment, The Iliad,* and *Animal Farm.* Doyne Halbritter had helped me understand why these books prompted such a negative response. He had talked about the psyche of Appalachia: the distrust of outsiders, the fear of change, the balm of the New Testament.

When Vivian McConnell, an English teacher at Terra Alta High School, asked if I could help with her journalism class during the 1975–76 school year, I immediately said yes. When I talked to her that fall, she made sure I knew that she disagreed with the fundamentalists in Kanawha County. She was a force in Terra Alta. I had photographed her directing choruses at the high school and the Methodist Church, one hand on the piano keys, the other jabbing the air. She had cropped gray hair, oversize glasses, and the respect of almost everyone in town. Her late husband had been the long-time county agricultural extension agent; her son now held that job.

When I showed up the first time to volunteer, I noticed that the classroom probably hadn't changed much in fifty years, but a half century of paint layers softened its angles. The students in front of me in the classroom were just a few years younger than me. I shifted from foot to foot on the wooden floor and told students that journalism gave them the right to be nosy, to ask questions. To be present, to witness history. To matter. In front of that audience, I justified my life. I also told them that to be writers, they needed to be readers. A week later I brought in a stack of my own paperbacks to supplement the school's meager library and asked each student to read one book and write a review. Some of my books were on Kanawha County's banned list; two, *The Wind in the Willows* and *Of Mice and Men,* had also been scorned by Preston County, although I don't recall seeing its specific list of banned books. My slightly subversive act was thrilling. I was a volunteer; the board couldn't fire me. One of the poorer students—her family lacked money and any interest in education—picked up my battered *Of Mice and Men,* "because it's the shortest," she said, making brief eye contact.

When she handed it back to me some days later, her eyes were shining. "I liked it," she said, her voice full of surprise. "It was sad, though." She crossed her arms on her desk and sat straight. "It's the first book I ever read all the way through."

At the time, the percentage of students in Preston County who went on to college was pretty low. Teachers' children and lawyers' children continued their education beyond high school. But the children of coal miners, builders, and merchants often did not. Why should they? A coal miner made more money than a teacher. A lot more. A man with a back-hoe could support a family and have enough money left over to vacation in Myrtle Beach and buy nice vehicles. Teachers often needed summer jobs to supplement their income.

The best salaries in the county were in the coal industry, at the power plant in Albright, the gas plant in Terra Alta, the manganese plant by the Cheat River, the bronze plant in Kingwood, or the railroad. The timber industry was thriving, but it paid owners well, not workers. If someone had political connections, he or she worked for the state road department, in one of the better jobs at Hopemont, a hospital for the chronically ill, or, depending upon who sat on the school board, the schools. Farmers found part-time work driving school buses.

◆

In the spring of 1976, the county was moving toward consolidation. Hundreds of angry citizens from communities that were losing their schools gathered in front of the board of education office. They formed a semicircle on the dark lawn, held signs, and chanted, their faces twisted by passion. As I walked past on my way into the board meeting, I flinched from their fury. "Yankee, Go Home!" one woman screamed, glaring at me with hate. The hand-lettered sign she carried said, "Save Our School." My stomach clenched with fear and my hands trembled. But I walked toward the woman and stood opposite her, guts roiling and heart pounding.

"Missouri was a border state," I said. "West Virginia is West Virginia because it was Union. *You* are the Yankee." What I didn't say, what I wanted to say, was if she had had access to a good education, she might know this fact. She stopped her chant, quit waving her sign. The noise of the crowd surrounded us. Did she see that I was close to tears?

The boardroom was so crowded that I had to squeeze myself into a small space on the floor, nearly underneath a table. At some point in the meeting, the protesters began to stomp their feet; the boom, boom rhythm shook the floor. An architect hired by the board to design school additions stood, his arms raised in a plea for quiet. "If this continues," he said, his voice high with stress, "this building could collapse." His announcement was greeted by derision from some of the protesters, who renewed their stomping with vigor. But the board was alarmed. Jesse Jennings, a member of the board's anti-consolidation minority, stood and the room quieted. The crowd respected him: he was a soldier, a farmer, a leader. I respected him too. He had been my guide during the War Games in 1974. Jesse assured the protesters that their opinions mattered. And they did. The board appeased the opposition by promising to put forward yet another school bond. This one, called the deconsolidation bond, would fund seven high schools.

Between that scary March and the May 1976 bond election, both pro-consolidation and deconsolidation forces used the media to try to sway voters. Guest editorials and letters to the editor filled *The News*'s opinion page. The deconsolidation forces had found a small-school proponent, an academic in Boston, and we ran his lengthy arguments. He and his followers praised "community schools." I couldn't dispute his reasoning: small was better; students received more attention. After all, I had chosen to live in a rural community, to be a big fish in a small pond. But I couldn't get past the fact that few students here had real choices, that they were not exposed to a wide curriculum. How could they choose a career if they hadn't been introduced to a wide variety of subjects? No one could imagine the Internet then; options were limited.

When the only underground newspaper in the area, a pro-labor paper published in neighboring Marion County, started running stories supporting deconsolidation, I despaired. That paper was a strong voice for the underserved. I had always considered myself to be a liberal, a champion of the beleaguered. But here I was on the other side.

My writing failed to change anyone's mind. Instead, it prompted vituperative attacks. That woman's voice, the cry of "Yankee, Go Home," stayed with me. I sympathized with much of the opposition. Who could be against "community schools"? But I was sure that consolidation would benefit a greater number of students. The newspaper took an editorial stance against the deconsolidation bond. When it failed and the board continued its plans to merge high schools, the fight persisted.

◆

In October 1976, a bouquet of flowers was delivered to the newspaper office. Annie carried them to me. "For you," she said. I pulled the small card from its envelope. "In Sympathy," it said on the front. I looked at the signature, "Union District." Aurora.

"That's weird," Annie said. I held the card, puzzled. Who was it from? In sympathy for what? I looked at the bright flowers and shuddered. Could this be a threat? I called the florist. Could there have been some mistake? No. The flowers were paid for with cash and the clerk couldn't tell me who had ordered them. In a column the next week, I pleaded for answers. "Whoever you are in Union District, thank you (I think). If you meant to please me, you did. If you meant to scare me, you did. But, most of all, you confused me. Please let me in on your secret. I want to give thanks where (and if) thanks are due."

No one responded.

◆

Protesters were pretty quiet during the months in which the state-funded school building program constructed new facilities and improved old schools in Preston County. But when the newly consolidated schools opened in the fall of 1977, irate citizens broke windshields on four buses with shotgun blasts and rocks, crimes committed while the buses were parked. They slashed tires. They blocked buses traveling from Newburg, Aurora, and Fellowsville with cars, farm machinery, and trees that had been deliberately felled. A small crowd stood on the bridge to the Fellowsville school to prevent access. Many students stayed home. Deconsolidation proponents continued their vigil at board of education meetings, pleaded for their schools to be returned.

In the spring of 1978, Jerry decided that the only way to change politics in West Virginia was to run for office. He filed for a seat in the West Virginia State Senate and ran in the May primary election. He asked for my help. "You're going to have to take over some of my duties," he said. "Like the county commission. More meetings." I nodded assent.

The deconsolidation forces had the same idea: change from within. In that May election, the county chose members of the school board. For years, the board had a pro-consolidation majority. After the election, though, the power shifted. Two vocal opponents of consolidation joined Jesse Jennings to shift the power to a new three-to-two majority. Jesse was elected board president. In one of its first acts, the board voted to deconsolidate. But the state rejected its plan.

◆

Throughout the school consolidation battle, Jerry had theorized that Bob Cline, a local power broker, was pulling strings behind the scenes. Cline, a Rowlesburg resident, didn't hold elected office but he had connections to state politicians. That meant he could place friends in state jobs—in the department of highways, at Hopemont State Hospital, in work programs. Jerry despised Bob Cline. He considered Bob to be emblematic of all that was wrong with West Virginia politics—he considered it to be a system based on rewarding individuals who delivered votes, not public service; a system based on nepotism; a system that diverted West Virginia's meager dollars into the pockets of a few. Power, in West Virginia, meant jobs. Although Bob Cline's wife was a teacher, and a good one, he did not control the school system. That is, until the war over consolidation awarded him power.

In that same May election that turned the board's power structure upside down Jerry won the Democratic nomination. While he was out campaigning, I attended every board of education meeting. So did Bob Cline. Bob was a large, pale man, bald and doughy looking. He didn't speak often, but when he did, his voice was soft and low and occasionally sinister. His wrists were wrapped with elastic bandages that people said covered nitroglycerin cream. When Jerry first told me that Bob Cline had a bad heart, I didn't know that was a literal statement, not a judgment.

Jerry lost the general election in November 1978. It was not a surprise; his six-county district was heavily Republican. But his defeat in Preston County was a real blow. Jerry knew his pro-consolidation stance would hurt him, but he thought he had made enough friends, championed enough causes, to win support from his community.

◆

Phil had started covering the board in 1979, just as the deconsolidation board took control. The newly powerful trio wreaked havoc with Preston County schools. Teachers were in an uproar; many of them were not sure where they would be working that fall. When the pro-consolidation forces discovered that one of the leading candidates for the superintendent's job was a man who had worked with Bob Cline under former governor Hulett Smith, they protested that politics had infected the school system.

The board retreated behind closed doors to consider their choices for superintendent. We four members of the Preston County press corps played poker to pass the time. Phil leaned his large frame back in the chair and considered his hand. "Three cards," he said. His new cards were an obvious disappointment.

"Two cards," I said. For once I had a good hand. But our game ended when the door opened. Board members announced that they were hiring a new superintendent. His résumé wasn't as blatantly political as the first candidate's, but he too had ties to Bob Cline. Phil scooped up the cough drops and we murmured our disappointment. In the spring of 1980, the board decided to hire a second assistant superintendent, creating a new job that threatened the very capable current assistant superintendent. The new guy's résumé amused our cadre of journalists. He had spent the past three years working for truck dealerships. Three years before that he had been an assistant football coach and instructor in the athletic department at a small college. He had been a math teacher at two high schools, but always in conjunction with coaching.

We in the press corps were outraged. Our schools needed academic help, not political patronage. In a fury, I returned to *The News* office to write my story and paste it into the hole I had left on the front page. The headline stretched across three columns at the top of the paper: "Truck salesman named 2nd assistant superintendent." Scorn fairly dripped from the thirty-six point font. I know now, maybe I knew it then, that this was a cheap shot. Blatant editorializing on the front page. Wrong, wrong, wrong.

But I believed in democracy. Although the majority of Preston County voters thought that consolidated schools would be better schools, they let a minority of angry voters take over the board of education. Preston County schools were hijacked in much the same way that the entire country would be hijacked early in the twenty-first century when a motivated minority took advantage of the majority's complacency, paving the way for George W. Bush and Donald Trump to become president in spite of losing the popular vote.

Jerry Ash continued his political career. He ran again for state senate in 1980 and this time he won. He worked hard and earned the respect of his constituents, but he was wrong about one prediction: In the 1990s, Preston County high schools were consolidated into a single school. Preston High is located in Kingwood.

✺ **21** ✺

✦ ✦ ✦

DEER DEAR FRIEND

———

IT WAS 1977, early December. The dogs led us to the doe. She lay where the woods met the hayfield behind our house. It was obvious that she had been down a while. Her hooves had torn divots from the ground, had released the smell of damp earth. I ordered the dogs back, knelt beside her, and trickled water into her mouth. I stroked her ears, sung the tuneless chant I had used to soothe horses. But she was a wild thing; her brown eyes widened with fear and she flinched at my touch.

Wilford squatted beside me. "What's up, girl?" he crooned as he stroked her smooth side. The deer lifted her nose; her shallow, labored breaths were visible in the cool air. Neither Wilford nor I could find an obvious cause for her distress. Wilford kept a hand on her flank as he turned to me. "She's bad off," he said. "But I can't do anything." A picture came to me: my father carrying our ancient collie out of the house, to the vet. To be "put to sleep." Not sleep. Death. I felt dread. Pain. Sorrow. Those feelings spilled into tears as Wilford and I walked toward the house. I had already called the local game officer. He came as soon as he was able, but the sun had set. Wilford and I led the way with a flashlight. The officer knelt beside the doe. "She's sick," he said. "Maybe run by dogs?" He got to his feet. "I'm going to put her down."

Wilford put his arm across my shoulders. "I'll walk you back to the house," he said. I leaned into him, grateful. He had been in my life less than a year but his presence was essential. I turned the television up loud to mask the gunshot. Lights disappeared down the driveway. When Wilford opened the door, he opened his arms, folded me against his chest.

"It's crazy to be so sad about a wild animal," I sobbed. Wilford cupped the back of my head, comforted me without words. For months we had watched a herd of does and their fawns graze in the field behind the house, had admired their graceful form, their alert way. We believed that we knew this doe.

A few days later, the officer told me that the autopsy had revealed a twenty-two caliber bullet near the doe's spine, probably from a rifle. The wound itself, nearly invisible, was not serious. The doe died from a massive infection, he said. I couldn't imagine how long she had been in agony. I was furious. "Isn't it illegal to hunt deer with a twenty-two?" My voice was shrill.

"Yes," the officer said.

I thought of the doe, of her slow, miserable death, and raged. Then I wrote a column about her, ending with a few paragraphs critical of hunters. The headline: "Grief begets anger" had this subhead, or kicker, "Doe's agonizing death should be lesson for so-called hunters."

In early January, 1978, several weeks after the column was published, a woman walked into the newspaper office. "I want to meet the person who wrote about the deer," she said. "That column made me cry."

That is how Ann, blue-eyed, freckled, and smart, joined our circle of friends. She had come to Preston County from Massachusetts. "From Boston to Bruceton," she liked to say. She was a nurse-practitioner who specialized in women's health, a liberal, a feminist, a reader. She had much in common with Phil, Frances, Michael, and me. Like all of us, she had chosen to live in Preston County. Ann worked for the health council, the organization whose mission was to bring health care to Preston County. Ann helped women make reproductive choices. She prevented pregnancies and celebrated them. She knew how to relax, too. Ann was unashamed of her passion for television and movies. We spent hours deconstructing character and plot. Like me, she had moved to Preston County to make a difference. Like me, she would marry a man from Bruceton. Our sons are distant cousins. We are friends still.

22

HAPPY DAZE

WILFORD AND I SAT AT THE TOP JOINT, rotated on stools and nursed beers. Wilford's friend Chip sat next to him, elbows on the bar, hands wrapped around a cold bottle. Chip wasn't happy. He and Wilford had often hung out together until I came along. He teased Wilford. "You might as well be married," he said. "When *are* you getting married anyway?" Wilford swiveled to look at me, raised his eyebrows, waited for my answer.

"August, 1978," I said. "The second anniversary of the month we met." The words came out of my mouth, surprised me. It was late summer, 1977. Wilford and I had been together for a year. We shared a home. I wanted to be his wife, but I wanted him to ask me. I wasn't one of those girls who imagined a romantic proposal, a fantasy wedding. But I was old-fashioned. The man should ask. So the man, sort of, was Chip. Wilford jumped off his bar stool, grabbed my hand, and dropped to his knee. "My lady," he bowed. "We are engaged." The bar erupted in cheers.

My parents had always joked about weddings. They would shake their heads at the thought of paying for three galas. They suggested that their daughters forgo fancy ceremonies. "All you need is a lantern and a ladder," was their refrain, a joking reference to nineteenth-century elopements. I will never know what they really thought of Wilford, of my decision to marry this mountain man. My mother, after all, was a psychologist. She knew if she opposed my relationship with Wilford, I would stubbornly cling to him. So she adopted a philosophy that I have tried to emulate in my own life: If my child loves someone, I will do my best to love that person. And keep my mouth shut when criticism threatens to take voice. My mother praised Wilford's good manners. My parents recognized his charm. If they were dismayed by his lack of formal education, they never mentioned it.

◆

Wilford liked to be naked. And I liked him naked. He was a delight to behold: slim, with good shoulders. Translucent freckled skin. An architectural face and great hair. He had the loveliest, long penis.

Before he stepped out of the shower, Wilford ran curved hands like squeegees down his arms and legs to whisk the water off. "Then the towel doesn't get so wet," he explained. I handed him a towel. Thick, decorated with a butterfly. My parents had bought the set when I went off to college. Wilford swiveled to hang up the towel. Nice ass. My pretty man. He stepped close and I touched him.

A woman in her twenties is looking for a mate. Looking to mate. That's who I was, a package of skin and hormones. I had discovered sex in high school. Wow. What a great way to use your body. But I would hear a voice inside my head questioning my choices. "Don't!" "You're a slut." "Maybe just once, if you love him." "Well, I'm not a virgin anymore, what the heck." "It feels great." "Wow, it really feels great." That tiny pill every day was a miracle.

Wilford was a miracle. He was in perpetual motion. In cooler months, he spent hours working to keep us warm. He split logs, chopped kindling. He shoveled coal, cleaned ash from the stove, sprinkled cinders on the driveway. He polished my shoes, sharpened my knives, pitched in when I cleaned. Our division of labor seemed to work. I never had to ask Wilford for help. He did whatever work was needed. In warm months, he was bent in the garden, often naked. He cut the grass (clothed), tuned up the lawnmower. Eventually he welded a beer holder to his favorite mower. He always had a beer nearby, extras on ice.

◆

"Nance, come here!" Wilford's excited tone got my attention. I stopped doing the dinner dishes and joined him outside. The fall sun had set and dusk colored the yard a soft gray. Wilford sat on top of the picnic table, feet resting on the bench, knees together. His hands were cupped above his thighs. "It's a flying squirrel!" He looked at me, looked delighted. "The cat had him, but I got him in time. I think it's a young one." He parted his thumbs and there in his palms was a fairy creature, all pop eyes and soft fur. Still stunned from its encounter with our cat, the squirrel curled its front claws around Wilford's finger. He gently moved it enough to show me the furry membrane between its front and back legs.

"That may be the coolest animal I've ever seen." I touched the soft fur. "What are you going to do?"

"I need to let it go or it will die," Wilford said. "I'll put it in a tree but first you have to get the cat in the house."

"Here kitty kitty! Here kitty kitty!" The cat answered to canned food, not me, then settled on the couch. All traces of light had left the sky by the time we joined her there and turned on the television. Wilford had attached an antenna to the roof so now we could watch NBC, ABC, CBS, and PBS. He sat in front of the TV and flipped through the four channels. None of the fuzzy images captured our attention. Wilford glanced at me. "We could go outside and check." He grabbed a flashlight, then grabbed my hand. He led me to a big tree, swept the light up and down the thick trunk.

"He's gone." Wilford's voice was pitched low. "That's where I left him." He aimed the light six feet from the ground. We circled the tree, the light playing on its bark. So the fairy creature was safe.

"You saved him." I hugged my hero.

◆

Wilford was sometimes a pain in the ass. His vehicles were unreliable. I'd have to get up early and drive him to the top of Salt Lick, to the gas station, where he would catch a ride to work with a friend. I hated getting up early and was usually pretty grumpy. Wilford was all positive energy. He'd hop out of the car and pull his handkerchief from a back pocket to clean each headlight. He would blow me a kiss and tip his ball cap.

Cranky couldn't win against such charm. I was so attracted to this man. Wilford didn't complain when I buried my nose in a book and ignored him. Instead he found something else to do. Fueled by pot and beer, he swept the porch, tilled the garden, pulled weeds. He had a gift for finding four-leaf clovers; I pressed them between the pages of my dictionary.

While Wilford took charge outside, I claimed the kitchen. I felt domestic. If this was the adult version of playing house, it was time to learn to cook. My mother was eager to share recipes; food was our new common language. I studied cookbooks and conducted food experiments. Wilford would try any culinary creation. When I went through a tofu stage, he didn't complain. You couldn't buy tofu in Terra Alta (then or now). In Morgantown, the only place to find it was the hippie food co-op. *The Book of Tofu* encouraged me to make it myself. From raw soybeans. It was crazy. I had to cook the beans, crush the beans, squeeze soymilk from the beans. Wilford built a tofu press, a small wooden box for the curds I scooped from the whey. He did that even though the tofu dishes I made were not very exciting. He did it because I was enthusiastic. He did it to make me happy. He did it because he loved me.

If he wasn't at work he had a buzz on. Always. Pot. Beer. Cans and joints held in hands that would have been elegant if they hadn't been colored by labor. Hands that flew when he talked. And he loved to talk. He remembered jokes and would act them out, all loose-limbed entertainment. The more he drank, the longer and more complicated the stories would get. When he went on and on, I would roll my eyes and retreat. Enough, I said. Sometimes Wilford drank hard liquor—Jack Daniels was his favorite. When he did, his eyes narrowed and his words slurred. He got sloppy. He got stupid. This was different from his usual buzz. I didn't like this dark man, wounded and mean. But he didn't appear often. I didn't think it was a problem. Wilford would change. He would mature. Some of our friends partied to excess. Wasn't that just part of being young?

We surrounded ourselves with our friends. We spent time at Marian and Joe's home in Albright. Marian had been involved with the Women's Information Center. Joe was a great storyteller, a born comedian. He was a good guy, the kind of guy who saw a dead animal on the road, stopped, and moved the carcass. "I don't want kids to see that," he'd explain with a shrug. Marian, with her Italian father and Irish mother, was lively and warm. Literally warm. Her olive skin radiated heat, made every hug special. Marian and Joe collected friends, opened their home to other young couples: Ellen and Corky, Mickey and Crow, John and Terry. People would bring their kids and covered dishes and spend the day.

One Sunday at Marian and Joe's, I walked outside to escape the smoky kitchen and saw Wilford standing like the Pied Piper surrounded by children. He had used boxes, chairs, and boards to rig an obstacle course in the yard. "Follow me," he yelled, and got down on all fours to crawl through a tunnel of chair legs. Giggling kids pursued his skinny butt. This man would make a great father. I watched him and felt a warmth throughout my body. We would have freckled happy children.

◆

The rabbi in Morgantown wouldn't perform a mixed marriage, even though Wilford was not religious. When I had asked him to identify his religion, he shrugged. "Protestant?" It was a question.

"I'm sure you're Protestant," I said. "Which one? Methodist? Baptist?" I didn't think he was Lutheran.

"Methodist, I think." Wilford nodded his head. "But we'll get married however you want." So I planned a Jew-ish wedding. We found a rabbi in Uniontown, Pennsylvania, a man of Indian heritage and Scottish upbringing, to perform the ceremony. His Hebrew had a Highlands lilt, which amused some of my relatives from the Midwest. So in August 1978, true to the date I had announced the year before, Wilford and I built a huppah in the field behind the barn, covered it in pine boughs, and decorated it with flowers. I wore a white cotton dress with eyelet panels. It wasn't a real wedding dress but I had never dreamed of being a princess bride. I carried my grandfather's Hebrew prayer book, a family tradition.

Wilford's mother, accustomed to small weddings with receptions in church basements, had worried for weeks about our decision to have an outdoor ceremony. But the sun shone on our mountaintop that day. A hundred friends sat in chairs loaned to us by the funeral home. Wilford's parents escorted him to his place under the huppah. My parents flanked me as I joined him. Bill, the journalism professor who had sent me to West Virginia, had moved back to the state and was our photographer. Jerry had found a wonderful band, and their music—dulcimer, fiddle, bass, and guitar—serenaded the party. The ceremony, the first (and only) Jewish wedding most of the guests would attend, was short. The receiving line was long and great fun. Our eclectic guests were enjoying themselves. Terra Alta matriarchs chatted with our hippie friends. My relatives enjoyed the beauty of the mountains. My mother became the band's groupie for a day; she settled in a chair next to them and grinned with pleasure. We ate marvelous food. Kathleen Sisler, the cook at Terra Alta Elementary School, was our caterer.

◆

Kathleen was famous for her homemade rolls; her green beans bore the smoky touch of bacon, and her fried chicken drew paying customers to the elementary school. Kathleen was a widow when I met her, round-faced, her white hair braided and wrapped close to her head. An apron always covered her simple, cotton dresses; she could have stepped from a photo taken in the 1930s. I have a vivid recollection of the day I asked her to describe how she lived before plumbing. "I'll show you," Kathleen said. Like a teacher before a class, she stood in her cozy living room, scooped water from a pink-flowered ceramic washbasin to wet her face, then grabbed a washcloth, dipped it in the water, turned her back, and scrubbed each armpit in turn. When she faced me again, a triumphant grin lit her face.

Kathleen, Wilford's mother, and other Preston County matriarchs would have clutched their sides and howled with laughter if I had told them that in the beginning of the twenty-first century the way they dealt with food would have a new term and new cachet: locavore. Their milk came from the cows next door, their meat from chickens, pigs, cows, and deer in nearby fields, and their vegetables from a patch of land steps from the back porch.

We didn't have a dairy next door, but Wilford's mother taught me how to can, how to turn rows of green beans in the garden into rows of filled glass jars. I made plum jam. Mary Jane, the woman who had introduced me to Wilford, helped me can tomatoes and tomato juice. Wilford and I bought a side of beef from a neighbor, cut and wrapped venison. *The Mother Earth News* was a primer for the life I wanted to lead. Wilford hid the magazine from me once. He had been alarmed by the photos in the story, "How to Turn the Common Garden Snail into Escargot."

◆

We went to New York City on our honeymoon, a long weekend. The Finns, friends who had grown up near the city, were our escorts. We saw *Grease* and walked up the Avenue of the Americas. A snooty hostess deemed our dress inappropriate for the restaurant on top of Rockefeller Center and we ended up at a Scandinavian buffet next to huge men eating huge amounts of food. We checked into the Century Paramount Hotel near Times Square and Wilford announced that the Finns and Feathers had arrived. "And where is Mr. Fur?" the clerk joked. I stifled my impulse to blurt that I hadn't changed my name.

The decision to keep my birth name had some unexpected feedback. An older woman whom I had interviewed lamented changing her name when she married. "I'm a Dodge," she told me. "Everybody thinks I'm a Gibson but I'm a Dodge." Wilford's father disapproved of my decision. But I never considered taking my husband's name. My name was my name.

I did, however, consider motherhood. We wanted to make a baby. Our sex life, always good, got better. I'm certain I got pregnant when we visited my parents over the Christmas holidays. My first child, made in Missouri.

23

♦ ♦ ♦

WHY IS THIS NIGHT
DIFFERENT?

YOU COULD CALL ME JEWISH, but really I'm Jew-ish. My family was Jewish according to Hitler but by no other measure. We celebrated Christmas. Not the birth-of-Jesus Christmas, but the shopping Christmas, the Christmas of presents, pine smells, and prime rib. My religious education came from a cheap edition of *Bible Stories for Children* and a few years of Sunday school at a reform temple. My fellow students there had lovely clothes and shiny shoes. Modern art decorated the soaring sanctuary; I liked looking at the metal and glass shapes high above the bimah. In the classroom, smart was celebrated. This was my tribe. But my parents had no use for organized religion. They never went to temple, ignored the holidays. Why be Jewish? Give up bacon, shrimp, and lobster? Absurd! My maternal grandmother's family had dabbled in Christian Science in the early 1900s. She rejected that religion but didn't practice Judaism either. Instead, she celebrated any accomplishment by a Jew: the Salk vaccine, Danny Kaye's performances, Oppenheimer's bomb. She worshipped Sandy Koufax. My father's family was more traditional; both of his brothers had Jewish wives. But they were Reform Jews: nobody had a bar mitzvah. Instead we worshipped good deli: corned beef, knishes, and smoked salmon. My parents did have a bit of religious iconography in our home: foot-tall, anatomically correct statues of Adam and Eve that were displayed in a window next to the front door. The local Baptists, who visited often in a bid to save our souls, would stand in the doorway, cite scripture, and avert their eyes from Eve's pendulous breasts and Adam's equally pendulous penis.

When a friend of ours was killed in a car accident, my sister Julie and I attended her funeral, held at a small Catholic church. We covered our heads with lace circles from a basket by the door. The Catholic rituals were mysterious, the Latin as foreign as Hebrew. The priest stood at a simple altar, raised his arms, and spoke about our friend's brief time on earth. He said life was like a tapestry and we, the living, only view the back: the knots, the rough edges. Our friend was with God, with angels, he preached. She now saw the tapestry's beautiful side: the pattern, the colors. "Rejoice!" he said. I could not, would not. My friend was dead and that was a tragedy. Not God's will. A car, a moment of distraction, and a bridge abutment. I walked out of that church an atheist. Religion was a crutch, God a myth we invented for comfort.

In college, I returned to religion for a really bad reason. The Hillel at the University of Missouri sat in the middle of campus. If I joined, I would have a great parking place. I also was lured there by politics and art: the Yom Kippur War, the plight of Soviet Jewry, the photos of Roman Vishniac. Jews had played an important role in the Civil Rights Movement; we could be the good guys. The rabbi at the Hillel was young and charismatic. His Passover Seder was the first I had ever attended. It was fun, a ritual celebration of food and freedom. I should confess that once outside the Hillel walls I ignored the holiday's big rule: no leavened bread. I am a hypocrite. I follow the rules I like; ignore the ones I don't.

◆

My first West Virginia Seder, in the spring of 1976, was hosted by a Jewish woman who briefly worked for the county's other weekly newspaper. I bought *The Molly Goldberg Jewish Cookbook* and learned how to make chicken soup, chopped liver, and *charoseth* (a Passover concoction of chopped apples, walnuts, and sweet wine).

Simon, the doctor I had met through my friend at the health council, hosted Seder the following year. He and his girlfriend, a schoolteacher, transformed their tiny dining room into an intimate space that glowed with candles and reflective surfaces. In addition to Simon, his girlfriend, Wilford, and me, attendees included Judy, my stylish coworker, and her husband Chuck—longtime friends of Simon's girlfriend—and two Cuban brothers. Simon gathered us around the table and poured copious amounts of wine. Since Judy, Chuck, and the Cubans lived nearby, they had walked to the Seder—they were unafraid of drinking to excess. The Cubans had come to Preston County to manage their father's coal interests. They were dark and charming, the closest thing to playboys that existed in Preston County. We poured our wine glasses full and when Simon, Haggadah in hand, directed us to drink the first cup; we drained it. Simon led us through the rituals. By the time we finished the third cup of wine and welcomed dinner, the table was a blur. We were slaves. We were high. When the younger Cuban passed out before dessert, his head on his plate, we razzed his brother. "Cuban lightweights," we said. "It's Passover, not pass out."

◆

Wilford and I hosted our first Seder in the spring of 1978. We invited our hippie friends, Phil and Frances; Marian and her husband, Joe. We used a piece of plywood on sawhorses to extend the table. Candlelight made our rough cabin cozy. The evening had a celebratory vibe. We took turns reading from the Maxwell House Haggadah. Phil used his radio voice to do the Kiddush, the blessing of the wine, a stellar performance, and with a flourish he passed the book to Wilford. Wilford hunched his shoulders, then read. He paused at each word. "This . . . is . . . the . . . bread . . . of . . ." His voiced died.

Phil leaned over Wilford's shoulder. "Affliction," he said.

Wilford kept his eyes down. His voice was a monotone, "which our . . . ?"

"Ancestors," Phil offered.

"Ate in the land of . . . ?" Quiet. "Egypt." Wilford's eyes stayed on the Haggadah, did not lift to meet mine. I tried to will him the words, ached with the desire to help. Phil glanced at me, raised his eyebrows, and nodded. He put his big hand on Wilford's shoulder. His voice boomed. "Let all those who are hungry enter and eat thereof; and all who are in distress, come and celebrate the Passover."

Wilford kept his eyes down. Now everyone knew his secret: he could barely read. Wilford raised his head. "Sorry," he mumbled. He offered an excuse. "I never read anything like this." He passed the Haggadah to Marian, who read the four questions. We dipped parsley, a symbol of rebirth, into salt water, symbolic of tears. The ritual foods on our table had particular significance. Wilford's mother had made the pungent horseradish, had grown the root in her garden. The shank bone came from a lamb in Phil's flock. He had delivered it, herded it, and he and Wilford cut its throat. The tribe's sacrificial lamb. We continued through the ceremony, drank cup after cup of sweet wine and passed the Haggadah around the table. Every time Phil finished reading his part, he placed the book between himself and Wilford and the two of them read together, Wilford's voice coming a split second behind Phil's. We celebrated freedom, friendship, and the coming of spring. We ate and drank and talked and smoked. By the evening's end, we staggered, drunk and high, from the table and sprawled in the living room. Wilford and I had recently bought modular furniture, squishy taupe foam pieces whose bottoms unfolded to make close-to-the-floor mattresses. Wilford lay with his head in my lap. I pushed his hair back from his face and leaned over to kiss him, tipped that sharp chin toward my own. I could taste coffee liqueur and pot. Wilford was pale and quiet.

In a few days Phil would ask if I knew before the Seder that Wilford could barely read and I would hesitate before I answered. I finally admitted to Phil that I hadn't realized the extent of Wilford's problem. I had refused to see signals, my denial buoyed by an entire life among the literate. But that night, a night different from all other nights, a new truth entered our lives. Wilford was functionally illiterate. Holy Moses.

24

◆ ◆ ◆

BLACK POWER

———

IN 1979, *The Preston County News* produced a thirty-two-page tabloid on coal. Jerry wrote the introduction:

> We wanted this to be an important effort, not just a vehicle in which to sell advertising to coal interests, but a major attempt to learn and understand the past, the present and the future for coal and for Preston County. . . .
>
> All the questions were asked in Preston County, wishing to present the story as it is here, in the coal fields. So you will read no statements from state or national officials, no proclamations or justifications from those who make the decisions or apply the regulations. You will receive the story as it is perceived by your friends and neighbors who are the industry.
>
> Make no mistake about it, this report was conceived from the start to be biased, if bias means telling the industry side of the story. We had heard all the "cons," we wished to openly listen to the "pros."
>
> Yet, even as we admit our biases, we know that we are a "motley crew of reporters," a mixture of diverse and incongruous

elements—an admitted environmentalist, one who suspicioned he might be, another who strongly favored the industry point of view and another who had been fed a steady diet of "company propaganda" for years.

We put all our personal opinions aside, and listened. And we tried to accurately relate the stories we heard.

Now we hope this special supplement will provide you with many of those same things. May it lie upon your coffee table for many weeks.

◆

The "motley crew" began planning the issue long before its April publication. We met at Alpine Lake, a struggling resort just east of Terra Alta. Alpine's development in the late 1960s had paralleled the development of Deep Creek Lake Recreation Area just across the Maryland State Line. The mountains drew vacationers from wealthier areas: Washington, D.C., Baltimore, and Pittsburgh. By the mid-1970s, it was obvious that Alpine could not compete with Deep Creek, where skiing—snow and water—drew crowds. Alpine Lake wasn't big enough for motor boats. Its ski slope was short and unchallenging, the wobbly rope tow a throwback to the old days. Alpine's planners had more greed than taste; they divided the property into too many miniscule lots so houses were too close to one another. But Alpine had a golf course, a slightly rundown lodge, and a restaurant that aspired to some class. We sat around the table: Jerry, Michele, Judy, Bill (a part-time reporter who had been hired to work on the tabloid), and I.

Judy was enthusiastic about the special issue. She knew she could sell it. Because her husband was an engineer for one of the county's largest coal companies, she had connections. Bill had just moved to the area. Originally from Maine, he and his wife met as students at Macalester College. They were exactly my age, so a few years out of school. Bill's brother-in-law and sister-in-law were among the small cadre of hippies in the mountains. Bill and his wife lived in an unplumbed, heated-by-wood-stove cabin on property owned by a cabinetmaker and his wife. It was a great accident of timing that brought Bill to *The News* just as we needed another voice. In Jerry's introduction, Bill was the reporter who suspicioned he might be an environmentalist.

◆

I was the "admitted environmentalist." I had read *Silent Spring*; I knew that DDT was poison. All I knew about coal was that it was dirty. I wanted clean air and clean water. During my first summer in Preston County, I'd seen my first strip mine. A brown slash spilled across the hillside like a scar on a beautiful face. The vacant ground spoiled the vista, interrupted the repeating green waves of forests and valleys. When I realized that the ugly landscape was a coal mine, it was a personal affront. What kind of person would despoil nature so? I marched into *The News* office shortly after my discovery and loudly declared that strip mining should be outlawed. At the time, I would have been oblivious to the views of my audience: Jerry, Rich, Annie, and Michele. I was such a smart-ass twenty-something. So young, so unaware of my ignorance. I didn't know that coal made steel manufacturing possible, fueled the industrial age, electrified the country. I didn't know that coal was the sacred heart of West Virginia's economy.

Coal trains curled through Preston County, railroad car after railroad car piled high with black rock. Coal trucks roared down every highway, from mine to cleaning plant, cleaning plant to power plant. When they were full, those big trucks crawled up hills and, even on the straight stretches, never traveled much more than thirty miles an hour. Vehicles stacked up behind these ugly turtles. When the trucks were empty, they gained speed, their wide bodies treacherous on narrow roads. I liked to drive fast and eventually learned the location of every passing zone, every dotted yellow line in the county. I would downshift, gun the engine, and swoop around the truck.

Even Wilford's job was tied to coal. The lumber company he worked for produced posts to hold up mine roofs. And I knew others whose employment was tied to coal. Our friends Joe and Corky worked at the power plant. Charlie, the rock and roll musician, drove a coal truck. Carolyn, the leader of our softball team, was a draftsman for a coal company. Wilford's friend Chip operated a giant bulldozer on a strip mine. Coal supported other industries too: equipment dealers, machinists, and insurance salesmen. These jobs in turn supported retail businesses: grocery stores, restaurants, beauty parlors, and funeral homes. Bars. Thousands of families. Coal taxes supported the schools and local government. Miners in Preston County produced nearly three million tons of coal a year, most of it used to make electricity.

◆

Back at Alpine Lake Lodge, we divvied up the assignments for the coal issue. Jerry and Judy would sell advertising. Jerry would tell the history of coal in Preston County, what coal's value was during an energy crisis, and write a profile of a local pioneer of reclamation, who restored land that had been mined to its original contours. Bill would report how government regulation affected a local company. He would also do a story on renovations at the county's largest coal operation. Judy would ride with the owner of trucking fleet for a story. I would write about a reclamation program and find out what was required to become a coal miner. I would photograph miners and mines, trains and trucks, a coal broker, and a reclaimed field.

At this meeting, I was newly pregnant, in that delighted and slightly secretive gestational phase. As a result, I might have had a beer, or a glass of wine (back then experts preached moderation, not abstinence). The others at the table were not moderate in their alcohol consumption. I was soon the only one not under the influence. I even remember what I wore that evening, a loose, beige sweater dress. Under the table my left hand cupped my growing belly, the fabric of my dress soft beneath my fingers. Judy knew my secret. I don't remember when I told Jerry and Michele. I know that my thrill was tempered by their difficulties in conceiving a child.

◆

Milford Jenkins, the pioneer of reclamation Jerry wrote about, was one of the stars of the coal issue. He was a strip miner in Preston County, a successful businessman who felt responsible for the land that mining disturbed. Tall and lean, dark hair slicked back in a low pompadour,

Milford looked like Clark Gable. Milford was one of the richest men in Preston County but unlike some of the strutting blowhards I had met, he was a soft-spoken gentleman. I photographed him using a moderate telephoto lens, a three-quarter view of his handsome profile against a pale sky. A flattering portrait, though he wouldn't know that until the paper was published. Jerry had already wooed Milford for the coal issue. We needed the vantage point of his helicopter to illustrate our reclamation story. Several of the coal companies had helicopters; business was good and the war in Vietnam had created a supply of pilots, including Milford's son Mike. I quickly decided to make use of Mike's skills.

I had found out that a school bus route near Pisgah (pronounced PIZ-ghee), in the far northwest corner of Preston County, ran alongside a high wall—a remnant of the old days of strip mining, when damaged land was simply abandoned. The man-made cliff loomed over a tangle of rock and weeds. Twice a day, a school bus skirted that precipice, its wheels dangerously close to the sharp drop-off. The road the bus traveled, Laurel Run, had two-way traffic but was just one lane wide. No shoulders. No guardrails. When I tried to photograph the scene from the road, to illustrate the void next to the asphalt, it didn't read. I needed to get higher.

When I asked, Milford said Mike would be happy to take me up in the chopper, so on a chilly early spring afternoon we met at the company's headquarters. Two West Virginia Department of Natural Resources (DNR) officers were along for the ride; they wanted to see if the harsh winter had hurt the deer and turkey populations. We settled into comfortable seats under a clear dome. Mike, a friendly guy who was my age, adjusted his headphones and flipped switches. I was nervous because I had recently seen *Superman*, which included a vivid helicopter crash, but I did not share that information. In seconds we were airborne, the blades chopping the air into harsh sounds. From the air, the mountains flattened out; the leafless forests were a monochrome gray-brown. The ride was thrilling; I had not considered the novelty of this vantage point. Within minutes we were over a moonscape. Acres and acres of damaged land. No trees. No brush. Just mud and rock. This was what old strip mines looked like. These sites near Muddy Creek had given up their coal before reclamation laws came to be. I had no idea this terrain existed, hidden far back off of dirt roads. I was shocked by their expanse. Then quickly we were over wooded hills again. Below us, deer were dark shapes easily spotted. When they noticed a flock of turkeys clustered in a field, the DNR officers spoke with excitement. There would be a good spring gobbler season, they said.

◆

I had coordinated our fly-over with Mrs. King, the bus driver on Laurel Run. She drove past the Pisgah high wall twice a day. She knew exactly what time we needed to hover above. Even though I had asked her to drive slowly that afternoon, I would have just seconds to shoot my picture. The yellow bus was easy to see as it made its way toward the top of the cliff. Mike maneuvered the helicopter so I had a clear shot. I had no motor drive to automatically advance the film in the camera. Instead I had to press the shutter, then work the lever with my thumb. How many frames? I didn't count. Just bang, bang, bang until the bus passed the high wall.

I didn't know I had a problem until much later when I rewound the film. The tension on the film was momentary, not continuous, as was the norm. I knew what that meant: I had not loaded the camera properly. A rookie mistake, one I had made before and had vowed to never make again. All I had to do after I laced film though the sprockets and closed the back of the camera was flip up the rewind lever, then watch it turn as I advanced the film. That revolving motion proved that film was going through the camera. Something must have distracted me when I loaded the camera. I had not gotten one image on my helicopter ride. I was horrified. Chastened. Sickened by my mistake. Jerry was upset too but he saw that he couldn't make me feel worse than I already felt. I had to confess my sins to Milford, then ask for another ride. I had to call Mrs. King, admit to many people that I was an incompetent fool, that my confidence in myself was misplaced. On the second try, I got the picture.

"Coal '79: A look at Preston County's most important industry—the end of an era, the edge of the future" was published to great enthusiasm. West Virginia secretary of state A. James Manchin loved the publication. He gave us certificates proclaiming each of us a "Commodore of the Ship of State." Judy had hers framed. I still have mine, its edges nibbled by silverfish. A. James Manchin was a real character. He had helped John Kennedy win West Virginia, a campaign that earned close examination. He established a political dynasty that flourishes to this day. In a poster prominently displayed in our office at *The News*, A. James posed next to a discarded car, a scythe over his shoulder. He wore a fancy coat and a fedora. The caption read, "We must purge these proud peaks of these jumbled jungles of junkery." Thousands of abandoned cars were removed from the landscape because of his efforts. No one trusted A. James Manchin, but everyone loved him.

The coal issue won awards from the West Virginia Press Association. Clips from Bill's stories won him a job at a bigger newspaper. He eventually worked for the *Charleston Gazette*, a wonderful newspaper. He then went on to work for West Virginia University, its medical center, and the governor of West Virginia.

Within a year after its picture appeared, the high wall at Pisgah was fixed.

25

◆ ◆ ◆

THE MURDERER AND ME

———

IN NOVEMBER 1975, an early blizzard changed the landscape. I wanted a photo and headed across the Aurora Pike. Not far out of town, I saw a two-story farmhouse on the side of a hill. Melting snow had carved the fields surrounding the house into a pattern of dark and light horizontal stripes. It was a simple, graphic scene. I pulled to the side of the road, not really out of the way, but I hoped I had enough time to jump out, shoot a quick photo, and move my truck before someone came around the curve and plowed into me. I shot the photo and drove on. The information for a caption would come later. I was sure someone at the office could identify a farm not more than three miles from town.

A few days later, I held up the print and asked, "Anybody know this house? It's off the Aurora Pike." Annie, Michele, and Jerry glanced at the photo and shook their heads. The typesetters shrugged. It was time to put the paper to bed, so I ran the photo with a caption about early winter's short-lived grip. The next day, postal clerk Charlie was looking at the newly printed front page when I dragged in a canvas bag filled with papers to be mailed. "That's the Mullenax house!" he said.

"Whose house?" I asked.

"Vonda Mullenax. She killed her husband there." Charlie pursed his mouth and shook his head, gestures that conveyed his superiority. He leaned on the counter; he was dying to tell the story.

"The Mullenaxes had a bunch of kids, ten maybe," Charlie began. "He was a janitor at the grade school. Folks said he wasn't a nice guy. It was the perfect crime and she would have gotten away with it if she hadn't confessed to some guy she dated later." He shook his head again. "The Mullenax house! On the front page of the paper!" Then he added, "You know, she escaped from jail three times!" (He was wrong; I later learned she had escaped eight times.)

Charlie was not the only one to gleefully identify the farmhouse. Everyone in town knew the Mullenax story. The crime had taken place more than a decade earlier, in 1965. I'm sure they were tickled by a newspaper so stupid that it not only publicized a notorious spot, but dared to call it artful.

I sat in the office, head squeezed between my hands, and cursed my ignorance. Would I ever belong here? I squinted at the photo, considered its real story. Annie faced me across our combined desks. Annie was a generous soul. I looked up when I heard her sigh. Her eyebrows were pursed in a V of regret.

"It's my fault," she said quietly. "I didn't really look at the picture." Annie moved around to look over my shoulder. She pointed to a dark smudge beside the house.

"That may be the trash pile where she burned him. There were rumors that he was—" Annie paused.

"Yes?" I prompted.

"Bad," is what she settled on. I waited to hear what else she would say.

"He used to bring men home to Vonda," Annie finally said, her voice low, as if she was sharing a secret. "To have sex. Everyone felt sorry for her."

What a story. That afternoon when I went to volunteer at the high school in Vivian McConnell's journalism class I couldn't wait to ask about the Mullenax murder. Vivian leaned against her desk, crossed her arms, and frowned. "They were poor," she recalled. Even in a town with few distinctions between the classes, poor was a pitiable ranking.

"Mr. Mullenax was a big man, quiet," she said. "But he had an eye that turned the wrong way and that made him look scary. He was a drinker, too." She took a breath. "There were ten children, but one drowned." Vivian's forehead wrinkled in concentration. "Before they moved to the farmhouse on the Aurora Pike, they lived down Salt Lick and the kids had to cross the creek to catch the bus. One of the little boys, too young for school, followed them, fell in the creek, and drowned. The rest of the kids didn't see him; they just got on the bus." She looked up, her eyes wide behind owlish glasses. The horror of her words hung in the air, silenced us both.

The family piqued my interest, so I did some research. Back issues of *The News* were bound into huge, heavy, dusty books, the size of a newspaper broadsheet. I plopped 1966, the year of Vonda's trial, on the counter and turned the yellowed pages. The correspondence from each community—reports from Homemakers and 4-H clubs—was nearly identical to what ran in the current newspaper.

The Mullenax murder wasn't hard to find. The trial was front-page news that spring. Someone showed me a crime magazine that called it "the perfect crime." The story began when Ray Mullenax failed to show up in magistrate's court in Terra Alta for a bad debt charge just before Christmas 1965. Local authorities started asking questions. Vonda told them that the last time she had seen Ray, he was heading to Terra Alta. The sheriff didn't believe her. He suspected that Ray had skipped town to evade paying his debts. He would stay gone just long enough for Vonda to qualify for welfare. The sheriff had seen men do this before. But deputies considered the possibility that Mullenax might have had an accident. They searched the snowy hills. They knew if they didn't find him right away, snow would cover any clues until spring. They found nothing.

A couple of months after Ray vanished, a local man named Gank, an ex-con, told a police officer a wild story. Ray Mullenax hadn't run away, he said. Ray's wife Vonda had killed him. She had confessed to Gank when he told her he was worried Ray would come home and catch them together. Vonda promised Gank that Ray was no threat. She had killed him, she said. Gank told the deputy that he wanted to tell him the story because he was worried that he would be accused of killing Ray. But Gank had been drinking the night he told the tale. He had a history of drunken lying, so the officer didn't believe he was telling the truth.

A month later Gank visited the sheriff's office again, this time to complain that his truck windows had been broken out. Sober this time, Gank accused Vonda's other boyfriend, also an ex-con, of the vandalism. Gank again told the deputy that Vonda had killed her husband. This time, the deputy asked him to elaborate. Gank sat down with several officers. During questioning he suggested that the officers talk to Vonda. "She's outside in the truck," he said. Although they suspected Gank of the murder, deputies brought Vonda into the stone building that housed the jail. After just a few questions, Vonda, obviously frightened, blurted a confession. "I killed him!" she said. The deputies were shocked. They never actually imagined a woman, a mother, could be capable of such an act.

Vonda was advised of her rights but said she didn't want a lawyer. She wanted to talk. She said she had slowly poisoned her husband with arsenic and when he was too weak to fight back, she strangled him. Later stories reported that the murder weapon was a piece of string Vonda had found. People also said that Vonda had loosened the fuses so her children couldn't turn on any lights and discover what she had done. Vonda told the deputies that she dragged Ray's body outside to the trash pile and started a fire. For days she returned to that site, contained by an old barn foundation. Over and over she burned what rubbish she could find, stopping only when a snowstorm buried the site.

The night she made her confession, the officers got a warrant and took Vonda to the farm, where they uncovered the trash pile and removed bags of blackened debris.

By the time the trial started a few months later, Vonda had changed her story. Again, she claimed Ray had deserted the family. Her lawyers tried to get her confession dismissed, but the judge wouldn't allow that.

Character witnesses testified that Vonda was a good mother, a hard worker. The jail wasn't really set up for female prisoners, so Vonda wasn't locked in a cell while she was on trial. She stayed in a room under the eaves on the top floor of the old stone building. (A decade after her stay, this is where the Preston County Women's Information Center would meet.) Unaccustomed to leisure, Vonda spent hours cleaning the jail. The sheriff testified that she was a model prisoner.

The prosecutor found a letter that he presented to prove motive. Vonda had written her mother to report that Ray had sold the family's cow. "My children need milk," Vonda wrote. "This is the last straw." A photograph of Vonda's note to her mother was on the front page of a musty copy of *The News*. Neat handwriting followed the lines on notebook paper.

The prosecutor called in a scientist from the Smithsonian. On the witness stand, he held out a small, blackened bone fragment and identified it as human. This tiny piece of evidence was all that remained of Ray Mullenax. The jury was awed by the scientist's expertise and his Washington job. So, in spite of widespread sympathy, Vonda was convicted in July and sentenced to life in prison.

The newspaper stories didn't report the fate of the nine Mullenax children. And although I looked through years of papers, there were no reports of Vonda's escapes. I asked around, but no one seemed to know the particulars. I didn't forget the story; I thought about Vonda every time I drove the Aurora Pike and passed the farmhouse. I wondered about the drowned child when I drove down Salt Lick. But the demands of daily life and work kept me away from the story.

◆

Two years later, in 1977, Charlie, the postal clerk, surprised me with an update.

"Vonda Mullenax is out of jail," he said. "She got out for good behavior. I hear she's living right across the state line in Maryland. That's news." He raised an eyebrow as if in a dare.

I tracked down a phone number and called. A woman's voice answered.

"Is this Vonda?" I asked.

"Yes."

"I'd like to interview you," I blurted. "People are interested in your story."

"No," she said. "I don't want to talk to the newspaper. I just want to be left alone. I just want to be with my children."

I wrote this story, then mailed it to Vonda:

Vonda Jean Mullenax, convicted in the 1965 murder of her husband, has been released from the state prison at Pence Springs, prison officials said.

Jack Nestor, superintendent of the West Virginia State Prison for Women, said Mrs. Mullenax was granted parole last Wednesday after serving nearly 11 years of a life sentence.

Despite a sensational trial in which the details of the grisly murder of Ray Lynn Mullenax, 39, unfolded, Nestor said he had "no indication" that persons in her home county feared her return. "It's just the opposite. People call and express their opinions the other way," he said.

Nestor described Mrs. Mullenax as a model prisoner while at Pence Springs although she escaped eight times, apparently to visit her children.

She was convicted by a Preston County Circuit Court jury in July, 1966, of first degree murder in the slaying of her husband whom she allegedly had poisoned for several months and then strangled to death and cremated.

Eight escapes! Ten children! What a story. But two more years would pass before I learned more.

◆

My own pregnancy in 1979 propelled me back toward Vonda. My made-in-Missouri baby was not due until September, but I asked Jerry if I could start my maternity leave in May. "I'm going to write a book about the Mullenax murder," I said.

Jerry chuckled. "We don't have a maternity leave policy," he said. "But I can lay you off." He nodded. "You can collect unemployment."

I already knew that the newspaper's health insurance policy excluded maternity care. (This was legal in 1979.) I imagined the lean budget in my future. A book, a *book*, could help us.

I called Vonda to set up an interview. This time I confessed that I was motivated by money. "I think a book about you would sell," I said. "Of course I would share the profits." I heard Vonda inhale. "I'm not sure I want to do this," she said, her breath a whisper. Her voice strengthened. "I read the clipping you sent me a while ago."

"Please, let's try," I said. "If it gets too hard, we'll stop."

She hesitated again, then in a soft voice said it would be okay if I visited her at work. She told me that she was taking care of Gank's father, who was suffering from black lung, a coal miner's affliction.

The older Gank lived in a tiny brown frame house in Hutton, Maryland, a town best known for its speed trap and rag shop. I stood on the porch next to a small stack of oxygen tanks and knocked on the screen door. In the living room, a television set glowed. A small, bald head shined over the back of a recliner and the hiss of oxygen competed with the turned-up volume of the TV. When Vonda came to the door her eyes slid from my face quickly down to my round belly.

"Hi," she said, holding the door open. Her voice was low and gentle. "When's your baby comin'?"

"September sixteenth," I said, and walked in. Vonda turned and headed to the back of the house, into the kitchen. She was tall and solidly built, a large woman who looked strong enough to move a body. Her short brown hair, cut in a style that was fashionable in the 1950s, framed her face in soft waves. She had gorgeous skin, with high color spotting her cheeks as she motioned for me to sit down. Vonda poured two cups of coffee. "Milk?" I nodded.

"This your first baby?" Vonda raised her eyebrows.

"Yes," I said. My eyes fell to her muscular forearms. I didn't know where to begin this interview. I was wary of appearing too eager, so I decided to ask about her children

"We're trying to get better acquainted," she said. "Six of them live around here. They were in foster homes while I was in jail. The two little girls went to my sister's in Washington, D.C." She paused for a moment, her eyes down, then took a deep breath. "My baby, little Robert; they let him be adopted." She raised her head and looked at me, her eyes shining. "I never gave no permission. He was my baby." She started to cry. "I went to see him as soon as I got out, but he was calling this other woman 'Momma.' She wouldn't give him back and I could see he wasn't mine no more."

She continued to cry quietly. I watched, helpless. The coffee was no longer hot, but I took a sip. The silence was broken only by the sounds coming from the living room, the hiss of the oxygen tank, the choppy sounds from the television. I changed the subject.

"I heard that you escaped from jail?"

She wiped her eyes with the back of her hand and met my gaze. "I had to see my children."

"Can you tell me what happened?"

She reached for her coffee, curled her fingers around the cup. "For the first two escapes, I was at Pence Springs." (A southern West Virginia prison for women.) "I just tied my sheets together, climbed out the window, and went over the fence. I was worried about wearing out my shoes, so I carried them. I stayed off the roads during the daytime so no one would see me."

I imagined Vonda barefoot, picking her way through brush, walking alone in the dark beside the two-lane blacktop, heading north.

"It must have been difficult," I offered.

She shrugged. "It took a while." She grasped the coffee cup. "The kids wrote me and they sounded sad. I had to make sure they was being treated right. On my second escape, it rained hard. I got pretty muddy.

"By the third escape, I had been moved to Alderson." (A federal prison for women.) "I hid in a laundry truck to get out. This time I went to Washington to see Christy and Susan, the youngest girls. They was at my sister's. That was a hard trip. I walked a long way."

Her forehead wrinkled. "It was good to see my baby girls," she said. "But I got caught right away. My own sister turned me in."

I was so shocked that I forgot to ask about the rest of her escapes. I scribbled in my notebook, distracted by a baby somersaulting in my belly, a baby who had already changed more than my body. In those stirrings deep inside me, I had discovered a new kind of love. All-encompassing. Overwhelming. Although I could not fathom the strength Vonda's journeys required, I understood the drive that gave her the energy to walk all those miles.

"Can you tell me how old your kids are?" I asked.

Vonda slumped in the chair, brought a hand to her chin. "Let's see," she said. "In 1952 I had Kathy, in 1953 I had Debbie, in 1954 I had John, in 1955 I had Michael, in 1956 I had Ronnie." She paused for breath. "In 1957 I didn't have a baby." Another breath. "In 1958 I had Linda, in 1959 I had David, in 1960 I had Susan, in 1961 I had Christy, and in 1962 I had Robert." When she stopped the recitation, I stared at her. Ten children in eleven years! I sat back, embarrassed, hands on the ball of my belly. I found my voice. "I live down Salt Lick on the old Martin farm," I said. "Your place was just down the road from me."

"I remember the Martin farm," she nodded. "It's pretty in that valley."

"You were across the creek?" I asked. Then I lowered my voice and my eyes. "I heard you lost one of your boys in Salt Lick."

"Yes," she said, her hands clasped on the table. "David fell into the creek and drowned. He had followed the others on their way to school. He was my only blond baby."

I looked down at the table, its surface scrubbed so hard that the pattern had disappeared in spots. I didn't know what to say. I was too soft-hearted to ask hard questions. But Vonda continued without any prompt.

"I remember it was 1962. I had just finished canning two hundred and twenty-two quarts of pears. I remember the number because it was two-two-two."

These numbers fell matter-of-fact from her mouth. We talked about canning, about the effort to grow and pick produce, clean it, slice it, boil it. It took me an entire day to put up eighteen quarts of peaches. I could not imagine 222 quarts of pears any more than I could imagine mothering ten children. How could I understand the woman sitting across the small table?

I visited twice more. I learned that Vonda met Ray when he stopped to give her a ride as she walked home with a Sunday paper. She told me what her children were doing. One afternoon as the sun dimmed into evening, she lowered her voice and her face and told me that Ray used to have sex with chickens. She explained how that was possible. She quietly talked about the men he brought home, how Ray turned her into a prostitute. I listened to her words, wrote in my notebook, and felt horror and unhappiness inhabit the kitchen. In 1979, she could have invoked a battered woman defense. During her trial in 1966, when Vonda needed it, that didn't exist.

I only asked about Ray's murder once. Vonda told me she had found the jar of arsenic when the family moved into the house. She looked me straight in the eye, crossed her arms, and said, "I told everyone he ran away." Her tone scared me. The cold, flat voice defied further questioning. I was dejected. How could I write a book if its subject wasn't forthcoming?

Vonda talked about Gank, how he had double-crossed her. Her voice bitter, Vonda said he had often visited her in prison, but he fell in love with another inmate. She had expected his help when she finished serving her time. Instead he married someone else. He hired her to take care of his father, a man whose lungs were crippled by coal dust, who sat in front of the television all day, who could not ever escape his oxygen tether. Vonda cooked, delivered meals to the living room on a tray, cleaned the house.

She wanted me to write her story, hoped it would bring in some money. But she wouldn't admit to the murder and although I framed my arguments several ways, I was not able to convince her that the book depended upon her confession. I could not be more forceful than a woman who canned 222 quarts of pears in order to feed her children. That summer my belly grew and I canned my own peaches, green beans, and tomatoes. I made elderberry jelly. I stacked rows of bright jars in my pantry. Not one jar of pears among them.

26

✦ ✦ ✦

BUCKWHEAT BABY

FOR FOUR DAYS EACH FALL, the Buckwheat Festival rules Preston County. The Friday of the festival is a school holiday. Many businesses close. Kingwood's elite abandon their offices to work in the hotdog stand or manage the crowds standing in line for buckwheat cakes—thin sourdough pancakes whose merits are judged just as oenologists evaluate wine: by nose, by mouthfeel, by the producer's pedigree. Buckwheat—brown, oddly shaped kernels—was a staple when Preston County was first settled. It matured quickly, thrived in the thin Appalachian soil, and could feed man and beast. I knew nothing about buckwheat until I moved to Terra Alta. I had never tasted kasha, a porridge of roasted buckwheat, a staple in the diet of my Jewish ancestors in Poland and Russia. In Preston County, by the 1970s, buckwheat was grown more for show than for profit. At the time, white bread was king. Whitetail deer loved buckwheat. They destroyed crops. Farmers complained that they couldn't keep deer out of their buckwheat fields.

In 1975, I paid three dollars for my first buckwheat cake dinner and stood in a long line outside the brick community building in Kingwood. Inside, rows of tables turned the space into a cafeteria crowded with citizens old and young, dressed in fine clothes and farm clothes. I joined the procession making its slow way along the inside perimeter. The screech of metal folding chairs announced customers coming and going. The line ended at a kitchen window; beyond the counter, men held giant spatulas like weapons, scraped griddles, then greased them with fatty pork skin. The volunteer cooks poured circles of thin batter from pitchers; smoke and sizzle filled the space; a noisy fan offered little relief. The pancakes cooked almost instantly and were flipped, a roan pattern now marking the top. A woman at the counter thrust a warm plate piled with three thin cakes and two patties of sausage into my hands. She said someone would bring coffee to my table. I scanned the crowded room for a familiar face and found none so I squeezed into a vacant spot.

Condiments were on the table: pats of margarine sandwiched between squares of cardboard and wax paper, plastic bottles of maple-flavored corn syrup, bowls of applesauce. Applesauce? That was curious. The first cake was delicious, slightly sour and chewy; the lace at its thin edge had a slight crunch. But I wished for real butter. And I had never liked fake maple syrup. I tried the next cake covered in applesauce. Yum. This was a symbiotic combination. Harvest food, stick-to-your-ribs sustenance. The sausage was a revelation—completely different from any meat I had ever tasted. I would soon learn that the Stalnaker men were the lords of sausage making. In the basement of the community building, they pushed pig parts through a grinder, mixed the fat and meat and spice in perfect proportions. Hundreds of pounds of pork, piles of pork, all to be turned into patties.

A server delivered hot coffee and asked me if I wanted more cakes. I could have as many as I wanted. Extra sausage cost a few cents. I don't remember if I had seconds, but I do remember that I ate four more buckwheat dinners at that festival, my first Buckwheat Festival. Five dinners in four days. I still love buckwheat cakes. I make them myself, although it took me years to perfect the process. I keep a sourdough starter going year round. I serve my cakes with real maple syrup, real butter, and, if I've had time, homemade applesauce.

The Buckwheat Festival was a big deal, a homecoming, a destination for tourists, a moneymaker. It supported the county's volunteer fire departments and civic groups. It celebrated the harvest and the county's agricultural roots. And it was fun: rides and contests and food and socializing. The fairgrounds smelled like sugar and animals. A juried crafts show occupied the space below the community building where fire trucks were normally housed. The back-to-the-land movement had brought artistic hippies to West Virginia and they were potters, woodworkers, toymakers, and jewelers. I bought my first piece of furniture, an oak rocking chair, from a bearded artist who seemed grateful to take my money.

Dulcimers tinkled in a space strewn with hay bales in the rear of the craft show. The Gardner brothers, Worley and Asel, wore red-checked shirts and string ties; white-haired men who championed lovely, authentic Appalachian music. Jerry wore a matching shirt and jammed along, the dulcimers ringing joy.

That first year, I was sure I would live in Preston County forever, that I would photograph every Buckwheat Festival, shoot each queen's coronation, each grand champion steer, each parade. As I wound through the crowd, hustling to photograph the cascade of events, I felt a sense of belonging. I often came face to face with people I knew, which was fun. But I didn't have much time to talk. Sometimes it felt as if I was missing the party—that observer versus participant tension.

My first four festivals whooshed by. They became distinctive for odd reasons: the queen who overplucked her eyebrows (I meticulously drew fake eyebrows on her photo with Spotone and a triple-zero paintbrush), the year I discovered the crunchy, salty corndogs sold by the county's sole black church, Love Chapel; the year the Powell boys got drunk and obnoxious and the police beat them into submission. Wilford knew the brothers and invited them to *The News* office so I could photograph their swollen faces. They claimed police brutality but after they left Wilford said he was sure they were guilty.

◆

My friend Ann, the nurse-practitioner who liked my writing, still denies that she brought family planning materials to my wedding. But she did. One of the brochures said the best age to have a first baby was twenty-six. That worked for me. I was a few weeks shy of twenty-five when I got married. Wilford and I had already talked about wanting to be parents. We put our fifth-grade school portraits next to each other: two long freckled faces. Wide smiles. We could have been cousins. I pictured our baby, a redhead named Sam. In the spring, when I announced my pregnancy and my due date, Jerry shot me a piercing look.

"So you'll miss the Buckwheat Festival."

"There will be other festivals," I said. Even though I loved the festival, I was looking forward to skipping its obligations for a year. "Sorry," I said. "I feel a little guilty."

My pregnancy made me feel exposed. My growing belly announced to everyone that I had had sex. It seemed so personal. So public. I was a different person. A mother. One secret I kept was that I had started wearing Wilford's underwear. The wide waist band and thick cotton fabric were so comfortable. Maternity underwear seemed an unnecessary expense.

Michael was back from his artist-in-residency gig in Illinois. Wilford and I helped him and Phil make hay on our farm and theirs. My pregnancy relegated me to the easy job of driving a big Ford flatbed truck through the field. First gear, lurch forward, then pause long enough for the men to stack bales behind me. Repeat. A battered copy of *The World According to Garp* was face down on the seat next to me and I would pick it up when I could. Garp became my model for parenthood.

Kathleen Sisler, our wedding caterer, and her daughter hosted our baby shower up Salt Lick in their shaded yard. Kathleen's daughter worked at the county hospital and had her mother's penchant for hard work. I hate to describe her as a spinster, but she had a way of viewing the world through sharp glances and lips pursed with what looked like disapproval. (She did eventually marry, for the first time, when she was in her sixties.) I had asked the Sislers if we could have a coed shower. Times were changing, I said. Men were labor coaches, active parents. I was an enthusiastic proponent of natural childbirth. I had it all figured out: I would have a drug-free labor, breastfeed my baby, and use cloth diapers. Wilford would be a hands-on dad. My friends Marian and Ellen were my role models. Marian was pregnant with her second baby;

Ellen's son was born just months after my wedding. I was surrounded by fecund women and their supportive men.

On a warm evening in August, the Sislers piled food on tables, directed silly games, and pretended not to notice when Wilford and a friend carried a cooler full of beer onto the lawn. "No beer at the baby shower," I had told Wilford earlier. Surely he and his friends could go a few hours without drinking. I suppose this should have been a giant, red-letter warning that I wasn't really in control of this whole baby thing. Or Wilford. But I ignored it. I thought I was jealous that he continued to drink and smoke pot while I mostly gave up intoxicants. If the Sislers were bothered by men and beer crashing their shower, they were too polite to tell me.

My September 16 due date came and went. In spite of increasing discomfort (I couldn't get out of the bathtub without help), I continued to believe that childbirth classes would lead to a drug-free birth, that my body, trained to handle pain, would cooperate. That the labor plan I wrote and discussed with Ann and Stephanie, my midwife, was gospel. Instead, reality got in the way. On the evening of September 19, I went into labor. Wilford drove me to the university hospital in Morgantown. Although we had sold the Jeep to buy a Subaru, one of those new, small four-wheel-drive vehicles, it was an uncomfortable ride for me.

The exam wasn't comfortable either. Stephanie looked up from between my legs. "Sorry," she said. "You're here too early." She patted my shoulder. "Come back when you can't smile."

But then she had an idea to speed things up. She and Ann took Wilford and me to a bar that featured a reggae band. It was a dive and I swear the floorboards creaked under my bloated body. I mimicked the motion of fun but soon gave up. Wilford drove me home. I tried to sleep, the rise and fall of the water bed doing nothing to salve the intermittent pain. I was miserable, unable to breathe away the agony. Early in the morning, we returned to Morgantown. At the hospital, a resident physician pulled rank over Stephanie, proclaimed "Redheads dehydrate!" and against my will inserted an intravenous line into my hand "just in case."

A photo mural of a deer in the woods covered an entire wall in the room where I labored. Ann, Stephanie, and Wilford circled the bed.

While Bambi's father peeked over their shoulders, they directed my breathing, rubbed my back, helped me into a warm shower. I agreed to let psychologists working on a research project with laboring mothers practice guided imagery on me. The soft words and strumming guitar were not much comfort. Finally, I begged for drugs. A little dose of a short-acting opiate (oh bliss!) helped me to relax and hours later, Sam was born. His hair was brown, not red, but he was perfect. Perfectly average. Average weight. Average length. I was exhausted. I was swollen in tender places, skeptical that I would ever again have sex. My swaddled son nursed with enthusiasm and fell asleep in my arms. I was in love; a golden glow that grew too large for my heart, filled the room, then spread across the universe.

My mother came to help after we came home. She announced that the baby would call her Deedy, her nickname, not Grandma. Deedy emphasized that she was there to cook and clean, not help with the baby. She had often shrugged her indifference to infants. "Babies are boring," she said. "Teenagers are interesting." She didn't ask to hold Sam. But she made my favorite meals, did the laundry, and squelched criticism of my homely little cabin.

Ellen and Marian came to visit. Ellen's son Logan was ten months old; Marian brought Ian, her three-year-old; her second son, Nathan, would be born six weeks later. My little house was full of adult women and little men.

My mother observed the chaos with a scientist's eye. "So many boys," she said, her eyebrows lifted. "There's going to be a war."

"I hope not!" Ellen said. "That would be terrible."

"But we love peace!" Marian exclaimed.

In my arms, Sam wailed, the high-pitched clamor of the hungry. As Ellen and Marian had taught, I cupped one breast then the other to gauge which was the fuller, then guided a nipple into Sam's mouth. I looked up to catch a rare, fleeting look of regret on my mother's face. Her eyes flicked to mine. "I wanted to nurse," she said. "No one encouraged me." Marian and Ellen clucked sympathy. I felt Sam tug my nipple and grunt with pleasure.

My mother stayed a week. She sat beside me as I drove to Kingwood to make a required stop at the unemployment office. Deedy was amazed by my nonchalance at driving up and down Caddell Mountain's steep curves. She sat at my kitchen table and worked through dozens of crossword puzzles. I watched my mother fill square after square and was surprised by my compassion for her. The anger that had always bubbled beneath her surface, an anger she diffused with cigarettes, now made sense. She had earned a master's degree in psychology from Washington University, had practiced her profession in a mental hospital. When the men returned from World War II, women were told to leave their jobs, get married, have children. My mother was isolated first in the St. Louis suburbs, later in the rural county. She felt trapped by three demanding daughters. A quarter of a century later, I had the choices she had been denied.

But it was a hard life. I had to go back to work. Even part-time I would earn much-needed money. I hadn't imagined how poor I would be when the unemployment checks stopped. I went back to work, covered meetings and other events. Wrote stories while Sam napped. Marian taught me to hand-express my breast milk; I don't remember anyone using a breast pump back then. This was my new life: a wide-eyed son, a helpful husband, and work. Friends with babies. Not enough hours in a day.

TOP: The Rutherfords pose for a picture with their new supply of coal.
BOTTOM: A news crew from the *Charleston Daily Mail* surrounds a
Gama Goat during the winter of 1977. That's me in the pom-pom hat
on the left. (Photo by Bill Tiernan.)

FRANCES'S HORSE, Lily, grazes in the farm's first bowl.

PHIL leads his flock.

R. DOYNE HALBRITTER preaches the virtues of history.

TOP: The consolidation of high schools in Preston County was strongly opposed in communities losing their schools. Here citizens picket outside the board of education office.

BOTTOM: Protesters crowd the meeting space inside the board office.

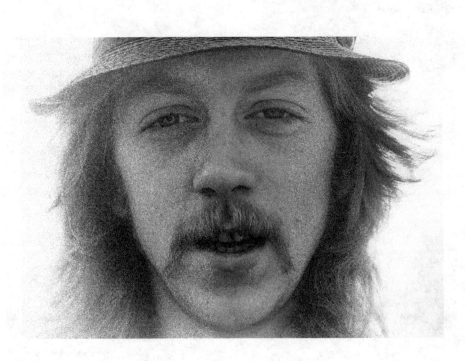

WILFORD'S collection of hats rarely included one in pristine condition. Not long after this picture was taken, a dentist fixed the spot between his teeth.

JUST MARRIED. (Photo by Bill Kuykendall.)

THREE MINERS at Reliable Coal Company pose for the cover
of "Coal '79."

A SCHOOL BUS skirts a high wall created by strip mining coal in pre-reclamation days.

MAN, BOY, dog, weed.

IT WAS BOB'S IDEA to do a story about a town "living on memories."
These boys pose in the Newburg Teen Center.

SAM AND SIMON in our pre-plumbing days. I carried this photo in my wallet for years.

THE MORE FORMAL PORTRAIT for our 1984 Christmas card was a disaster. At least in this picture everyone looks happy.

PHIL CONDUCTS AN INTERVIEW during Arthurdale's fiftieth
anniversary celebration.

GLENNA WILLIAMS leads the community in song.

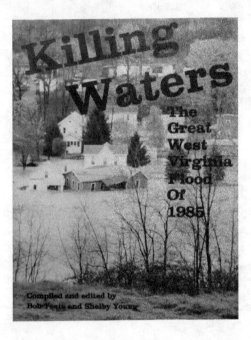

TOP: Near the peak of the November 1985 flood, the Cheat River crashes over the causeway to the Albright Power Plant.
BOTTOM: The Cheat River rips an Albright house from its foundation in this photo, the cover of *Killing Waters*, a book about the flood of 1985.

JUNE ISAAC rings the bell in the resurrected Albright Baptist Church.

❧ 27 ❧

✦ ✦ ✦

APPLE CIDER

JOHNNY APPLESEED may not be responsible for the old apple orchards in Preston County but he would be delighted by the number of old trees in the mountains that still bear fruit. Up until the middle of the twentieth century, dozens of homesteads could be found in Salt Lick Valley. Farming the steep hills required a Herculean effort—clearing the forests, removing rocks—tasks that had to be repeated endlessly. Until the blight in the early 1900s most of the structures in Appalachia were built of chestnut, a plentiful, magnificent wood. Water came from streams, springs, or hand-dug wells. Every farm had a garden, fruit trees, a few beef cattle, hogs, chickens, maybe a milk cow. Self-sufficiency wasn't just a matter of pride. It came from necessity. The farms were scattered on hilltops and up hollows, often miles from a road. In January and February, snow could isolate a family for weeks at a time.

By the time I came to West Virginia in the mid-1970s many of the remote farms had been deserted. It was sometimes hard to find even a trace of those previous lives. Houses and barns were torn down so the old chestnut lumber could be sold in cities back east. An apple orchard could be the only clue of a homestead's location unless you were lucky enough to be by in the springtime when lilacs and daffodils signaled previous domesticity. That's how Wilford and I found the old foundation beyond the hayfields on the farm where we lived. One year the plum trees planted by that family produced a bountiful harvest. I made plum cake and plum jam and returned the following year expecting more. The trees never bore fruit again.

In the 1940s, natural gas wells were drilled on farms throughout Salt Lick Valley. Although the wells no longer produce gas, the pipelines that linked them are still used to transport and store fuel. The gas company employees travel old roads to access and maintain this pump storage network. Miles and miles of gravel roads end at green tanks and orange pipes. The gas company employees don't usually pay much attention to the apple orchards they pass except to note the deer that are regular visitors.

In September, the apples start to ripen; first, the sweet, yellow transparents, good for pies and applesauce. Then the McIntoshes, red and tart. Good for eating right from the tree. Some communities hold apple butter festivals, cook apples in huge copper pots over wood fires. Women stir the mixture with paddles—sticks tipped with angled, pierced pieces of wood. These are specific tools, used only for apple butter. The women wear bonnets and long skirts to evoke the old times. They sell jars of caramel-colored apple butter to eager customers.

The apples found in Preston County's old orchards are usually small and blemished. Most trees are not tended. Certainly most are not sprayed. You could put an organic tag on them, but, even if it's true, the imperfect fruit is a product of neglect, not intent. Although they're small, it is easy to find enough apples for a few pies and some applesauce. The real adventure comes in the fall during cider time; bushels of apples are needed to make even a small amount of cider. On the old Washington Lantz farm, Michael took a long view. He envisioned an orchard; planted apple trees, pear trees, plum trees. He planted blueberry bushes. He planted nut trees. Even though he was often away from the farm, he was committed to that land. He was confident that he would be there for the duration, for the decades it would take for the bounty to grow.

◆

While we waited for the apple orchard at the farm to mature, we scavenged apples wherever we could. On a clear fall day in 1980, I strapped one-year-old Sam into his car seat and Phil and I piled into the Subaru. We were familiar with the back roads and the families that lived there. No one wanted the ugly little apples we were after. When we spotted a tree drooping with fruit, we made our way toward it through brush and brambles. Phil tossed a rope knotted around a rock over a branch loaded with apples then pulled it taut. "Watch your head!" he warned, then yanked the rope as if he were ringing a bell. The tree shook and released its apples, which thudded onto the ground. We loaded buckets and dragged them to the car; poured the fruit into feed sacks or trash bags. Then we were on to the next tree, repeating the process until we were exhausted. Although apples were our goal, the autumn hills also won our attention: auburn and gold and green, a crazy calico quilt of nature. Holy and wholly beautiful.

The car was nearly full, but Phil wanted to look for one more orchard. Someone had told him about a grove of apple trees behind a farm a mile up Salt Lick. We turned off the blacktop onto a narrow rocky road and crossed Salt Lick Creek on the gas company's sturdy, concrete bridge. Except during hunting season few people came back here. The gas company had miles of roads like this to cover, two gravel grooves separated by a long grassy strip. Phil and I were in no hurry, so we chatted and shared sandwiches and admired how the sun turned the fall colors into lit-from-behind stained glass. At every fork we chose the route that headed uphill. We splashed through puddles, slowed to look for apple trees. Near what looked to be the summit, I warily approached a particularly long wet spot. "I have a vision of driving into one of those holes and not driving out," I told Phil. By the time the words were out of my mouth we were stuck. I had tried to drive close to one side of the hole; it looked safer. But somehow I had managed to sink my left front wheel into one deep hole while the right wheels dangled helplessly in the water. The left side was sunk so deep that I couldn't even open my door. And it wasn't simple mud that held us hostage; it was slimy, smelly gunk.

I shifted into reverse: more spinning. I tried rocking the car, shifted back and forth between reverse and first gear. That didn't work either. Phil stepped into the slime and tried to push the car free. But it wouldn't move. The Subaru was high centered. Four-wheel-drive doesn't help when the wheels can't dig in.

If cell phones had existed then, or if I'd had a CB radio, I would have called Ray Spahr for a tow. Phil and I looked at one another and shrugged. It was unlikely that the gas company would be by any time soon. So I climbed into the back, freed Sam from his car seat and we started walking back the way we had come. We took turns carrying Sam in the backpack. We ate apples and walked, always heading downhill. Phil assured me that he knew the way out. How long did it take us to get to the hardtop, three miles away? I have no idea. Once we reached Salt Lick Road, we knocked on the door of the closest house and asked if we could call for a tow. We hung out by the road and waved when we saw Ray Spahr and his 1948 Chevy, a growling hulk of rust and winches. Ray was amused; he liked it when we outsiders had to ask for help. He also liked taking our money. Phil and I climbed into the cab. On my lap Sam bounced with delight, his eyes huge with the thrill of a ride in a big truck.

Ray steered up the road, shook his head at our tale of apple foraging. As we burrowed farther into the woods, he marveled at the distance from the paved road. The car, when we came upon it, seemed to float in the mud. A sump hole, Ray announced. When the gas wells are emptied of gas, they're filled with water. When the company is ready to use them for gas again, the water is pumped out. So this was a monstrous, manufactured hole. Ray made a three-point turn, a masterful maneuver in the narrow space. He hooked the winch to the underside of the Subaru and with sucking and grinding sounds wrenched the car free. The charge would be added to my tab at his gas station, he said. He watched in the mirror as I turned around, and we followed him out of the woods. At the hardtop he turned right, toward town, and we headed the other way, down Salt Lick.

A few weeks later, Ray retired the Chevy. It was too hard to get parts for it and on paved roads its speed topped out at just forty-five miles per hour, not quite fast enough. The Chevy's retirement merited a front page story, a photo of my own rescue, and a column.

◆

The ancient cider press at the farm, made of iron and wood, probably weighed two hundred pounds. About four feet tall, three feet long, and eighteen inches wide, it was cumbersome. Phil and Michael, young and strong as they were, struggled to move it out of the shed. We washed the apples, poured them into the wood hopper, turned the crank that fed them through the metal-toothed grinder, and filled the slatted, wooden bucket underneath with apple chunks. The sweet smell of the crushed fruit summoned yellow jackets, black and gold and determined. When the bucket was full, a wooden disk topped the mash, and we slid the bucket forward underneath a large iron screw, like an upside down car jack. I laced a smooth club through the eye of the screw and started turning. Amber-colored juice trickled into a metal bowl. As the disk was forced lower, Phil leaned forward to help me, then took over. When Phil could no longer budge the screw, Michael grabbed the other end of the stick and the two men worked together. Their effort rocked the press. Finally, they could turn no more. Michael squatted, dipped a coffee mug into the bowl, and took a drink. He closed his eyes with pleasure.

"It's very sweet this year," he said. He handed the cup to me and I drank the golden liquid. If autumn had a taste, this was it: a tart perfume. I refilled the cup and offered it to Phil. He laced a finger through the handle and raised the mug.

"To Johnny Appleseed," he said. He looked down at me, waved the cup higher. "And adventure." He bowed toward Michael. "And to our orchard."

Was the cider that year worth our effort? That depends. By the time we paid for the tow truck, we probably would have been better off buying cider in the store. But that wasn't the point. We needed to be frugal; all of us were poor. But our goal was more complicated: we aimed for self-sufficiency. We wanted organic, natural, unsullied cider. We wanted that connection to the land, to our labor. When we brought that cider to our lips, we knew what we were drinking, what it required from us. We swallowed that holy elixir, inhaled its essence. Appreciated every drop.

28

❖ ❖ ❖

BUSTED

———

I LIKE MARIJUANA. Ever since my first toke at the age of fourteen, I've used pot to make life more entertaining. My deflowering, or should I call it my flowering, occurred during my sophomore year in high school when someone in a carful of kids handed me a joint. The herbal stink put me off; the fire-tipped scrunchy white cylinder smelled nothing like my mother's menthol Belairs. Although I remembered that the cigarettes I had filched from my mother had made me nauseous, I didn't hesitate before I inhaled from the joint. Pot was alluring, primarily because it was illegal and illicit. I don't remember getting high in that car. But late that night, when I arrived home, my mother sat at the kitchen table, a cigarette burning in the ashtray in front of her. This was completely unexpected. My parents never waited up for me. My sisters and I had no curfew. Our friends thought this proved my parents' social permissiveness. The reality was they couldn't stay awake past ten thirty.

"What did you do tonight?" my mother asked, her eyes lifted to mine.

I couldn't lie. Not to her. My mother had the best bullshit meter of anyone I've ever known. And, like her grandfather, she had episodes of extrasensory perception: knew who was on the phone when it rang, bought extra groceries before unexpected company showed up, was transcendently calm in the face of emergencies.

"I smoked pot for the first time," I said.

She looked at me closely. "And . . . ?"

"I think it stinks." I shrugged.

She lifted her eyebrows and stubbed out the cigarette. "I had a feeling," she said. That was it.

My mother never preached abstinence. Instead, she declared that if my sisters or I screwed up—got pregnant or arrested—she would not bail us out. And we knew she meant it. She expected us to be honest and responsible. And we were.

I tried pot several other times early in high school. But it was on a date with a fellow redhead that I finally got high. Giggling high. My rebel guide's older sister was the hippie queen of the high school: her long hair was held in place by a horizontal headband, her clothes floated around her like signal flags. My guide sat in the back of classrooms and made snide comments, a behavior that attracted me. I sat in the front of the room, a smart girl, and became a cliché—falling for the bad boy. We smoked a joint on the way to a movie. I don't remember anything about the film, but I can vividly recall that I laughed so hard that my sides ached the next day.

◆

Alcohol never made me feel as good as pot did. The few times I drank enough to lose control, the spinning room and the eventual retching were so unpleasant that I vowed to be more cautious. Drinking dulled my senses and made me nauseous. Pot brightened the world and made me laugh. It softened my critical bent. Bad television became amusing and junk food delicious. So what that pot was illegal? I'd just be discreet. And careful. Of course, careful defined by a twenty-something is not the same careful I now consider. In the mid-1970s I drove stoned. I worked stoned. I had sex stoned. I shopped stoned. I was foolish and lucky. And I had fun. Pot was the great antidote to boredom, a smoky detour from reality. It made the world more colorful, softened rough edges so that they gave off burnished vapors. My body felt wholly mine but of another world. Pot turned Preston County into an alternate universe, gave it a luminescent glow.

The best pot, and back then I defined "best" as free, was the pot Wilford and I grew. We started seeds in little peat pots, then hid the young plants in between rows of corn in our garden. During our wedding, my cousin's husband tipped his head toward the green rows and with a stage whisper told my brother-in-law, "Yes, I do believe that's marijuana." Our plants struggled in Terra Alta's cool and often overcast summers. But we managed to harvest enough pot to supplement what we bought from friends. Enough pot to keep me happy.

We threw the empty peat pots into a heap next to the barn. In the spring of 1980, we noticed a marijuana plant emerging from the crumbly pile. The hardy volunteer thrived, solitary, facing south and protected by the barn from the north wind. Wilford pinched it back and it grew bushy and lush. Its very exposure was the source of its strength, but it put us at risk.

During the war games that summer, our landlord gave the Army permission to use the back field as a drop zone. Wilford held Sam in his arms and we watched the soldiers fall from the sky and march down the driveway. Wilford had parked his truck in front of the plant, and we waved from the garden across the way to try to distract the soldiers' attention, but some of them spotted our volunteer. They nudged one another, pointed, and smiled.

Bob Shrout, the caretaker our absentee landlord paid to maintain the property, had also noticed the plant. In hindsight, we probably should have been more wary; our relationship was barely civil. Until I moved there in 1975, Mr. Shrout had enjoyed exclusive access to the farm. He resented our presence on the property. We believed he was responsible for shooting the suffering doe we had found in the fall of 1977. We thought we had seen Mr. Shrout spotlighting deer on the property, a nighttime hunting method that blinds deer with light, making them easier to shoot, and had asked the DNR officer to help us stop him. That officer told us that he suspected Mr. Shrout and his son were responsible for a small explosion in Salt Lick Creek that had killed a number of fish. It wasn't so hard back then for people to get their hands on explosives; they were used to blast coal out of the ground. A charge dropped into a stream freshly stocked with trout could yield enough fish to feed a family. Mr. Shrout and his children seemed well fed, even a little heavy. Maybe he had suffered from hunger as a child and now worried that his family would starve. Maybe I should have been more sympathetic. But he was hostile from the first day I met him. When I moved into that little house, I had effectively ended Mr. Shrout's reign over those two hundred acres. He didn't know that Wilford wasn't much of a hunter; he considered him competition. Every time Mr. Shrout rattled up the hill in his old truck, he glared at both of us. He didn't try to hide his disdain.

Tire tracks in the mud proved that he often visited the place when we weren't there. I felt violated, uneasy. In 1979, when our cat had kittens, adorable balls of gray fur, and two of them disappeared, I knew Mr. Shrout had taken them. I called the sheriff.

"There's no law against stealing cats," he told me. Dogs had to be licensed, so they were considered property. Not cats. The magistrate confirmed those facts. I'm sure both men thought I was nuts. But I wanted to keep one of those kittens, and the other had been promised to a friend. They were my cats and I wanted them back. The magistrate suggested that I go to Mr. Shrout's house. It would look better if I took along someone who appeared to be professional, he said. Annie, my coworker at *The News*, stood beside me when I knocked on the door. I was trembling but when a woman answered, I blurted that I had spoken to the sheriff and the magistrate and I wanted my kittens back.

She stiffened, pressed her lips together to form a frown. "I'll get them," she said. Minutes later the kittens were in our arms. Their mewling serenaded our victory.

◆

By late September, the marijuana plant was a giant, towering over Wilford, who was two inches shy of six feet. We could not join hands and reach around it. Instead, we danced in front of our miracle plant, fueled by its dried and smoked leaves. Hidden behind photos in our wedding album was a photo of Wilford with the plant, Sam solemn in the backpack slung from his dad's shoulders. A lovely family portrait: father, son, and marijuana.

In October, Wilford uprooted the plant and hung it from the rafters in the barn. On a perfect autumn day Sam, just over a year old and beginning to walk, played on a blanket in the yard as I washed the car. The early afternoon light filtered through the pine trees in front of our little house. A row of cloth diapers hung from the clothesline, squares of white blowing in the warm breeze. We heard the car before it pulled up and when I recognized the Department of Natural Resources cruiser I expected to see the officer who had previously been on the property. But two other officers were in the front seat, their faces familiar but not friendly. I picked Sam up, settled him on my hip, and walked over to the car to say hello. I was surprised to see Butch O'Hagan, a deputy sheriff, in the back seat.

"Hi," I said. "What brings you up here?"

"We hear there's a marijuana plant in your barn," Butch said.

It was as if I had been struck hard in the chest. I sucked in my breath, straightened up, and hitched Sam higher. My mind raced. I can't go to jail, I'm a nursing mother. Then, somehow, my brain worked.

"It's not my barn," I said. "We just rent the house."

The cruiser rolled past me and parked next to the barn. One of the DNR officers climbed into the loft. He pulled out a knife to cut the rope that secured the plant to a beam then tossed the marijuana onto the concrete floor, where it landed with a scratchy noise in a puff of dust.

I'd like to say I remember exactly what was said. But I don't. Did the men admire the size of the plant? Did I speak? I know I was scared, my heart pumping blood so hard that I felt lightheaded.

They opened the trunk of the cruiser and stuffed the plant inside, snapping branches so it would fit. The dried leaves sprinkled the spare tire. I waited for them to arrest me, to say the words I'd heard on television: "You have the right . . ." But they smiled and chatted among themselves, got back into the cruiser, and drove away.

They never glanced at the two rows of pot in the garden.

My whole body shook. Sam absorbed my distress and fussed to nurse. How did I ever relax enough for my milk to let down? Maybe I chanted: I can't go to jail. I can't go to jail.

I called Wilford, sobbing. Then I called Michael. "We got busted!" I cried. "Pull all your plants!" I ran to the garden and wrenched the stubby pot plants from the rocky dirt. I stuffed them into garbage bags along with all our paraphernalia: pipes, papers, roach clips.

Wilford and I took the bag to our friend Ellen's house. Her father was a retired state trooper and she lived next door to him. We thought that would be the last place cops would search. Then we waited.

I dreaded telling Jerry. He was making his second bid for a seat in the state senate and the election was just weeks away. I had taken over many of his duties, had become a well-known representative of his newspaper. I stood before his desk and stammered my story. When I ran out of words, Jerry tugged at his beard, and turned away. His shoulders sagged. Then he turned back to me. "Bob Cline was behind this," he said. Cline was his political enemy. Jerry's words came in a burst. "Shrout must be working for him." He paced, pausing every now and then to look at me and sigh.

Phil and Michael also were freaked out. They were afraid of being busted. Phil used his reporting skills and contacts to discover that warrants for my arrest and Wilford's had been issued. Deputies planned to seize me during Monday's county commission meeting, he said. That very public act was planned to maximize damage to Jerry's campaign. But Jerry figured out how to subvert those intentions. He called the magistrate and arranged for Wilford and me to come in before Monday. We would post bail, make our pleas. Jerry helped us find a lawyer. Bill was just a little older than we were. Like me, he was an outsider married to a native West Virginian.

Bill listened to our story and asked one question: "Did they have a search warrant?"

"No," I answered. "I never saw one."

When he heard that, Bill took our case. He accompanied Wilford and me to the magistrate's office, a squat building that had once been a small grocery store. I was deeply embarrassed and scared. But Bill had given us hope that the lack of a search warrant would help us escape this mess. We pleaded not guilty. The magistrate said he would set a date for our trial.

My fellow journalists believed that my arrest was political and sat on the story. I was grateful for the collusion but so ashamed. These were people I respected and because of me they practiced bad journalism.

Still, plenty of people knew about the charges. Bob Cline's rumor mill put out word that Jerry Ash's employee had been caught selling cocaine and the media had conspired to cover up the charges. Like nearly every rumor I pursued as a reporter, this had enough truth behind it to be believable. But the damage must have been confined to Preston County. Although Jerry lost there, he won the election, the first Democrat elected in the six-county region in more than fifty years.

◆

In addition to the damage to my career and Jerry's, the bust had financial repercussions. In the fall of 1980, I was only working part-time at *The News*. Jerry and Michele understood that I wanted to spend time with my son, so they allowed me to fashion a schedule. To supplement our meager income, I did some substitute teaching. It paid better than the newspaper and I enjoyed the work. My mother had been a substitute at my high school; in the 1970s both of my parents began teaching in community colleges. They were gifted teachers who were happy to offer advice.

But no one could have prepared me for my day with a Rowlesburg kindergarten class. We were by ourselves in an old house that was never intended to be a school. The wood trim was dark with old shellac and the floors creaked. The teacher hadn't left a lesson plan and the five-year-olds at my feet cried for their old routine. At rest time, one little girl screamed that the boy next to her was trying to lift up her dress.

I did better with older students. I spent a full week substituting for Vivian McConnell at the high school in Terra Alta. Every once in a while the kids would act up. When I restored control one little voice piped up. "You gonna write about us?"

"No," I said. That turned out to be a lie. I wrote a column.

I substituted on average one day a week. I had begun the work simply for the additional income; but I enjoyed my time in the classroom and particularly appreciated the inside look at the county school system.

The pending drug charges ended my new career. Bob Cline had a strong influence on the members of the school board and the battle to deconsolidate the schools had ceded him even more power. *The News* had editorialized against the superintendent of schools, hired at Cline's behest. And I had called the assistant superintendent a truck salesman in a front-page headline. I should not have been surprised when the director of personnel, a man I respected, called to say I would not be able to serve in the classroom until my case was resolved.

So I was humbled and poor. Our lawyer cost more than a month's wages; I'm sure we paid him in installments. Wilford and I together earned less than $18,000 a year. We lived a frugal life. Sam's clothes came from yard sales except for two pairs of Osh Kosh B'gosh overalls that I had bought at a discount store in Morgantown. I rationalized that purchase by dividing the price in two: our next child could wear them. We had our garden and I had learned to preserve the food that we grew. We bought bulk beef and pork from local farmers. And we heated with wood and coal, cheap fuels. I tried to save money—ten dollars or twenty dollars from every paycheck—so that we could eventually buy a house.

Our big luxury was our Subaru, bought the month before Sam was born. Wilford drove an ancient Ford truck, a rusty red hulk that shimmied around curves and demanded constant maintenance. Our driveway took a fierce toll on both vehicles and I learned the language of suspension: struts, DOJ joints, and differentials. Wilford tried to do the work himself but often we had to pay for repairs, putting a strain on our budget, and our marriage. We didn't have money to do anything fun, to buy any extras.

One Sunday I kissed Sam and Wilford good-bye and went to town to work in the darkroom. Afterward I stopped at the store to buy a gallon of milk. I took out my wallet, but all my cash was gone. (This was a big deal because there were no debit cards in those days.) I hadn't been anywhere; I knew the money hadn't been stolen. Then I remembered that Wilford had gone out the night before. He had to have taken it. Shit! I blushed, mumbled an excuse, and put the milk back. I hurled down Salt Lick, anger growing by the minute. Wilford was under his truck when I pulled up to the house. Sam was nowhere in sight; it was his naptime.

"Wilford!" My voice was a shriek. "Did you take my money? I

stopped for milk and I didn't have any money!" My face was a grimace. Heat rose from my neck to my temples. Wilford eased from beneath the truck. His eyes were wide. My hands were on my hips and I was close to tears.

Wilford straightened up to face me. He frowned. "It's wasn't much." His defense. "I just bought a little beer."

I held my palms over my eyes. My voice rose higher. "Jesus! You just bought beer. Did you need more? Shit! Can't you go a day without beer?"

Wilford narrowed his eyes. "Hey! I work hard and I deserve some beer. You think you're so smart, bossing me around. I can't do anything. Can't have any fun." He slumped against his truck, crossed his arms, and gave me a look that I had not seen before: defiance crossed with shame. I turned and marched into the house, actively crying. I hated being the bad guy, the responsible one.

We were still nursing that anger a few weeks later when Ellen invited us to dinner at her house. She and her husband had split up; she craved adult company. While Ellen fixed dinner, her son, Logan, and Sam played. We sat around her small table; Ellen's kitchen was always immaculate.

"I can't stay long. Phil is picking me up to go to a county commission meeting," I said.

"You'll stay longer next time," Ellen said. "Wilford will help me clean up."

Wilford had a beer in front of him. "I'm going to take our stuff home," he said. Our garbage bags of pot and paraphernalia were in Ellen's basement. I thought of our giant plant, how the leaves crumbled into dust when the officers crammed its branches into their car. I had been so scared.

"Be careful," I said as Phil and I left for the meeting.

◆

The meeting was well underway when the heavy wooden door to the commission office swung open and two police officers walked in. The commissioners fell silent; the officers headed my way. I nearly peed in my pants. One officer leaned over to me and whispered that Wilford had wrecked the car. Nobody was hurt, he quickly said, but they suspected he had been drinking. He and Sam were at the sheriff's office next door.

My baby. My husband. My car. My drugs. My concerns brought me to my feet. Phil joined me; he kept his hand on my shoulder as if he could literally hold me together and in a low voice he pleaded with me to be cool. The sheriff's office was a warren of desks, equipment, and deputies. Wilford slumped in a chair; I could tell with a glance that he was drunk. Liquor, not just beer. Whiskey narrowed and reddened his eyes and twisted his sweet countenance into drooping melancholy. Drinking seemed to loosen his skin, the folds under his eyes dragged down by gravity. Wilford was misery in human form. Across the room Sam was all lightning toddler. He was dressed in a fuzzy blue Winnie the Pooh sleeper and careened from desk to desk. He stood in front of a police radio, twisted the dials, and giggled. The buzzing fluorescent lights turned his hazel eyes bright green. I grabbed his soft, blue form and burst into tears. There wasn't a mark on him. He had been securely fastened in his car seat. I glared across the room at Wilford. Poisonous words threatened to erupt from my mouth. Phil grabbed my arm and shook his head. When an officer said we could leave, Phil walked over to Wilford, put an arm around his shoulder, and guided him toward the door. As soon as we were in Phil's car, far from the deputies, I started to shriek.

"How could you have been so stupid? How could you have put Sam in such danger? How did you get so drunk? What happened to the garbage bags filled with pot?"

Time felt both speeded up and slowed down. I was freaked out. I clutched Sam; Phil didn't have a car seat.

"Jesus, Wilford," Phil said, and headed up the mountain.

"I wasn't that drunk," Wilford spoke slowly, carefully, without conviction. "I swerved to avoid a skunk and ran into a field." His voice was a monotone, an effort. "I emptied the bags and threw everything into the field before the cops came." I started to cry. Sam fell asleep in my lap. We ascended the mountain in silence. Just outside the Terra Alta town limits, Wilford pointed to the site of his wreck. I could see that instead of guiding the car around the left hand curve Wilford had kept going straight: through the ditch, then the fence, and into the pasture.

There had been no skunk. Alcohol caused this disaster. This new pattern: drinking, driving, and lying would poison our marriage.

The next day, Wilford found our paraphernalia in the field: our bong, our pipes, our roach clips. He found the garbage bags. But he didn't recover any pot. We drove by the spot and looked at the cows. None of them looked happy either.

◆

Wilford pleaded guilty to driving under the influence. Our car insurance rates doubled. I didn't know it then, but our real problems were just beginning.

Our trial for possession was held in February. Wilford and I stood on one side of the small courtroom; the officers who had confiscated the marijuana plant stood across the aisle. The magistrate nodded at me as he took his seat. Within minutes he asked the officers if they had had a search warrant. No, they admitted.

"Charges dismissed." The magistrate brought down his gavel. And that was it. I hugged our lawyer before I hugged Wilford. Although I was relieved I didn't feel like celebrating.

29

◆ ◆ ◆

DILETTANTE

IN SPITE OF BOB CLINE'S EFFORT to taint Jerry's campaign with
my possession charge, Jerry was elected to the West Virginia State
Senate in 1980. His pro-business platform won Republican votes and
his government-can-help belief won the Democrats. *The Preston County
News* was a valuable training ground for a politician. Jerry's column,
the folksy "Dear Preston," won him a local audience. That audience
expanded when friends of his in the West Virginia Press Association
started printing his new column, "Jerry Ash on the Mountain State."
Jerry wrote about the state budget, the death penalty, public works,
education, and tourism. He decried overregulation of the coal industry. His job in the senate was part-time work; Jerry kept his office in
the back of the *News* building, his desk separated from the Heidelberg
press by reams of blank paper. I often wandered back there to talk
politics. Our arguments would echo off the high ceiling. When the
train roared past, the vibrations worked their way from my feet to my
head. Hands on my hips, I spouted my liberal beliefs. I argued for gun
control; insisted that handguns be banned. I proclaimed the death
penalty barbaric.

"Courts convict innocent men," I said.

Jerry pointed to popular opinion. "It's what the people want," he countered. In a column, he lamented a legislative process that allowed a handful of politicians to block the death penalty from even coming to a vote. I cheered this process.

But the topic closest to his heart was abortion. The United States Supreme Court decision that women had the right to obtain an abortion was less than ten years old and Jerry hated it. He wanted West Virginia to make abortion illegal. He was unapologetically pro-life. The first time we discussed abortion, Jerry reclined in his big chair, placed his hands on top of his head, and let me prattle on about a woman's right to choose.

"Government has no business telling women what to do with their bodies," I said. "Women have always sought abortions; this law makes that option safe." Jerry dropped his hands to his knees; his chair squeaked as he leaned forward.

"I'm adopted," he said, his voice low. "If abortion had been legal in the 1940s, I wouldn't be here." He folded his arms and sat straight, triumphant. How could I argue with that? In addition, Jerry and Michele were adoptive parents. They had flown to El Salvador and came back with Libby, a little girl with a classic Central American profile and an observant gaze. She called Jerry's campaign billboards "big vote-for-Daddy cards."

◆

In 1981, a year after Jerry was elected, he summoned me to his office. He looked at my face, took a deep breath, and said, "I'm selling the paper." His thick eyebrows rose as if the announcement was a question. "I'd like to offer it to you first," he said. I stared at him. I thought my heart rhythm might be visible. The worn wooden planks beneath my feet were a tightrope. I stared at them and struggled for balance. Jerry knew I didn't have any money. He paid me six dollars an hour. Wilford earned four dollars an hour, sixty-five cents more than minimum wage.

"I can't afford the paper," I said. "I've been working for you." I grinned to defuse the criticism. He knew I had gradually increased my hours until I was back to working full-time. He didn't know that Wilford earned less than I did. "I'm grateful that you offered it to me first," I said.

◆

"Put down the beer," I said. Wilford and I were on the porch swing. "I have to talk to you." Wilford tucked the beer between his legs. I told him about Jerry's offer. "I wish I had the money," I said. I didn't know that Wilford heard that as an accusation. He picked up the beer and took a drink.

"I'm no help to you," he said. "I'm worthless." He stopped the swing and went into the house. I heard him open another beer.

Later I wondered if Jerry had already discussed the sale of *The News* with the man who would become its new owner: Bob Teets, the owner of Teets General Store and brother to House of Delegates member Jim Teets. His family had money; his grandfather had owned Terra Alta's first Ford dealership; his father, Clem, had owned the local Pennzoil franchise. Jim now ran Teets Oil Company. Bob had been contributing occasional folksy essays to *The News* for several months. He had a degree in journalism from West Virginia University and since his store had gone out of business the year before, Bob had time on his hands. He was a writer and a businessman: Jerry's perfect heir. They announced the paper's sale in November 1981. They promised, in print, that this was swell.

Bob occupied the editor's desk as if it were a throne. He smoked long brown cigarettes that he clenched in his teeth, lit end angled toward the ceiling. He had to have been imitating Franklin Delano Roosevelt. Bob was what passed for aristocracy in Terra Alta. His father had made a fortune when folks switched from coal heat to fuel oil furnaces. His mother, Ruth, and her family had turned a Ford dealership into a small empire. I met her when I was new to Terra Alta. Jerry had sent me to take a picture of the winner of a contest sponsored by Teets Oil Company. The prize surprised me: the old Ford four-wheel-drive was long past its prime, its body patched and roughly painted. The winner must have expected a better vehicle, though all she did was correctly guess the number of beans in a jar. In the picture she is smiling as she accepts keys from Ruth Teets. Business was a mostly male realm back then, but Ruth, a widow, was accepted in the club. She was respected. She was on the board of directors of one of the two banks in Terra Alta and she was active in the Methodist Church.

Ruth and her late husband had collected antiques: farm implements, buggies, the obsolete contents of an entire general store, old clothes, books, and furniture. They had opened their collection to the public as the Americana Museum. "Discover your roots," was the marketing slogan. The museum was open just one day a week, although it also accommodated schoolchildren on field trips. The last time I visited the Americana Museum was in the late 1990s with a group of people from the farm on Salt Lick. Ruth was on the verge of losing her mind to dementia. She slowly led us through the warren of log and metal buildings, all sinking into disrepair. The gravel floor of the largest building had been breached by groundhogs; decrepit mannequins in dresses whose hems had been gnawed away seemed to stand guard over the access to the burrows. The air bore the scent of mildew and dust. The dehumidifiers that littered the grounds were full, their red lights blinking as if to summon help. A few years after our visit, the contents were auctioned off.

◆

When Bob took over *The News*, the bank (his mother was on the board) ran a full-page ad with "Congratulations!" scrawled across it in ninety-six-point type. Below the headline was a photo: Bob in a grand leather chair, hands clasped in his lap, his legs angled to his right. His wide grin tilts slightly up on one side. Behind him is the all-woman *News* staff, our expressions mostly inscrutable although Angie, a typesetter and the youngest person on the payroll, looks pleasant. I'm on the left, arms crossed, chin down; the corners of my mouth barely turn up. I recognize the attitude: a Missouri "show me" dare.

Something about Bob made me nervous. It was like he was our new stepdad and trying too hard. His grin and jovial manner seemed a mask. Who was this man whose previous business failed after five years, who put out his brother's eye in a farm accident when they were young, who did not seem happy in spite of his good fortune? He was a board member of the West Virginia Writers organization. The stories he had written for *The News* in the past were good. He had brought the typewritten pages into the office, had handed them off to the typesetter as if turning over a cherished belonging. He was tall and blond and rich, but he projected insecurity and need. I remember our first fight after he took ownership. I was being pissy, whining about some assignment I didn't want to do, a check-passing photo. I had tried for years to educate organizations. Call me to photograph your fundraising events, not the checks, I'd say. I wanted to photograph group activities, not people lined up in rows. But Bob had promised to give readers what they wanted. He wanted to please them. He didn't need to please me.

During that fight I faced Bob, my arms flailing to punctuate my words. Bob sat in his massive chair, his usual smile absent, his head bowed. When I said, "You don't pay me enough to do that," Bob exploded out of his chair and in one step, loomed over me. He sputtered with rage.

"Jerry gave everyone a raise just before he turned the paper over," Bob shouted. "After we made a deal." My wages had gone up twenty-five cents an hour, less than ten dollars a week. I sagged in defeat. I understood that this fight didn't have anything to do with theories of journalism. I was just a stepchild Bob had inherited. He thought I was expensive. I thought I worked cheap.

Bob's first Christmas at *The News* was tense. Jerry had always distributed bonuses of a week's salary in our early December paychecks, and he canceled the issue between Christmas and New Year's so we could all take a week off. With pay. We waited to see what Bob would do. The December pay envelope contained no bonus. The Christmas party was a potluck lunch, not dinner (Jerry's treat) in a restaurant. After we ate the food we had brought in, we rolled our office chairs into a semicircle around an artificial tree decorated with miniature stockings, one for each of us, our names written in glitter. Bob wore a Santa hat as he handed out the stockings. Each contained a crisp fifty-dollar bill. Not a week's salary. Bob's grin seemed unnatural, like a clown had painted it. Had our office manager told him about Jerry's generosity?

Bob ducked his head, swallowed the smile. "We're not going to skip the issue between Christmas and New Year's," he said with forced enthusiasm. We greeted this announcement with silence. I felt beaten down and hopeless. Work had turned into drudgery. The outside world was falling apart. Ronald Reagan had taken office. My optimistic outlook— that forward-thinking citizens would lead the country into progressive times, that solid, professional work would prompt change in my community, that I could be a good wife, a good mother, and a good journalist simultaneously—now seemed a fantasy.

My new situation would have been unbearable had Bob been a bad writer. But he had talent. He had ideas and he was a good editor. He encouraged creativity, suggested improvements. He shook up the paper's routine and made me a better writer, a fact I wouldn't appreciate for years. I thought he was a dilettante, the first real dilettante I had ever met. I resented his attitude, the way he strolled into the office at ten and boomed, "Is everything copacetic?" He never waited for an answer. He often took a two-hour lunch, then at three announced that he was beat and heading home. His air of entitlement rankled, but it was his inherent distrust of the staff that bothered me the most.

When the newspaper moved out of the rambling storefront on Washington Street into a cozy bungalow on Route 7, Bob moved closer to us. His office was just off of the living room-dining room space the rest of us shared. Bob was now privy to our chatter and it drove him crazy, particularly when we took phone calls unrelated to work, usually about our children. He came up with new timesheets, split into five-minute intervals, and created an elaborate set of codes for our tasks. We were to keep careful track of our work, and deduct the minutes we spent on personal phone calls or in the bathroom. I found the policy confusing. Was I on the clock when someone stopped me in the grocery store to give me a news tip? What if I came up with an idea for a column while washing dishes at home? What was fair? How to get to copacetic?

$\approx$ **30** $\approx$

$\blacklozenge \ \blacklozenge \ \blacklozenge$

THE NESTING INSTINCT

"**COME IN. COME IN.**" Frances held a glass of wine in one hand and waved with the other. In the spring of 1982 she and Phil had moved into the house below the farm, right on Salt Lick. We had the same landlord. In fact, I had asked Mr. Smith to rent me the very house I was stepping into.

"Sorry. No," he had said. "I like to stay there when I come up to visit." How had Frances gotten him to say yes? I'm sure she was both persistent and charming. We have been friends now for forty years; I know how skilled Frances can be at getting others to bend to her will. I give up too easily; I'm too polite.

The kitchen was tiny with no counter space. Frances had moved a rough narrow table next to the sink. So functional and it looked nice. I followed Wilford, carrying Sam, into the next room, and put my bag next to a heavy wooden chair. The room was lovely. An oriental rug was centered underneath a massive oak table. A carved sideboard occupied the far wall. Big, comfortable chairs were grouped together. The colors, the arrangement of objects, were pleasing. "You can see I like green and red together." Frances moved into the room. "They're complementary colors you know." I didn't know. She pointed to the shades covering the windows. "I found this fabric at the rag store." I nodded my approval. "Cherokee Red, Frank Lloyd Wright's favorite color," she said.

"It looks great." I put my hand on the back of a chair. "Really nice. Where did you get the furniture?"

"Oh, it's family stuff." Frances shrugged. "My brother and I drove to Highlands in North Carolina and picked it up." Frances had talked about her family home in the southern mountains. She walked over to the sideboard and patted its curved side. "I think this is from Spain, from the sixteenth century." She took a drink of wine. "Who knows?" The more she drank, the more Southern she sounded. Frances grew up in Memphis but had spent a lot of time at her grandmother's home in Highlands. There had been a grand house and servants, private school, and drinks on the veranda. There had been a long, slow depletion of family funds. In my family, my mother's family, the family fortune disappeared in the 1929 stock market crash, a sudden tragedy for the Kahns of Chicago, or so I was told. My grandmother Vera once told me with great pride that she had never washed her own hair.

Frances never earned money growing flowers in West Virginia, as had been her original plan. Instead she endured a series of menial jobs, then went back to school to become an art teacher. She switched on a lamp, a beautiful brass fixture. "I remember this lamp in a corner of the big house in Highlands," she said. "It needed the space around it." She patted its side, a beautiful patina. "This house doesn't do it justice."

"This is really nice." I sat in a big oak chair and admired the room. My parents had longed for nice things but never had the money to buy what they wanted: modern furniture. I remember a Nelson bench (or a knockoff) and turquoise couches. This room wasn't modern; it was classic. Frances patted the cushion next to her. "Sam, come sit on the sofa with me," she said.

Sofa? I called it a couch. Was that a sign that I lacked class? Sam, suddenly shy, ran over to me and I pulled him up on my lap. He quickly wiggled off.

"We're going to have babies together," Frances announced. "Let us know when you're ready for number two."

"Three and a half years apart," I said. "I think that's what Ann said." I counted on my fingers. "Soon."

So it came to be. Our babies were due six weeks apart: mine in March and hers in April 1983.

◆

At a Halloween party in Kingwood in the fall of 1982, I was a just-showing pregnant bride with Wilford my shotgun-carrying "father." Real wedding gown, real gun (unloaded), fake blacked-out tooth. Frances was a bear tamer, Phil the bear. Frances's skimpy outfit highlighted her curves. She carried a whip made of a stick and a red cord. Her tiara kept tilting in her thick hair. Frances and I were the only sober dancers. When someone came in with news of a big fire in Terra Alta, Phil and I left to head back up the mountain. The warehouse down the street from *The News* office was on fire. By the time Phil and I arrived on the scene, the flames danced into the sky, an orgy of orange and sparks and terrible noise. Fire trucks from at least four towns blocked the street. I made my way carefully around equipment and men, glad I had changed from my wedding dress into sweats. Phil had removed his bear ears and covered his furry costume with a pea coat. We approached a row of Terra Alta firemen as they aimed a hose at the roof of the building.

"We can't save it," the fire chief yelled. "But we can try to keep it from spreading. The firefighter manning the nozzle was a clown. Or had been a clown. He had a smeared white face and a wide red smiling mouth. Other firefighters had painted faces under their helmets. Such a surreal scene (and I knew about surrealism because of Frances).

◆

Wilford and I hosted Thanksgiving dinner that year. We smoked a turkey. In a Weber kettle, not a bong. Phil and Frances and Michael joined us, as did Marian and her family: husband, Joe, and sons, Ian and Nathan. We were their second dinner of the day. The three little boys played with plastic dinosaurs; the four big boys watched football (and the turkey).

Frances and I were both pregnant. She leaned against the counter. "This is better than a couple of years ago," she said. "Remember?"

"I don't think so," I said.

"Yes, you do," Frances nodded. "You, Wilford, and Sam came up to the farm and the turkey was still raw." Frances frowned. "You were so mad."

"Oh, Nance. I think you told me about that." Marian stopped cleaning up the kitchen and gave me a hug.

"It was our fault," Frances said. "We told you dinner was at five and of course we spaced out and didn't get the turkey in the oven."

I remembered. But it wasn't the turkey that had set me off that day. It was Wilford. He had started drinking early and I was too distracted by pie- and bread-making and toddler-wrangling to pay attention. By the time we were ready to leave for the farm, I didn't trust him to carry Sam. Or the pies. Sam and I, accustomed to eating early, were peckish. Our family was doomed before we even got to the farm.

This Thanksgiving was better. Wilford was intoxicated but no more than the other guests. He stopped short of the stupor I had been seeing more and more. What a relief. The smoked turkey was spectacular, as were the pies. We were surrounded by good food and good friends. Grateful for the bounty.

◆

Frances had talked me into taking a prenatal yoga class that winter. We made a half-hour drive to Oakland, Maryland, where we climbed the stairs to the second floor of an old school and eased onto the creaky wooden floor of a long-abandoned classroom. Our teacher, a physical therapist who had moved to Terra Alta with her fiddler husband, had a musical voice and positive mien. I struggled to follow her lead. When I looked over at Frances, she was blissful in child's pose.

"This is what I want to do," she declared, happy to ignore the instructions.

◆

Bob Teets had been my boss for a year and a half when my second son, Simon, was born in the middle of March. That spring, our tiny cabin overflowed with diapers, toddler paraphernalia, and hormones. My three-and-a-half-year-old was alternately helpful to me or a threat to his brother. I had taken to wrapping the phone in a towel and putting it into a cupboard to keep its ringing from waking Simon. When it rang one morning in April, the cord tethered me to the wall as I whispered hello. At the same time, Sam grabbed my legs, desperate for attention.

"I need you to come back to work," Bob said. "My father-in-law died and I have to go to Beckley. I don't know how long I'll be gone." I was a jelly mass of exhaustion, all quiver on the verge of meltdown. Before I could stutter my answer, he quickly added, "You can bring the baby." I thought about the six-week maternity leave I had planned. Unpaid of course. But we needed money. A second-time mother, I was a little more relaxed about this baby. I wouldn't go back to work for Bob, I told myself. I would do it for our readers. So three weeks after giving birth, I returned to work. Simon napped in a bassinette beside my desk, and I retreated to a quiet space when he demanded to be nursed. By the time Bob returned to Terra Alta at the end of April, I had settled into my old forty-hour-a-week routine. Simon stayed with me for another couple of months. He went with me when I covered a trial and when the testimony dragged, I jiggled him awake so his baby sounds would give me a reason to leave the courtroom. Eventually he joined his brother, Sam, at a babysitter's house.

◆

Every week that spring and summer I scanned "for rent" ads in the paper. Our family of four plus two big dogs overflowed the twenty-four-foot by twenty-four-foot cabin. And the driveway was still a nightmare. The few places we looked at weren't much better: what was available in our price range was depressing and squalid.

Then, at the end of the summer, Bob's wife, Preston County's first female realtor, presented an option: an old white farmhouse on thirteen acres. On Salt Lick. It had no indoor plumbing, but it was a sweet place on a flat plot next to the creek. An older couple had been living there, but they moved to town after selling the place to Bob and his brother Jim. Bob's wife urged us to buy it from them. I wish I could say with certainty how much we paid for the house and thirteen acres— six flat, seven on a steep hillside—but it must have been around thirty thousand dollars. We were able to make a miniscule down payment and we signed a deed of trust.

So what if the new house had no running water and we had very little money? No problem. Wilford could install plumbing, he assured me. We rented a floor sander for two days, all that we could afford, and during the Buckwheat Festival, just after Sam's fourth birthday, we ground layers of paint off the wide pine planks on the second floor. The machine bucked across the boards; I wrestled with its handles as if it were a live bronco. I would get so far, then abandon the machine, make the half-hour dash down the mountain to Kingwood, and photograph events at the festival. I'd then hurry back to Salt Lick and pick up where I left off. We painted the plywood floors downstairs Cherokee Red and ignored the fact that the kitchen floor sloped downhill from the sink. Shortly after, we moved in, just as the leaves blazed their autumn show.

Although I had never lived without plumbing, I imagined I could rough it for a while. Our well and pump were outside and we brought water into the house in heavy buckets. We were able to flush the toilet by pouring water into the tank. We filled the bathtub with water we heated on top of the King O Heat. If this was a test, I was passing. If my parents were wary of my new adventure, they didn't let on. Maybe they still carried a little guilt for tearing me from my beloved Wild Horse Creek Valley.

My father still occasionally questioned my decision to live in West Virginia. "Can't you find a job in the Midwest?" he would ask. "I don't want to," I would reply. "I like West Virginia." My mother, the psychologist, kept her mouth shut.

On their first visit to West Virginia, in 1976, my parents had actually driven a motor home up the steep, rocky, nearly impassable road to my cabin. Instead of being horrified by that experience, or by my tiny home, they had instead been distracted by my joy at that day's discovery of Lady Slippers, wild orchids, around my house. If they had voiced any criticism of my life in West Virginia, I would have ignored them. In my twenties and well into my thirties I carried my choices like chips on my shoulder; I danced to keep them balanced there. When anyone asked why I stayed in Preston County, I had an answer. I praised the beauty of the mountains, made my "I like being a big fish in a small pond" argument. I didn't tell them that a little voice inside my head kept saying I could *afford* West Virginia. I didn't make much money but I didn't need much money. This was a place where I could have it all: satisfying work, a marriage, children, beautiful views. Saying it out loud made it so.

◆

Wilford and I spent what money we had on bathroom fixtures, appliances, and a septic system. In the weeks that fall when Wilford and our friend Bennie worked on the plumbing, I learned that although my husband was an incredibly hardworking man and a skilled machinist, he was actually a pretty poor plumber. I was grateful for Bennie. We didn't know him very well; he was our friend Ellen's new beau. Bennie was sort of odd looking, with a head shaped like a big toe and hair that spiked from circular patches. He wore glasses that made his eyes look small and beady. But he was a cheerful guy and not at all bothered that his invitation to visit included an obligation to work. I'm sure Ellen had convinced him it would be fun. I remember that it was. Beer and pot were plentiful. The music was loud and varied. Ellen's son, Logan, played happily with Sam, and she and I took turns with the adorable redheaded Simon. And I cooked, something I have always done with passion and, if I might say, some skill. When Bennie and Wilford hooked enough pipes together to get water to the kitchen and bathroom sinks and to the toilet, we were thrilled. Cold running water. So welcomed.

We called the gas company to request that natural gas service be resumed. Men I knew, men who had plowed the driveway to our cabin and rescued our runaway dogs, walked through the field and shook their heads. They pointed to a visible orange hose, the gas line. It should have been buried, they said. Can't turn on the gas until it is. That bad news came in December and the ground was frozen solid. This meant that the two gas heaters in the house, one in the living room and one in the bathroom, wouldn't work. We burned wood and coal in the old King O Heat stove, which made the kitchen warm. Enough warm air rose to keep the two bedrooms on the second floor tolerable. The living room and playroom, though, were frigid. Both the cooking stove and water heater we had bought were gas, useless. So I cooked with a medley of appliances: a hot plate, a slow cooker, an electric skillet, a toaster oven, and a microwave. When we craved a hot shower, we visited Phil and Frances down the road. Their daughter, Becca, was six weeks younger than Simon. Not only did they have running water, they had a miraculous machine, a VCR. We could watch movies.

I was a militant proponent of cloth diapers and I still sometimes joke that between my two babies, I had my hands in a toilet for five years. Lest you think of me as a noble, breast-feeding, cloth-diaper-using Mother Earth figure, you should know that my environment-friendly attitude was also prompted by our poverty. Wilford had become a machinist, but his shop was nonunion. He didn't make much money. And I worked for cheapskate Bob Teets. Still, we drank bottled water like famous people I read about in magazines. Only our bottles were recycled milk jugs that we hauled to and from a spring on Caddell Mountain, eight miles away. The water there is clear and cold, the mountains in liquid form.

◆

That Christmas we again smoked our turkey on the Weber. We had mashed potatoes cooked on the hot plate, refrigerated rolls baked a few at a time in the toaster oven. I'm sure I was grateful that the dishes could be rinsed under running water. I'm also sure that I was grateful that we could flush the toilet at will. I wouldn't know for months that the running hot water I craved would smell like rotten eggs. Our well, like many in Salt Lick Valley, produced extremely hard water, safe, but filled with minerals, including sulfates. I also wouldn't know for years that the family who had lived in our house in the 1960s destroyed a nearby spring that produced clear, clean water because they didn't like the folks who were replacing them as tenants.

The temperature had plunged to twenty-six degrees below zero on the day after Christmas, a Monday, usually my busiest day at work, but I had put the paper to bed early. Simon straddled my hip and I was doing what I call the "mother dance," swaying from foot to foot by the kitchen sink, providing just enough motion to coax calm from my overtired baby. Four-year-old Sam was nearby playing with his new He-Man plastic figures. Wilford was wedged in the crawlspace underneath the kitchen sink with my hair-dryer blasting our newly installed plastic pipes with warm air in an attempt to keep them from freezing and breaking. We only had cold running water and it seemed too cruel that Mother Nature would Grinch-like steal that away at Christmas. While the King O Heat radiated warmth throughout the kitchen, it couldn't offset the extreme cold that penetrated the exposed area underneath the house, where those precious white pipes angled.

In fact, the kitchen itself was so warm that the boys and I were wearing T-shirts. I had a love-hate relationship with the King O Heat, which was about the height of a ten-year-old child and the circumference of a hug. Sam had learned early on to respect the stove. We sometimes giggled together when we rotated alongside of it whenever we needed a quick infusion of heat. A large teakettle on the flat top provided a steady supply of hot water and humidity. But every time Wilford or I poked the fire, a necessity whenever we added wood or coal, black clouds of smoke and noxious sulfurous fumes roiled from the cylinder. Wilford had taught me to poke, then duck to avoid the whoosh of ignited fumes.

The warm kitchen belied the weather outside. Twenty-six degrees below zero didn't even factor in the windchill. The air was so brutal that a short trip to the shed to get more wood or coal was a trial. My fingers quickly ached inside my gloves; the air froze the hairs in my nose with an immediacy that was shocking. The dogs never once whined to go outside. Thick waves of ice coated the bottom half of each window.

When the phone suddenly rang that afternoon, I crossed the room. I expected a holiday greeting from a friend. I was surprised to hear Bob's voice—I knew he had gone to the Bahamas before Christmas, then stopped at his in-laws in southern West Virginia for the holiday.

"Hey. Merry Christmas." Did I imagine that his voice had a catch of insincerity?

"Merry Christmas," I said. "I hope it's warmer in Beckley than it is here," I said. "It's really cold, twenty-six below zero." I could hear the blow-dryer whistling below my feet. I did not say, "What do *you* want?"

"That's why I'm calling," Bob said. "Jim tells me Joe Stiles's house burned down."

I said I had heard that too. The radio and the daily newspaper in Morgantown had reported that the fire apparently was related to electrical problems caused by the extreme weather. Joe was one of Terra Alta's two police officers, a baby-faced man a couple of years younger than I was. Joe was always polite to me, and I waved and smiled when I saw him around town, but I wasn't comfortable around him. Although Joe had not been the officer who accused Wilford and me of possession of marijuana or the officer who had arrested Wilford that same year for driving while intoxicated (both infractions were outside the city limits), he knew who we were. I knew he could cause trouble. But I was sorry that Joe's house had burned down. His wife was a lovely person; I didn't wish them ill.

"Is there a story in the paper?" Bob asked. I knew he meant our paper, the issue between Christmas and New Years, the paper Jerry had always canceled.

"No," I replied. "I finished the paper on Friday. Joe's house burned down Saturday." I shifted Simon to my other hip. I felt my heart beat a little faster. I knew where this conversation was headed.

"You need to go in and change the front page," Bob said, his voice rising in pitch. I imagined his vacation in the Bahamas, Bob lounging in the sun, a straw hat on his head and a long brown cigarette attached to his lip. I pictured him at his in-laws,' at leisure.

Simon started to whimper. He grabbed my shirt in his fists and banged his head gently on my shoulder. He wanted a nap; he wanted to nurse. He didn't care about my boss or my job. He was a difficult baby, a challenge to soothe. Hypersensitive to touch, if I suffered from agita, he was bothered tenfold. I remember precisely how Bob's words made me feel: dread settled across my shoulders like a weight, guilt whispered into my ear, anger flushed my cheeks. I became a little hysterical.

"It's the day after Christmas," I whined into the phone. "Wilford is under the house trying to keep the pipes from freezing. The story has already been in the daily newspaper and on the radio. By the time our paper comes out, it will be old news." I didn't want to go to work. I had earned that day off, and not just because of the extra effort I had made the week before. I believed that I worked hard every week: my goal was to put out the best paper possible. My standards were high. "Perfect is almost good enough," has been my motto for too much of my life. I wrote most of the news stories on the front page. I shot, processed, and printed all the photographs. I wrote a weekly column, rewrote press releases, edited the contents of the entire paper. I waxed ribbons of copy and with help from others, arranged them on twelve or sixteen pages every week. I worked evenings and spent most Sunday afternoons in the darkroom. Still, I knew that I should do as Bob asked.

"I can't," I said. "If Wilford has to take care of the boys, the pipes will freeze."

"I really wish you would," Bob said. His tone contained a threat.

"I'm sorry," I said. "I can't." Simon started to wail. I wanted to wail too. In that warm kitchen, on that cold, cold day, I started to hate my job and I started to hate Bob Teets for making me hate my job. That day, that afternoon, I started thinking about leaving *The Preston County News*. Until Bob's phone call, I had suppressed my doubts about my life. I had managed to fulfill one goal—combining career and family—but I had failed to fulfill my bigger ambitions. At this rate, I would never be William Allen White. I would never be Margaret Bourke-White. I wasn't going to save Preston County, but maybe, just maybe, I could save myself.

I wish I could say that I acted immediately, but I didn't. I had a four-year-old son who brought me great joy, a cranky baby, and an often-intoxicated husband. We had thirteen acres along a creek in a valley. I wasn't ready to leave, to disrupt my family. It was time to find a good story, to be distracted.

31

✦ ✦ ✦

EXPERIMENTS WITH UTOPIA

"You know Glenna Williams?" Phil asked. I nodded. He nodded faster. "Everyone knows Glenna." We were in his living room, Simon and Becca, now near the ten-month mark, under our care. "Today she charged into my office and announced, 'We're going to do a play!' Not, 'Are you interested in doing a play?'" He paused. "'*We* are putting on a play.'" He pulled Becca onto his lap. "About Arthurdale."

"Tell me more." I could picture Glenna, a tiny older woman, wound tight with energy. Cat-eye glasses. She was a vocal champion of Arthurdale, a community in western Preston County established as part of Franklin Delano Roosevelt's New Deal.

"Arthurdale is celebrating its fiftieth anniversary in July. They're going to have a reunion, a party, and we're going to do a readers' theater." Phil straightened his posture. "Glenna said, 'We used to do theater and we're going to do it again.' It was like an order."

Phil beamed. "The thee-ah-ter!" His actor's voice made Becca and Simon turn to look at him.

✦

"*This* is the story of Arthurdale." Phil wagged a manuscript in the air, as if to tease me. We were headed to a board of education meeting, one of its marathon March budget sessions. I climbed into his Scout and took the sheaf of papers. The cardboard cover was stained, the pages wrinkled. "Arthurdale: An Experiment in Community Planning," Stephen Haid's 1975 dissertation, had become Phil's latest obsession. He shifted into gear and headed up Salt Lick. "Man, what a place! I can't believe no one knows about it." As he drove us toward Kingwood; the seat springs sang in protest as the Scout bounced through potholes. "I drove around Arthurdale with Glenna this week." He made quick eye contact. "Don't worry; I cleaned the Scout first. Man, it was great!" Glenna had shown him the original Arthurdale houses, he said. "The feds built three styles. Most of them have been remodeled, but you can still see the original lines." His voice rose. "All hundred and sixty-five are still inhabited! All of them! That's amazing!" His Buddha face crinkled with glee. "The feds, *the feds*, took the poorest of the poor out of shacks and put them in nice houses. Coal miners, farmers, carpenters. This was a rescue like no other rescue."

For the thirty-minute drive down the mountain, I was Phil's captive audience. He steered through turns one-handed so his free hand could punctuate this sermon. One miracle had him cackling with delight: Eleanor Roosevelt's trip to Scott's Run in 1933 just happened to coincide with the development of a subsistence garden program by the American Friends Service Committee and West Virginia University. Bushrod Grimes, the university extension agent who led the subsistence project, talked to Eleanor and, within a week, he was looking for a tract of land for what would become the country's first planned federal community. "Bushrod!" Phil stabbed an index finger in the air. "Bushrod! What a name! What a place!" He took his eyes off the road and met mine. "And Eleanor? She was amazing. She was really involved. She made sure this happened." He ranted all the way to Kingwood. He turned off the engine; the Scout convulsed. "Glenna took me to the old administration building." Phil whistled softly. "It's in terrible shape. The roof leaks; the place is falling down. It's filled end to end with junk.

Filthy." He clenched the steering wheel, shook it a little. "The disregard for historical value is astounding!"

Bob Teets did not share that disregard. Although he came from a long line of Republicans, he admired what FDR had accomplished in Preston County. He promised to print a four-page tabloid about the July 1984 event.

◆

The story of Arthurdale is a story about rescue. About idealism. The Great Depression eviscerated coal mining communities, and Scott's Run, across the Monongahela River from Morgantown, was among the worst of the worst affected. The coal-dusted houses that stair-stepped deep ravines were ugly in good times. Hard times turned them truly squalid. Coal companies let out-of-work miners live in the shacks just to keep the structures from being dismantled for firewood. Children were starving. Lorena Hickok, an Associated Press writer, toured the area and then wrote this to her friend Eleanor Roosevelt. "In a gutter, along the main street through the town, there was stagnant, filthy water, which the inhabitants used for drinking, cooking, washing, and everything else imaginable. On either side of the street were ramshackle houses . . . which most Americans would not have considered fit for pigs. And in those houses every night children went to sleep hungry, on piles of bug-infested rags, spread out on the floor."

These were the families that Eleanor would save. She would build a community—Arthurdale—and it would change people's lives.

◆

Glenna knew of Phil's work with a local theater group. She knew of his leadership abilities. And she was right. Phil's passion was contagious. The theater group tackled the project, though they had problems with the script Glenna had given them. They added dialogue from Haid's dissertation, from diaries, letters, news stories, government records, and interviews. "Arthurdale: Land of Beginning Again," the play they developed, began to take shape. Michael too was caught up in the project. Phil would do words; Michael would do pictures, a slide show running concurrent with the play. Michael suspected there was a treasure trove of Arthurdale photos. The government had paid talented artists to document America during the Depression. Works Progress Administration photographers had often visited Appalachia. Michael and a part-time resident of the farm named William combed through the West Virginia Collection at West Virginia University and culled slides. "Hundreds of images!" Michael's voice vibrated with excitement during a phone conversation. "You have to see. William and I will put it together." His voice accelerated, raised in pitch. "We'll do a premiere at the farm."

In June 1984, springtime at the farm was an explosion of green—a palette of chartreuse, olive, and moss. Mud was a counterpoint to the beauty. Boots were de rigueur costume for our celebratory dinner: soup, homemade bread, last year's jelly from the elderberry bushes below the house. The compact audience—Phil, Frances, Becca, Wilford, Sam, Simon, and I—squeezed together in the small living room. We circled the humming projector and waited for the show. William sat quietly, but Michael, one hand on the Kodak Carousel, couldn't disguise his joy. His smile electrified his face, lit him like a preacher. "There was a ton of stuff. More photos than I imagined. Great photographers: Lewis Hine, Walker Evans, Marion Post Wolcott, Ben Shahn." The room smelled of damp dog. Mud stuck to our clothes, rimmed our nails, splattered the floor. Michael flipped a switch and we quieted, even Simon, who had been squirming on my lap. The projector fan whirred and the first slide dropped with a click. Scott's Run, its misery a lamentation in black and white. Shacks. Miners. Dirty children. The slides fell and images appeared on a pitted whitish wall not quite big enough to display them. A doorway rippled each image. These were the photos that were in my head in 1974, the year I first considered West Virginia. Exactly ten years before. I realized I had been in Preston County a decade.

"We found lots of black families in the early photographs," Michael said. "But they wouldn't take blacks in Arthurdale so we didn't include them." His shoulders sagged. "Geez." A sigh. "I guess when you're accused of communism, it's okay to be guilty of racism?"

"That's it. That's Arthurdale," Phil's voice was nearly a shout. "It's all about contradictions. Good and bad. This was a big deal, the federal government's first *invented* community. FDR's critics were watching, ready to pounce on every mistake. And there were mistakes. Lots of them. The first houses were totally inadequate. Resort cottages on foundations the wrong size." He raised a hand to smooth nonexistent hair, a habit of his, and grinned. "And they're all still standing! Fifty years later!" He laughed, joy crinkling his narrow eyes. "Here in Preston County, where fires happen all the time, where coal stoves get too hot, where houses become ash, these houses are still standing! That means something." He leaned back in the one chair in the living room that could bear his big frame. "Yes, there was blatant bigotry. No blacks. No immigrants." Again the hand on top of his head. "It's remarkable they were able to create this thing. The feds could never do it again."

Michael pushed a button and we were in Arthurdale. The original Arthur mansion, a grand Victorian, faced a great empty field. Click. Homesteaders, all men, lined up on the fancy front porch for a portrait. "Look," Michael said. "They have new work clothes on. Bushrod Grimes arranged for them to get credit at a store in Morgantown." The men hold hats, their faces grim. Michael paused. "Man, this is something. These were the lucky ones, but they were ashamed." Two chefs, their white aprons drawing my eye, have crossed arms and scowls. Did I know those faces? Click. Photos of houses under construction; the straight vertical and horizontal lines reveal the skill of a professional photographer. "Here's a Hodgson house," Michael said. "They were pre-fab and when they got there they didn't fit the foundations. People freaked out."

"That wasn't the only problem," Phil interjected. "These were Cape Cod vacation homes. They weren't designed for Preston County winters. They ended up costing thousands more than expected." He laughed. "And they were considered luxurious. They had electricity, running water, and refrigerators. Only rich folks in Preston County had indoor plumbing back then."

A photo showed a pine-paneled living room, a rug, a stool, a chair, a breakfront, two shelves. "Eleanor helped with the interior design," Michael said. "This is like the best of Arthurdale. The furniture was made by the Mountaineer Craftsmen's Cooperative there. Every family got beds, chairs, and dressers. They even got cribs if they needed them. Beautiful stuff!" His voice rose to reveal his enthusiasm. "Those rugs were made in Arthurdale. That pottery." Images appeared and vanished. Every click, every soft whoosh, delivered another vision of the very type of society Michael, Phil, and Frances sought for the farm: artistic, community-minded, agricultural, independent. A photo of the forge drew Michael's cry. "They even made the hinges used everywhere!" Michael drew a deep breath. "This community was *designed*," he said. "Every home had space for some chickens, a cow, a pig. The government even dug root cellars. Amazing!" In another photo, one young girl churns butter while another cards wool. "Oh my God. The school!" He fairly vibrated with the pleasure of his message. "It was incredible. Elsie Clapp, who ran the school, was a disciple of John Dewey. They believed in progressive education, learning by doing, linking education to community. They were so far ahead of their time!" Another photo showed children building small shacks.

"Their own little village." William sat cross-legged, his back straight. "You know Arthurdale became known as Eleanor's Little Village." A woman and two men smile at a scale model of the proposed school campus. "Elsie wanted the school to be the center of activity in the community," William said.

Simon was getting restless. He arched out of my arms onto the dirty floor and crawled toward Sam, who ran an orange plastic bulldozer across the carpet. Becca sucked her index finger; her tilted blue eyes narrowed as if she were calculating the likelihood of a fight. Sam gripped the bulldozer; Simon would be denied this toy.

Wilford was already moving toward the boys. "Hey, Trouble," he crooned as he plucked Simon from the floor. He glanced at me, made sure I was watching. Skin hung in loose, bruised-looking bags under his red-streaked eyes. He looked whipped, beaten. The night before he had come home shitfaced. I had shrieked until my throat hurt and I was exhausted enough to sleep, red-faced and wounded. The entire day had been tense. We were on our best behavior at the farm. Wilford swung Simon onto his hip and headed into the kitchen.

Michael clicked to another photo. "This is my favorite," he said, his eyes lifted toward the phantasm on the wall. Eleanor's dress was a vivid floral print as she stepped slightly ahead of her dance partner, both of them facing the camera, both smiling. I recognized the Arthurdale gymnasium, where I had photographed Girl Scouts and basketball players.

"She loved to do the Virginia Reel," William said. Click. Eleanor trailed by a parade of media and visitors. Click. Eleanor surrounded by young men and women in caps and gowns. "She invited classes to the White House," William said. Click. Again, the Arthurdale gym. FDR sits in a wheelchair, the braces on his legs visible.

"The president gave the commencement address to the class of thirty-eight," said Michael. "This is a rare photo. The press never showed his braces."

"Eleanor's wearing the same dress as in the dance," Frances said. She always noticed what people were wearing. She was a master of accessories. The next click revealed a square of luminescence: the end.

"That was great!" Frances smiled, sincerity lighting her face. Becca leaned into her mother's chest and closed her eyes. In the doorway, Simon clutched Wilford, handfuls of shirt in each fist. He gently banged his forehead against his father's shoulder, a slow rhythm that warned of an impending tantrum.

◆

Blue skies, sunshine: a prize of a summer day. Immense trees shaded houses hastily built half a century before in an open meadow, formed a regal line next to the decrepit administration building. Across the highway at the Arthurdale School, Glenna Williams, the celebration's champion, and her team put on a glorious party. I photographed homesteaders and their families as they lined up for a formal portrait (to be taken by someone else). The sun was too high in the sky for the light to be pleasing, but the photo's narrative made up for its weak aesthetics. A banner across the top of the frame said:

> *The Arthurdale Dream, Then & Now*
> *"Celebrating 50 Years as a Community"*
> *July 13–15*

Beneath the sign, Elliott Roosevelt, third son of Franklin and Eleanor, dipped his tall frame to speak to an elderly woman. I had followed Roosevelt most of the day. He was greeted as a hero, his hands grasped and arms patted. All because a half century before, his mother had plucked families from gray, vertical hills and planted them in green rolling fields.

When it was time for the theater performance, light streamed through the open doors of the Arthurdale gym and bounced off the honeyed oak floors. It set the faces of the audience aglow. The doors closed and the room turned sepia. The murmuring crowd sat in a room their families built and listened to words drawn from letters, news stories, government records, and interviews. The slide show offered ghostly images of proof. On stage an actress spoke the words of a visitor to Scott's Run. "I watched a small boy cradle a pet rabbit in his arms. His sister tugged at my skirt. 'My little brother doesn't think we're going to cook that rabbit but we are.'" The room hushed. In another scene a homesteader spoke about Arthurdale's first community Christmas tree. She recalled the previous year, a holiday without presents, without hope. The photos whispered as they changed. They said "this happened." The audience traveled through time; some recognized their own family stories and images. When an actress declared that her move from Scott's Run to Arthurdale was like leaving a black and white world to enter Technicolor, heads nodded.

Phil sat in a wheelchair in a square of light. Dancing molecules of dust hovered in the air like a benediction. He channeled Franklin Delano Roosevelt, sat in the very spot, on the very board, and spoke the very words of that wise, generous president. Phil's voice was thick with emotion, its timbre low and melodious. I was moved to tears.

◆

There were a lot of tears in Arthurdale that day. Wendell Lund, who had been in charge of selecting families to settle in Arthurdale, stood in front of a cheering crowd and congratulated his choices and their descendants for proving that "compassion, whether on the part of an individual or on the part of government, is a very great thing." U.S. Senator Jennings Randolph, in 1984 the only member of Congress who held office during FDR's famous first hundred days, stood to greet the crowd. I eavesdropped, took notes, and made photographs.

"My daddy was the barber," one woman told Senator Randolph. "I believe he cut your hair."

"I believe I had more of it then," Randolph joked. The senator was an enthusiastic storyteller. He had often driven to Arthurdale with Eleanor Roosevelt, he said. He recalled one trip across U.S. 50 with Mrs. Roosevelt and Doris Duke. They had stopped to eat at a Romney hotel and then, he said with his voice lowered, "There I was with the wife of the president of the United States and a rich heiress and I had thirty-four cents in my pocket." He said he excused himself from the dining table and made arrangements to send the bill to his Washington office. He remembered Eleanor fondly. "Eleanor Roosevelt came to Arthurdale more than twenty times. I asked her if she was registered to vote here. Ha!" He had a laugh that used his whole body. The senator called FDR "the man that repaired America." His voice full of emotion, Randolph said, "This may be the last time I speak in Arthurdale as a member of the Senate." (That was true; he stepped down and in November 1984. Jay Rockefeller took his seat.)

Elliott Roosevelt reminded attendees of their history. "America was on its knees in 1932," he said. "The United States is a capitalist nation and many capitalists rant and rave about the New Deal. Well, it was the New Deal that preserved the capitalist system for them."

Eleanor Seagraves, granddaughter of Franklin and Eleanor, accepted the emotional outpouring, all the thank-yous from people who shook her hand and recalled her grandmother. At Saturday's Homesteaders Dinner, she looked at the 150 faces before her and held out a portrait of Eleanor, a gift to the Commemorative Committee.

"There have been many changes since my grandmother drove here in an open car," Seagraves said. "Today, what first lady could do that?" Then she added, "My grandmother wasn't afraid of change. She always said, 'Changes are coming anyway so it's up to us to be ready.'" Seagraves smiled. "Fifty years ago you sent a message of hope all across the country. On the fiftieth anniversary of Arthurdale you send another message of hope."

I photographed Milford Mott, Arthurdale's last federal manager, who had been on duty in April 1947 when the federal subsidies stopped. Mott recalled that when he came to Arthurdale in 1941, the houses needed painting. The government had sent some paint, mostly white, but also a few colors. Homesteaders were on the verge of owning their homes, but they still sought Mott's advice. "I told them they could paint their houses checkerboard if they wanted, but they were pretty conservative." He flashed a brief smile.

A woman tapped me on the shoulder. "Hi," she said. "Remember me?" I nodded. I had done a story on the post office in Independence, where her husband was postmaster, my first summer in Preston County. Now she had another story for me: memories of her childhood in Arthurdale. "We were very fortunate," she told me. "We really got involved with our school and our community." She spoke with pride. "I never would have gotten to meet the president's wife, never gotten to shake her hand, if not for Arthurdale." She recalled the beauty of the community. "Everything was painted white; it all looked so clean and new." Tears filled her eyes and her voice cracked. "Not very long ago when my mother died, we painted her house white again."

Throughout the weekend, as the sun shone hard against the still-white school buildings, people carefully scrutinized faces and nametags. Shouts of pleasure filled the air as homesteaders linked with their past. In a gymnasium packed with people, Glenna Williams led an inspired version of "Happy Birthday." Her index finger jabbed high as she changed the familiar chorus, "to us!" Joyful voices celebrated the anniversary of a radical, federal experiment that founded a community.

That Saturday I watched the sun set from the back porch of one of the original homes. Its occupant, one of the original homesteaders, had raised six children in Arthurdale. "I can't see how some people can call Arthurdale a failure," she told me. She gazed toward the purple sky, looked across her yard at green fields, lush gardens, good neighbors. "It's a wonderful place to live."

32

❖ ❖ ❖

CHANGES IN ALTITUDE

How **did** I **learn** in 1985 that the newspaper in Morgantown was looking for a photographer? Maybe Ron, the *Dominion Post*'s chief photographer, stood next to me at some event—a ribbon-cutting or a basketball game—and told me the newspaper was going to add a photographer to work a Sunday through Thursday shift. Maybe Kathy, the new chief of the *Dominion Post*'s Preston County bureau and a former *Preston County News* employee, suggested I apply. I read the *Dominion Post* every day, worked alongside its photographers and reporters. The paper used photos well most of the time. The writing and editing were inconsistent; I sometimes made fun of the spelling and grammatical errors that found their way into print. I was less than enthusiastic about the newspaper's politics. It was privately owned (and still is), controlled by a family that made its fortune in coal, steel, and limestone, then used that money to expand into the radio and newspaper business, and politics. The publisher was a conservative Republican. The *Dominion Post*'s editorial page made me cringe. But its front page was often dominated by a large color photograph. Color! When I was in journalism school, my professors had expressed certainty that newspapers wouldn't graduate from black and white photos to color anytime soon. They were wrong.

Did a voice inside my head say "you can be a photographer again"? If so, this was followed quickly by a realization: What would I use for a portfolio? I hadn't put together a collection of prints for years. How could I do that project and keep my job application secret? I was not accustomed to keeping secrets. That's why I became a journalist: to trumpet what I saw, what I knew. I wish I could remember the days before my interview. I do recall standing in front of the editor of the *Dominion Post*, Ron at my side. The newsroom was filled with matching furniture, new carpeting, and computers. Computers! Bob had bought a computer and I spent hours and hours trying to figure out how to get copy from it directly to the typesetter. It never worked. That morning Ron had a grin on his face that he tried in vain to suppress. Behind me, Ron later said, Sandi, the Lifestyles editor and a former Preston County reporter, mouthed the words "hire her." I got the job: third photographer, noon to 8:30 on Sunday; 11:00 a.m. to 7:30 p.m. Monday through Thursday. I would start in two weeks. My salary almost doubled.

When I gave Bob my notice, his eyes widened and his lips shifted into a disapproving line. "Good for you," he said, sounding unconvinced. I stood in my office at *The Preston County News* and faced what passed for our newsroom, a handful of desks in a former dining room/living room. My coworkers greeted the news with a mixture of applause and tears. I had been at *The News* for a decade, nearly a third of my life. I felt as though I was abandoning my family. My going away party was a solemn affair. Even the balloons seemed a little deflated. We ate cake and quickly went back to work.

Bob was kind enough to let me take my negatives with me. I also took a collection of cards and photos I had flattened under the glass top of my desk: A pink postcard that proclaimed, "If your mother says she loves you check it out." A postcard of a two-headed calf given to me by a man who owned a steam-driven sawmill. A square of paper with the saying, "If you can't dazzle them with brilliance, baffle them with bullshit."

◆

In April 1985, on my first day at the *Dominion Post*, I opened the door to the newsroom at noon; heavy plastic sheeting covered the cubicles, dripped from the ceiling. Legs emerged from holes above me; a man in a white plastic suit bent over, peered at me through a windowed hood, and waved me away. I backed through the door. He followed. "Asbestos abatement," he explained. "You shouldn't come in that room for a while." Great. I swallow my liberal leanings and go to work for a right-wing paper only to be greeted by poison. Served me right. Then Ron showed up and presented me with a Domke bag and two Nikons. My first motor drives. It was like Christmas. "There aren't any assignments," he said. The reporters and editors wouldn't show up until two or three. "Find a picture. Take the company car." He dangled a set of keys. "Can you drive a stick?" Whoo-hoo! This was living: new cameras, shiny car, and a big swath of time to look for pictures. Enterprise pictures, we used to call these. Found photos that capture a day: the weather, a neighborhood, people, animals. Something interesting and, if I was lucky, artistic to decorate the front page.

In time I would arrive at work with a photo ready to submit. Well, ready after some darkroom time. The forty-four mile commute from Salt Lick Valley over the top of the mountain to the lower-altitude Morgantown offered plenty of creative opportunities. The trip took a solid hour, longer if I ended up trailing a loaded coal truck on curving, narrow, impossible-to-pass-on roads. I often took a longer route to work just to avoid coal trucks, winding my Subaru across the ridge top along the Brandonville Pike, darting across the Prison Road shortcut, then speeding down the recently completed Interstate 68. Two photos from that commute are among the framed prints I have in my home today: a mamma pig nose to nose with one of her babies and a winter scene featuring a bicyclist on the Prison Road.

Winter actually made me unpopular at my new job. I had lived in snow country for a decade. My Subaru navigated all but the deepest drifts. I wasn't exactly fearless, but I was ultimately responsible. If I was supposed to work, I'd be there. Occasionally, Morgantown would suffer a blizzard and I would show up, even though Terra Alta had twice the snow. I would straggle into the newsroom and stomp the snow from my black rubber zip-over-my-shoes boots. The phone would be ringing and the editor would answer. He'd be silent a minute and then he'd say, "Well Nancy's here from Terra Alta." I was sometimes directed to go pick up a reporter who lived nearby. If not for me, she might have taken a snow day.

Ron and the paper's other photographer, Dale, each had a specialty. Ron loved spot news, Dale sports. They rolled their eyes at assignments from Sandi's Lifestyles section. But they didn't see what was happening. "Society" news no longer dominated the space. Feminism had changed the world and Sandi was enthusiastic about the transformation. She was full of ideas and enjoyed alternating serious content with fashion or food stories. When she did a feature story on female Vietnam War veterans, I went with her to shoot portraits of the women she interviewed. I had never considered that angle to the war. Sandi and I were an odd couple: she was close to six feet tall, curvaceous, and prone to wear ruffles. I was nearly a foot shorter, stocky, and my wardrobe choices matched the stories to which I was assigned: jeans for sports, tailored outfits for serious proceedings, and a black suit, white shirt combo for formal events. (I wanted to look like a wait person.) I tried to find clothes that allowed me to blend in with the subjects I photographed. Sandi was born and raised in Preston County, so she put on no airs, but she enjoyed mingling with the moneyed people of Morgantown.

When West Virginia University held its first cancer center fundraiser at the Greenbrier, a five-star resort in the southern part of the state, Sandi convinced our publisher that the event merited coverage. Even though I was the least senior photographer, I was tapped to go because Sandi and I could share a room. My babysitter made me a dress to wear to the ball: apricot satin with spaghetti straps, a draped bodice, and flowing skirt. I felt like Cinderella. The nearly four-hour journey to the Greenbrier (in the newspaper's Pontiac, not a pumpkin) was via Route 19, then a tortuous two-lane that wound up and down forested mountains, curled around the New River, and slowed through tired, gray towns. The Greenbrier appeared as if a mirage, like the Tara I had imagined: a grand white edifice surrounded by lawn and gardens, impossibly green grass and thousands of tulips that laid stripes of bright color. Sandi and I stepped into the past when we stepped into the lobby. Nearly all of the workers were black and uniformed and they bowed and ma'am'd us as if we were honored guests, not tolerated observers. I felt as if I had gone through the mirror to another land. Even in my father's restaurant world, I had never eaten so well. The lunch buffet nearly made me cry with its glistening seafood, gourmet salads, and exquisite pastries. Since the room charge included breakfast and dinner (we paid for the lunch buffet), I ate all I could. I should have foundered on the famous Greenbrier peaches nearly hidden under billowing piles of real whipped cream. I photographed golf, tennis, and gardens. I covered dozens of events, from fashion shows to cooking classes. I was on my feet with my cameras from dawn until midnight. When the grand finale, the formal ball, was over, I finally put down my Nikons and Sandi and I joined some of the other late-night revelers in the bar. One of them, Gaston Caperton, was a youthful, enthusiastic dancer who charmed all of us. A couple of years later, I photographed him at a groundbreaking event at West Virginia University. Afterward I approached him. "Is that your father running for governor?" I asked.

He put his head back and laughed. "Honey, that's the sweetest thing I've ever heard," he said. I was mortified. This youthful man (I later found out he was forty-five) was the Gaston Caperton who would become West Virginia's thirty-first governor. I don't know that I've presumed to guess anyone's age since.

◆

Most of my assignments were not so glamorous. The treacherous roads claimed many victims and I often was sent to gruesome accident scenes. The one most vivid in my memory was on Interstate 68, on the long descent from the top of the mountain at Coopers Rock State Forest to Cheat Lake. After several horrific accidents, the state had carved a truck escape ramp into the side of the hill. Over time, the soft bed of gravel designed to stop trucks had settled. It failed to slow a tractor trailer full of fabric softener. The truck shot along a cliff face, then rolled down toward the highway, breaking apart. Blue plastic bottles decorated by teddy bears were scattered across the mountain; the air was cloying with the sweet chemical smell. And there, on a ledge, was the dead driver.

The week before Christmas, the newsroom's police scanner picked up a terrible car accident, multiple fatalities, in southwestern Preston County. "Shoot that," Ron said. Then he changed his mind. "Go home," he said. "Be careful." The roads were icy. At the four-way stop in Reedsville, I had looked to my right, down Route 92, and thought about the crash a few miles away. How sad to lose someone during the holidays. My friend Marian had buried her sister around New Years and every subsequent year's celebration had a crushed edge for her. I navigated through Kingwood, over the Cheat River, up Caddell Mountain, down Salt Lick. I stomped snow from my boots and opened the door. Wilford was in tears. "It's Mary Jane," he said. "She's been killed. And both her kids." Mary Jane? Not Mary Jane, with her wide laugh and teasing ways. Not the woman who introduced me to my husband. We clung to each other and cried.

33

◆ ◆ ◆

THE CHEAT 1

———

BEFORE I MET MARY JANE, before I met Wilford, I got to know the Cheat River. The 1974 whitewater races had introduced me to the Cheat Narrows, a lovely stretch of whitewater that I had learned to kayak in 1975. In 1976, while working for *The Preston County News*, I was introduced to a new view of the Cheat.

June Isaac lived between Caddell and Albright. She could see the Cheat River from her window. The river flooded occasionally and her trailer sat in the flood plain. But June was not often concerned about high water. What troubled her was black water. The quiet Cheat was a deep green. The rain-swelled Cheat was caramel. Black water meant that someone upstream had intentionally polluted the river. June suspected Kleen Coal, a few hundred yards upstream, was the culprit. At its plant, coal was "washed" to remove some of its sulfur. The dirty water was impounded in a settling pond, but June was sure the company regularly breached the dam to release its overflow. June had complained to the state but was told it would be next to impossible to prove Kleen Coal's culpability. So she called *The News*. At the time, her daughter was one of our typesetters, a hard worker, quick to laugh, my eventual babysitter/gown maker. June was a force. She talked fast and could be charming, even when she complained about the coal company, about the state regulators. She had told me she would call me the next time the river was running black. And she did.

"Come now!" she urged one Sunday morning as spring turned into summer. I raced down Caddell Mountain and knocked on the door to her trailer. Her home, like June herself, was perfectly in order. We walked to the edge of the river. It appeared to be darker, with a suspicious sheen in places.

"This won't work," I said. "A black and white photo won't prove anything."

"We have to do something," June said.

"I'll call the DNR," I said.

So I did. Their water pollution expert listened to my story, then admitted it was almost impossible to catch polluters. Before I could interrupt him with my protest, he said the damage I saw was nothing in comparison to the pollution of past decades.

"Meet me by the Cheat next week," he said.

When I did, he led me on a hike far above the river, downstream from June. He showed me a breach in a rock face where water slowly seeped. "There's an old coal mine behind this wall," he said.

This expert explained that in the 1940s, companies took out all the coal in a seam. Water easily breached the thin buffer of rock left behind. He said the county was littered with old deep mines filled with water, water that became acidic from its collision with coal and coal waste and oxygen. Some mines, like the one he showed me, dripped slowly; they had poisoned the Cheat below them for half a century and would continue the affront. Stained orange rocks coated with "yellow boy" announced the insult. Once in a while, water in an old mine would burst through a wall and that sudden rush would wreak havoc wherever gravity led it. In the late 1970s, water burst from a hillside, roared down a hill, and swept through a beer joint. I did a story for *The Preston County News* and got clever with the headline "Who gets the shaft?"

◆

Even unpolluted water and gravity can wage a cruel assault. Altitude can contribute to the problem. The tops of the mountains in Preston County trap storms; clouds hover and drop vast amounts of precipitation. Snow piles up, but water follows a downhill course—along every fold in the rocky ground, into foot-wide ditches that lead to wider runs, which intersect with creeks, then empty into the river. Like the circulation system of a living being. Heavy rains sometimes washed away the earth around culverts and imperiled the roads. Flash floods, small disasters, occurred often enough to be no surprise. I remember the Cheat River overwhelming the Rowlesburg Park on several occasions in the 1970s and 1980s. It was an inconvenience, not a tragedy.

Everything changed in November 1985, the year of catastrophe, of the Great Flood. No one is entirely sure how it happened. Meteorologists have a theory: In the days before the flood, Hurricane Juan struck the gulf coast. It weakened, then revived by sucking moisture from the Atlantic. That storm collided with a storm stalled over the Appalachian front. Rain fell. Lots of rain. Fast. In West Virginia all that water followed the law of gravity, from run to creek to river.

On Monday, November 4, more rain fell on Shaver's Fork, a Tucker County tributary of the Cheat, than anyone had ever seen before. I had worked at the *Dominion Post* in Morgantown for seven months. That Monday, I stayed past quitting time to do a favor for a friend. Eleven years before, I had interviewed a woman for the tabloid *The News* did on the doctor shortage. I later did a story about her husband, who had gone from being president of a bank to professional toymaker. He called me at work that Monday to tell me that his mother-in-law had died suddenly while on vacation in Burma. The body had been cremated; the family needed a photo for a memorial service. Could I copy an old photo and make a large print? I said I would. Doing so kept me in Morgantown until well after 10 p.m.

When at last I dashed for the car, I was immediately drenched. The rain was relentless; the whole world seemed liquid. I navigated my Subaru over forty miles of curves and hills, through sheets of water. The windshield wipers beat a furious rhythm that drowned out the radio. I had never experienced such a deluge. I couldn't see beyond my headlights; everything had gone dark and fluid. By the time I headed down Salt Lick Road, I was exhausted. Five miles to go, then two, when I saw the water. Irish Run, normally quiet, was out of its banks, merging with Salt Lick Creek. The muddy torrent had breached a culvert to form a thirty-foot-wide barrier across the road. My headlights illuminated roiling waves. I had driven forty-two miles; home was so close. I did something stupid: I put the car into low gear and drove into the water. I clutched the hard plastic steering wheel with both hands and willed control. And made it across. It was impossible to distinguish whether the roaring in my ears was the sound of the water or my body's reaction to an adrenaline rush. My heart drummed a frantic rhythm as I continued down Salt Lick; my headlights reflecting off the monster that most days was a meandering, clear creek. Now it boiled and flung itself against its banks, an angry, powerful force.

I need to talk to Phil, I thought, when I finally got home. This is news. The house was quiet when I walked in. Wilford and the boys were asleep.

◆

When I called Phil, he described that night's sequence of events. He said that Rich Wolfe, director of emergency services for the county, had called him around nine or ten to ask him to check Salt Lick Road below us. Emergency responders had been in that area earlier to evacuate a family who lived beside the creek. No one died, but several of the rescuers were washed downstream and had to be rescued themselves. Phil drove as far as Kinsinger Run, but that culvert, like the one at Irish Run, was overwhelmed so he turned back. From the bridge on the S curve bridge below my house, Phil saw a creek that looked utterly foreign. When we traded information that night, Phil told me that was the point he understood how serious the situation was. His low voice filled my ear as I twirled the phone cord nervously.

"What if the water reaches our house?" I asked.

"We're all in trouble then," Phil replied.

I hung up the phone and woke Wilford. We could hear the roar of Salt Lick through the closed windows. I slid the kitchen window open and that awful sound invaded our home. Wilford and I looked at each other; his face was wide with alarm. He leaned out of the window and swept the flashlight in an arc. The creek was just beyond the beam, but its thunder filled the valley. My rat-a-tat-tat heartbeat started up again, prodded by "what if" thoughts. After the boys, what would I grab? Wilford put his arms around me. I felt the strength in his wiry body. "I'll take first watch, Hon," he said. "You go to sleep." So the night passed, a nightmare of angry water.

◆

Phil called before dawn. "I'm in Kingwood," he said. "I couldn't see the river in the dark, but Rich says this is big. Interstate Lumber is on fire." I relayed that news to Wilford, then Phil's voice rose. "I'm going up with the National Guard as soon as it's light. Fred Snider and his son are missing and the Guard's going to look for them." I had met Fred Snider and his wife. This tragedy had a face.

As soon as I hung up, the phone rang again. My friend Marian lived in Albright, normally a sleepy town on a calm river. Her husband worked at the power plant there. "Nance, you have to get down here," she said. "Houses are washing away." The enormity of the disaster triggered an immediate response. My shift didn't start until late morning but I needed to work now. I threw on clothes, grabbed my green raincoat and black rubber boots. In the murk of predawn, our back field was a café au lait sea that stopped a foot from our house. The rain had slowed to a drizzle. I turned to Wilford. "Can you take the boys?" He nodded.

I headed south. The creek was still a boiling, brown assault; it must have crested during the night. Flattened, muddy foliage lined its sides. At Kinsinger Run, the road vanished, the blacktop peeled away in jagged chunks. A muddy void gaped where the culvert had been. I turned around. The road followed the creek up the valley; in spots the water's destructive force had undercut the asphalt, which collapsed. I drove on the wrong side of the road. Fast.

My memories of that day come in flashes: images, conversations. I do not remember listening to the radio, but I must have tuned in to the local station, to Phil. While I was on the ground, Phil was in a National Guard helicopter with a couple of soldiers. No one had a camera. Phil had a tape recorder and a primitive version of a cell phone. The Cheat River Valley, visible as soon as the chopper flew over the ridge, took Phil's breath away. The river was vast, muddy, and ferocious. The wide, flat valley below the Cheat Narrows, home to the Preston Country Club, to Camp Dawson, had been swallowed by water. The chopper followed a two-lane highway up the Cheat to Rowlesburg. Every place the river curved, the highway was gone, the blacktop stripped away, the road bed collapsed.

At Rowlesburg, Phil struggled to get his bearings. Both the railroad and concrete bridges had collapsed. The water was up to the second floor of the school, normally a hundred yards from the river. The chopper flew past, up the river to Wolf Creek. Four children huddled on the roof of a house surrounded by water. The soldiers dropped Phil in a nearby field to lighten the helicopter's load. From there he watched the pilot hover close enough to the house for a soldier to grab the children. "I don't know how the hell the pilot did that," Phil said later. The crew left the children with a neighbor, picked up Phil, and in seconds they spotted Fred Snider and his son Adam clinging to trees above the muddy water. Again the soldiers dropped Phil at a farm across the river. From there he watched a soldier descend the rope and grab Adam Snider from the tree. They came back toward Phil and dropped Adam into his arms. Phil took him into the farmhouse, where a woman wrapped the boy in a blanket. By the time Phil came back outside, the soldiers had rescued Fred. Phil remembers catching him too. "He was as cold and stiff as anyone I had ever seen," Phil said.

The new concrete bridge high over the Cheat at Caddell was intact. It straddled a river gone impossibly wide. I stopped there to shoot pictures of Interstate Lumber, ruined by flood and fire, but I couldn't stay long. I needed to get to Albright, downriver. The St. Joe Road was flooded between Caddell and Albright. I wondered how June Isaac was faring. I drove up to Kingwood, then circled back toward the river on Route 26. A crowd had gathered at a vantage point above the town; the road into Albright was closed. The river was like something enraged, it roiled and roared, brown and violent. Giant, explosive waves marked the spot where it breached the causeway into the power plant. It had stopped just short of the plant itself. I started shooting.

The river pounded a row of houses; with a boom, one tore from its foundation and crashed into its neighbor downstream. A gas station garage twirled in the water, was upended and, instantly disappeared. I shot as much film as I dared; I needed to make sure I had enough for the rest of the day. I went to find a phone. I don't remember who answered the call in the *Dominion Post* newsroom. She told me Ron was in Point Marion, where the Monongahela River was up; Dale was photographing a flooded trailer in Granville. "You don't understand!" I yelled. "The world has ended up here. Send everyone."

I called Kathy, the *Dominion Post*'s bureau chief in Kingwood. She understood the magnitude of the disaster, had spoken to Rich Wolfe. She sent me to the hospital to photograph Fred Snider. I can see his face still: grim, shadowed with terror. Adam was in good spirits; he flashed a broad grin. Their survival was a miracle. They had been at their camp on Seven Islands in the Cheat when the water's sudden rise cut off their escape. The phone line was intact so Fred was able to call his family; he told them that he and Adam would ride out the storm in the barn. The water drove them into the loft and kept rising. When the timbers started to groan, Fred lashed together a pair of coolers. When the barn collapsed, they jumped into the water. Fred pushed Adam into a tree and grabbed another tree downstream. They clung to those branches, wet and cold, for five hours.

At the country club, the water had already receded. The golf course was strewn with drowned night crawlers, limp dark worms. Here and there a carpet of mud, smooth, unblemished, glistened. I paused in front of a home; the door was open and I could see floors covered in mud. I started shooting, then I heard shouting. "Go away! Get out!" I recognized the shouting man, a businessman. "No pictures!" he yelled. I begged for access, but he continued to shriek. Later, I found out that he had called the paper to complain that I had trespassed on his property. I probably did, though not with malicious intent. Now I understand that he was in shock, that he was really angry at the river, not me. I headed to Rowlesburg, but didn't get far. Route 72 disappeared, black asphalt dropped off the side of the hill. The detour on an unpaved road via Tunnelton would take hours. I shot what I could, used up my film, and headed for Morgantown.

◆

In those days, we developed color film by hand. Ektachrome slide film. The first eighteen minutes or so were spent in complete darkness, the stack of reels dipped into tanks: one solution, then water, then other solutions. All done by touch. To develop film, we followed a recipe. Time and chemistry and temperature had to be exact. So did the film's exposure. I was always worried that I would screw that up. I bracketed exposures whenever possible, shooting three frames of each photo: one overexposed, one underexposed and one (oh please oh please) just right. I didn't remember bracketing on the river bank. I needed to see the photos of the flood in Albright. Ron had already told me that I was the only photographer who had witnessed the flood's crest. I sat in the dark and prayed for a salvageable image.

In the photo the river has engulfed houses and trees. It has shoved a large blue house against a smaller, white dwelling. The brown water foams against the second story windows. In the background, the Albright school sits above the flood, untouched. The *Dominion Post* never ran that photo, although black and white photos that I shot that day ran on inside pages. One of those photos went out over the wire. When my former boss Bob Teets decided to publish a book, *Killing Waters: The Great West Virginia Flood of 1985*, he chose my color photo for the cover.

This was no ordinary flood; it was sudden, powerful, and historic. Twenty-nine counties in West Virginia were affected. Damages were estimated to be nearly six million dollars. Forty-seven people died, two in Preston County—an elderly man at the country club and an elderly woman in Albright. In Rowlesburg, the iron railroad bridge had trapped debris that had washed down from Parsons and Saint George and Macomber. That bridge, an engineering marvel when it was built in the 1850s, had been targeted by the Confederacy during the Civil War. Those thick steel struts survived the war. But the night of November 4, the bridge became a dam. When it finally gave way in a shriek of metal, water burst through the town then crashed through the Cheat Narrows. Floodwaters moved boulders the size of houses. The disaster forever altered a river that nature had carved. It destroyed everything along its banks. When the water receded, debris littered the valley; clothes and fiberglass insulation draped tree branches twenty feet above the highway.

Back in Rowlesburg, in a ruined house, the water upended furniture, exploded walls. But a sugar bowl sat unharmed on a windowsill, a faceted chalice of muddy water. In the Rowlesburg Park, a set of dishes looked as if they had been carefully arranged: someone's good china, pink-flowered plates glistening on a wide carpet of brown mud. Ten feet to the left, the road was gone, whole pieces of asphalt torn away. Houses sat at odd angles; one had landed in the middle of the road. People gawked. A couple moved as in a nightmare, posed for photographs on a concrete slab, the only remnant of their home. Looters snuck in and added to the misery.

As days passed, mold bloomed. Condemned buildings were marked with roughly painted red x's. Volunteers arrived. Senator Ted Kennedy strode through Albright and declared that the government would help. Crews worked to restore roads and bridges. Rowlesburg students had class in temporary quarters in Kingwood. They posed behind a mural covered with green frogs and these words: "We're so happy we could just croak." Rowlesburg lost a sawmill, a factory that made hardwood flooring, and, ironically, a whitewater rafting company.

It took months to clean up, to rebuild the bridges. But Rowlesburg had been fundamentally changed. The high school was gone forever. The new elementary school was built far from town on the other side of the river. Citizens tried to be positive. They planted flowers, planned events to draw in tourists, fixed up the old school and turned it into a small World War II museum. But the once-thriving railroad town, a community whose annual Ox Roast once prompted Senator Robert C. Byrd to take out his fiddle and play, is a ghost of itself today.

Albright hasn't fared much better. The power plant is closed, the school abandoned. There are churches, though. Less than a year after the deluge, the Albright Baptist Church welcomed worshippers back to a rebuilt sanctuary. June Isaac, one of its members (the woman who had enlisted my help years before to catch polluters), asked me to do a story on the resurrection of their congregation. In one of the photos, the church's Bible, undamaged, rests on the communion table. An elderly man, a member of the church for nearly forty years, said when the water came, the whole table floated; the flood never touched the Bible's tissue-thin pages. When he found the Bible, it was open to the end of Haggai and the beginning of Zechariah. Both prophets speak of the rebuilding of the temple at Jerusalem. In another photo June rings the church bell. Her grandfathers had built the church that the flood ruined. She salvaged wood from the wrecked sanctuary and had a clock made. June herself is gone now. I wonder if her clock still keeps time.

◆

In the mid-1970s, when I first came to Preston County, I thought it was poor. But I was wrong. That was the best of times. Coal boomed thanks to the Arab oil embargo. Preston County had a shoe factory, a bronze plant, a pajama factory, a manganese plant. Coal trucks clogged the highways. Kingwood had Chevy, Plymouth, Dodge, Ford, and Chrysler dealerships and another dealer who sold big trucks. Terra Alta and Masontown had Ford dealerships, small businesses, grocery stores. Kingwood had a Pizza Hut and a Hardees. The flood was only partly responsible for the county's change in fortune. When coal hit hard times, when mining required fewer workers, when people realized coal's incineration hastened climate change, the decline extended beyond the river. Except for the areas close to Morgantown, where houses sprout in former pastures and forests, the decline continues.

34

❖ ❖ ❖

THE CHEAT 2

THE NEW REPORTER WAS CUTE. Tall, broad-shouldered with a shock of dark hair that fell into a pleasing diagonal line across his forehead. Adam was from the suburbs of Washington, D.C., a fraternity boy who played lacrosse. The easy entitlement of the affluent middle class was like a cardigan flung across lovely shoulders. He had a brand-new journalism degree from West Virginia University and he had ambition.

On a hot August evening in 1986, the police scanner squawked news of a shooting. Adam and I were out the door immediately. I drove the paper's little Ford Escort as if it were a sports car, violated several traffic laws, and screeched to a stop outside the Big B Supermarket. Large windows framed the scene: a woman on the floor, bloody cloth pressed against her neck. Blue lights pulsed from police cars and bounced off all that glass, interrupting the summer evening like a sudden electrical storm. The ambulance hadn't arrived.

Morgantown's usual news was about local government, the university, and vehicular tragedies. I spent much of my time photographing groups of people promoting events and fundraisers. In the decade I spent at *The Preston County News*, I had never come close to the scene of a shooting. And I should mention here that in all those years there was only one shooting that didn't involve people who had at one time loved one another.

Then the ambulance was there, the onlookers (including us) chased away. We went to magistrate's court to see if the shooter had been arrested. He had. Police said the man had shot his ex-wife three times with a thirty-two caliber revolver. Although critically wounded, she would survive. I shot a photo of the accused. The image is of a man possessed by demons, his eyes wide and fierce.

◆

"Hey, fraternity boy, time to do 'Man on the Street.'" I stood at Adam's computer. He was scrolling through Associated Press wire stories. The two of us were the skeleton crew on Sundays, when the newsroom was deserted, all gray screens and empty cubicles. "Man on the Street" was a sure-thing package to anchor a section front—six portraits and six quotes under a banner headline like one of these: "Is the 911 emergency system worth an extra $1.35 per month on your phone bill?" (Six yeses, with one responder noting how much easier it was to remember three digits rather than seven.) "Do you believe surrogate mother contracts should be permitted?" (Three nos, three yeses.) "Do you agree with the ruling to uphold affirmative action?" (Six nos.)

"Should we go downtown, knock this thing out?" I said.

Adam picked up his reporter's notebook, unfolded his long legs, and followed me out the door. Our search for six "victims" to ambush often took us downtown. If the weather was lousy, we went to the mall. Adam and I strolled together, pausing to invade the privacy of strangers. In the months we had worked together I learned that Adam was passionate about the sea. He talked about sailing, said that he knew he would eventually settle near the Atlantic. I talked about my decade in Preston County. We entertained each other with our stories, argued politics. Adam was a Republican, a Bush supporter; his father worked for a conservative agency in the government. I had campaigned for Eugene McCarthy, still actively hated Richard Nixon. Adam should have been the enemy; instead he charmed me. It helped that he was handsome and talented and fun to work with.

◆

Five hundred people crowded the gymnasium in Arthurdale in early spring 1987; they were there to support an injunction to close the Preston County landfill. Although the landfill was established to serve county residents, as many as a hundred garbage trucks from Pennsylvania, New York, and New Jersey were arriving each day. Those trucks caused several accidents; in one, a local man died. The people in the gym suspected hazardous materials, including asbestos, were hidden in the garbage.

Bill, the lawyer who had kept Wilford and me out of jail when we were charged with marijuana possession, was the attorney for West Virginians Against Out-of-State Garbage and Waste. He stepped to the microphone and said thousands of tons of hazardous material were being dumped in the landfill every week. The audience cheered for him and waved signs.

Adam's story and my photos occupied the top third of the front page of the *Dominion Post*. Another story and more photos were on the local section front. An editorial supported the effort to ban out-of-state garbage. When the Department of Natural Resources later that week restricted the amount of garbage the landfill could accept, Adam's story again topped the front page. A week later, he reported that the landfill had closed. I cheered his accomplishments, applauded his growing clip file. If I considered myself his teacher, then he was my star pupil.

Another young reporter also drew my attention. Like Adam, Hope was ambitious. She wanted to be a capital W Writer and she had talent, but her work, like Hope herself, could be overexuberant. She was Jewish, voluptuous, and a little giddy. But she wanted to get better. She sought my opinion on her work. How many people can resist the joy of requested criticism? Not me. When a person with talent asks me for feedback, it's flattering, energizing, fun. For years, this has been my ambition: to be solicited as an expert. Ask my opinion on a photograph, on a piece of writing and I will tell you. Just don't ask me to tell you what you want to hear. I cannot lie. Except when I did.

◆

Hope had a crush on Adam. They had gone out a couple of times but she knew he didn't like her as much as she liked him. He wasn't interested in a relationship. I knew that too; Adam had told me as much. One Monday, Hope pulled me into the deserted photo studio. "I'm in love with him," Hope whined, "but he'll never love me." She dropped onto a stool and buried her head in her hands.

"Why is that?" I asked.

Hope raised her face, met my eyes. "Because he's in love with *you*." She pushed off the stool, brushed past me, and was gone. I leaned against the wall, my heart suddenly loud in my ears. Adam loved me? Oh no. Oh no. This couldn't be. I'm married, a mother. I'm ten years older than he is. Then a wide burst of joy. A surprise. He loves *me!* I am loved. I sat on the stool Hope had vacated. Shame and thrill vied for my attention.

I kept the secret inside me, a glow I could access during the long drive between Morgantown and Salt Lick, while I cooked for my family and did laundry and other household chores. Wilford took care of our boys every evening. I got home just in time to participate in the nightly ritual: bath, book, bed. Those gorgeous boys: Sam's hazel eyes shining from beneath thick bangs, Simon's red curls. Their joy greeted me when I stepped into our house. Later, exhausted, I considered the man asleep next to me. My husband. He smelled of metal and beer, of soap and tobacco. I knew he loved me. I knew he admired my work. I knew he drank too much. I knew he needed me to navigate the paperwork of modern life. But did I need him?

◆

The bar was a dive: badly painted plywood walls and a faint smell of mildew. But it was close to the newspaper, had a pool table and dart boards. It was crowded with friends from the *Dominion Post*. I sat a safe distance from the dart board; Adam was across the room. He had announced that he was leaving the newspaper. He was going to travel for a while, then find another job. He would leave in a month. Whenever I looked up, his eyes met mine. The air in the room felt different. Charged. Dangerous. I'm married, I told myself. I have two little boys. I love my husband. A quiet voice in my head said, "Even if he is an alcoholic." I left the bar.

Oh, please don't groan at this, but Adam copied the lyrics to Peter Gabriel's "In Your Eyes" and left the folded paper in my darkroom. He made me a mix tape that included the Psychedelic Furs and Suzanne Vega. No one had ever given me such gifts. I caved. I made a conscious decision to have an affair. I lied to my husband; a friend provided an alibi and a diaphragm. Late after work I parked near a frame house in a student neighborhood. Adam wrapped me in his arms and pulled me through the doorway. We kissed. Kissed more. Kissed like I had never been kissed, or have since. Kisses gentle and exploring. Hard and demanding. He had drawn a bath for me; scented blue water filled the tub. "Red." He touched my hair. "White." He touched my skin. "Blue." He nodded toward the water. I felt cherished, alive.

And guilty. Miserably guilty. It was as if I lived in a make-believe world, one that confused dreams with reality. I looked at my marriage and recognized a void. I had chosen Wilford because I wanted to belong in the mountains. He had attributes I lacked: an ease with machinery, survival skills, gene-deep intimacy with the land. But he had ended up more playmate than partner. Needy. Drunken. I wanted someone who challenged my smarty-pants attitude. Someone who respected my work. A critic. An equal. Adam filled that need. I was giddy with passion and foolish. I took Sam with me to Adam's lacrosse game. Sat on the sidelines among younger, more attractive women. One squatted next to me. "Your brother is really cute," she said, nodding toward my son.

I glimpsed Adam's world and I asked him to see mine. "Come to Salt Lick," I said. "If you care about me, you'll come to the farm." He did. On a raw spring day we climbed to the top of the hill. We wanted to lie under the broad sky, but it was cold and muddy. Instead we made love in my Subaru, a feat that required gymnastics and humor. A few nights later, on a warmer evening, we walked hand in hand toward a restaurant in a student neighborhood in Morgantown. Adam pulled me over to a wall where he sat on concrete warmed by the sun. He tugged me into the space between his legs and bent his head to kiss me. Our reckless behavior drew catcalls from a car stopped at a red light and we looked up to find one of the sports reporters staring at us. I heard him softly say, "Holy shit."

So my tawdry behavior was exposed. Now the newsroom would know that I was a tart, adulterous, a cheat. I was a bad country song. "No I'm not leaving my husband," I said, shame tinting my cheeks red. "This is just for fun." I repeated that sentence often, hoped I would believe it myself. I pointed out that my affair had an end date. Adam would leave and we would be done.

In my darkroom Adam fastened a thin chain around my neck. A small blue and yellow flag now hung in the notch between my collarbones. "It means you have sailed through rough waters," he said. He took me into his arms and our breath rose and fell together. The next day he was gone. I've since found that flag carries another meaning: I am maneuvering with difficulty; keep clear.

◆

Wilford slept; the comforter rose and fell with his breath. The room was dark; the sun wouldn't rise for another hour. I lay face up, arms rigid at my sides. Guilt was a physical torment, a weight on my chest, a knot in my guts. Tears trickled from my eyes, dripped into my ears. I loved this man, the boys sleeping on the other side of the wall. What had I done? When Wilford opened his eyes, reached for me. I curved into him and sobbed. I confessed, apologized, demanded punishment. Wilford pushed me away, his arms stiff. "Are you leaving me?"

I shook my head. "I love you," I said. "I want to be here." He rolled away so our bodies no longer touched.

"We'll see," he said.

We had boys to raise, a garden to plant, friends to visit. We settled into a new routine. I had been humbled and I tried to make up for my sin. I stopped nagging Wilford about his drinking, kept my mouth shut when he slurred his words and called me a college-educated bitch. Most of the time, we could have passed for happy. When Wilford was sober, he was sweet and generous. Forgiving. That April was like a scar, a ridge on my skin, both sensitive and foreign feeling.

Work was my distraction. Editors at the *Dominion Post* discovered I could write just as the paper decided in 1987 that it would expand into new territory, to gain footholds in nearby counties. They asked me to add feature writing to my duties. The paper had established bureaus in a couple of small towns and I picked up photo assignments from those offices. I looked for feature stories, stopped at interesting places along two-lane highways. One of the editors came up with a feature called The Personals: a portrait matched with the answers to fourteen questions. I now know that it was based on the Proust Questionnaire. I loved the questions, "If you could have dinner with anyone, living or dead, who would it be?" (Jesus was often the answer) and "Name something that's always in your refrigerator." This was like a new and much-improved "Man on the Street." Fun to do, a great excuse to loiter with interesting people. I interviewed a wide-mouthed older gentleman at his junk shop in Fairmont. His wish was to win the lottery. A week later, he did, a hundred thousand dollars.

◆

In the fall, the editor of the newspaper's Sunday magazine, *Panorama*, printed on newsprint as a tabloid, announced she was leaving to take a public relations job. *Panorama* was my favorite part of the paper. It covered arts and entertainment, excerpted books, and featured witty columnists. Early in my tenure at the *Dominion Post*, the editor had given me some fun assignments: eating and shooting my way through the Italian Heritage Festival, photographing wildflowers, and covering a Civil War reenactment.

"Why don't you apply for my job?" she said. So I did. I heard nothing from the publisher of the paper.

"You want that job, don't you?" the city editor asked. "You need to let them know how interested you are."

"I thought I did," I said. But I had never actually competed for a job. This was the time. I knocked on the door to the publisher's office, went in, and nervously made my case: *Panorama* was the perfect fit. I could be writer, editor, photographer, and designer. I would bring a fresh look to the magazine, write a column, publish interesting cover stories. A week later, I got the job. One of my coworkers congratulated me. "Welcome to day shift Monday through Friday."

✦

Soon after, an early winter storm made the roads treacherous. My headlights turned quarter-sized snowflakes into a dancing screen. The asphalt shone—a mirror of black ice. In a curve near Kingwood, next to a Pentecostal church, the road dipped sharply downhill. Sideways-turned cars blocked the way. I tapped the brakes and in a slow motion horror show slid toward the mess. My father's teaching and a decade of winter driving in Preston County again kept me safe. With a soft thump, the Subaru nosed into a ditch. I stayed there, tilted forward, heart pumping fast. One foot tapped, tapped, tapped on its own until my nervous system realized I was safe. One by one good Samaritans pushed the cars in trouble out of the way. A man in a truck stopped next to me. "I'll give you a tow?" he asked. When I nodded, he grabbed a chain from his truck bed and hauled me, ass end first, back onto the road. I had another fifteen tough mountain miles to go before I got home. Terror lurked around every blind curve. I stayed in second gear. I knew the boys would be in bed but I imagined their smell, their freshly bathed bodies, heads ripe for kisses.

The blue light of the television illuminated the living room. Wilford was passed out, sprawled on the floor, his pale face on a pillow. He smelled like liquor and cigarettes. Sam and Simon looked up at me, their eyes glazed with that manic up-past-bedtime look. "Mommy! Mommy!" Sam shouted. Simon was so exhausted that he ground his fist into his face. Sam held his breath, waited for my tantrum. I wanted to scream my frustration, vent the trauma of my drive. Instead I bent down to pick Simon up and nodded at Sam. "Time for a bath, then bed," I said. I sleepwalked through the routine, fatigue and agitation playing pinball in my skull. The sweet good-night kisses were a balm; they gave me strength.

Downstairs I stood over my husband. "Wilford," I said in a low voice. Then louder: "Wilford!" He slowly opened his eyes, and in one beat I saw the truth of my life. He was ashamed. He was weak. He was afraid. "I had a terrible drive home," I said. "I need a drink." I headed for the bottle of vodka in the kitchen. Wilford drank beer and whiskey; the vodka was there for my occasional bloody Mary. I had the bottle in my hand when Wilford appeared in the doorway. His chin drooped; it was like his neck had collapsed. "Don't drink that," he whispered.

"Why not?" I leaned against the sink. The bottle felt heavy; clear liquid ended in a line above the label.

Wilford kept his eyes on the floor. I smelled the vodka. Nothing. I put the bottle to my lips, tilted it straight up, and took a swallow. Water. Room temperature water. No burn.

It was at that moment, on that slanted red floor, that I decided to leave my husband. A minute before I had wanted to scream at him for passing out, for neglecting our sons. I had wanted to dance a fury on the living room rug. But my anger was gone, forced from my body by a weight, by a sadness that pulled like gravity, that turned my legs to lead and my heart to stone.

35

♦ ♦ ♦

THE CLIMB
FROM SALT LICK

I LEFT MY HUSBAND on Valentine's Day, 1988, in the year we would
have celebrated a decade of marriage. He and his friends loaded my
share of our belongings into his navy blue truck: bunk beds, the couch
we had bought for my parents' visit, the set of matching chairs I pur-
chased the month I was hired by the *Dominion Post*, toys and books and
spices and dishes. I tucked a blanket around my sole valuable antique,
the silver chest that had belonged to my grandmother. It had served
as the altar at our wedding. I took my stereo, bought with the money I
had made freelancing in New Ulm, Minnesota, just before I moved to
Preston County. All my albums.

"I want the Jimmy Buffet records," Wilford said. "You wouldn't
know about Jimmy Buffet if it hadn't been for me." He held the cardboard squares between his palms, as if he was holding the records themselves. *Changes in Latitudes, Changes in Attitudes; Havana Daydreamin',
Son of a Son of a Sailor*. Wilford didn't have a turntable; the albums
would become the bottom of a pile of put-aside belongings. I would

listen to Jimmy, keep his albums in the Bs so they could be easily found and enjoyed.

"I want them," I said. Wilford's blue eyes widened; pride and anger traveled across his handsome face. I backed down. "Keep them," I said. Wilford's friend walked by with a box in his arms. He swiveled his head to look down at me. "I would have broken them in half and thrown them at you," he said. Bitch. I heard the word even though it hadn't been uttered. An invisible shot to the gut. Pain I deserved. I had cheated on my husband and now I was abandoning him. Not because of anything he did. Worse. Because he was who he was: a sweet naïf, an impossible drunk. Wilford, Sam, Simon: My Three Sons. That was my joke, told often, a silly reference to a television show with the same name that was popular in my youth. An admission of the overwhelming responsibility I felt for my family.

I left Wilford on a day that applauded romance. I left him our home and our dogs. I had the boys and most of our furniture. I asked for no child support. That could come after he sold the house, had a little money. We had so little and the divorce lawyer was expensive. Morgantown rental properties were depressing. Back then, before developers built stacks of cheap apartments on every hillside in the university town, there were few options. One apartment smelled sour; another didn't even have space for a table.

A coworker soon to leave journalism for law school suggested I consider buying a place. I was skeptical, but she went with me to look at a little house in a working-class neighborhood close to downtown. "Globe Avenue," I said. "If I can't see the world at least I can live on it." It was the same, ugly avocado green color as the cabin on the hill. But it had a view. I sat on the deck and looked south across the valley: the Mountaineer Mall and Dorsey's Knob. Civilization and green hills. I would be okay. But could I afford the place?

"Ask your parents," suggested the realtor. "I'm sure they would be happy to help," she added. I was embarrassed to admit that I hadn't considered that option. Ask for help? Not my style. But I described the house in glowing terms, mentioned that it had an assumable Veterans Administration loan at the then enviable interest rate of 11 percent. A bargain in 1988. My parents mailed a check for the down payment. The house was mine.

I had brought the boys to Morgantown the week before we moved. I had introduced Sam to his new second-grade teacher and taken Simon to visit his daycare center. They seemed to accept without trauma the profound change in their lives. Wilford and I were no longer fighting. Instead, as he and his friends waited to bring in the furniture, we faced each other with sorrow. Regret is so much quieter than anger. Valentine's Day was cold; our breath made clouds as I unlocked the door, swung it wide, and waved the boys in. "We're home," I said.

Sam stood in the middle of the living room, rotated on the brown carpet. "Where's the stove?" he asked. I walked past him. "Here," I said, reaching toward the thermostat. Click. Such a small sound. Beneath my feet I heard the furnace rumble. Simon scooted toward a large metal grate in the floor. He sat on it, leaned his back against the wall. A smile split his face as warm air rushed from below. Sam looked up at me, raised his eyebrows in wonder, and scampered to join his brother. In our new life, we wouldn't have to chop kindling, haul coal, shovel ash. Still, we would be warm.

ACKNOWLEDGMENTS

THIS IS A WORK OF NONFICTION. The truth. But it's the truth as I remember it, and I understand that others may have their own versions of events. I have changed some names.

Many friends and colleagues made the work possible:

Bill Kuykendall, Jerry Ash, Michele Ash, and Rich Hopkins.

Keith Bringe, Jennifer Matesa, Susan Phillips, Sara Pritchard, Candis Litsey Young, and other valued readers; Luis Jaramillo and my other allies at The New School; Susan Cohen, Abby Freeland, Rebecca Rider, Carter Taylor Seaton, and Sarah Beth Childers.

Ann Dacey, Michael Patton, Phil Schenk, Frances Kenna, Brenda McGregor, and Cindy Hite.

Stan Einzig and Sam and Simon Feather.

Wilford Feather.

Thank you all.

CPSIA information can be obtained
at www.ICGtesting.com
Printed in the USA
FSHW01n1435230518
48389FS